The House of My Sojourn

The House of My Sojourn

Rhetoric, Women, and the Question of Authority

Jane S. Sutton

The University of Alabama Press

Tuscaloosa

Typeface: Goudy Old Style

∞

The paper on which this book is printed meets the minimum requirements of
American National Standard for Information Sciences-Permanence of Paper for
Printed Library Materials, ANSI Z39.48-1984.

Library of Congress Cataloging-in-Publication Data

Sutton, Jane S.
The house of my sojourn : rhetoric, women, and the question of authority / Jane
S. Sutton.
p. cm. — (Rhetoric, culture, and social critique)
Includes bibliographical references and index.
ISBN 978-0-8173-1715-7 (cloth : alk. paper) — ISBN 978-0-8173-8482-1 (electronic)
1. Women—Intellectual life. 2. Women—Social conditions. 3. Rhetoric. 4. Communication and culture. I. Title.
HQ1121.S9 2010
305.4201—dc22
2010017774

Cover: A. Johnson's Portrait Monument to Lucretia Mott, Elizabeth Cady
Stanton, and Susan B. Anthony, Washington, D.C. Photograph courtesy Dave
Swanson.

To my father, imaginary now
And to Jerry, through thick and thin

ORIENTATION

The props assist the house
Until the house is built,
And then the props withdraw—
And adequate, erect,
The house supports itself;
Ceasing to recollect
The auger and the carpenter.

—Emily Dickinson

I shall venture to ask, whether [speech] has any sex: and I shall venture to ask, whether they count for nothing, for something, or for everything, the influence of women in the deliberations and business of public life.

—Frances Wright

In the high heavens there is a roadway, which can be seen when the sky is clear. It is called the Milky Way, and it is famous for its whiteness.

—Ovid, *Metamorphoses*

Contents

Illustrations

Acknowledgments

I would like to express my gratitude to the Brooklyn Museum, New York, for permission to use Hiram S. Powers's *The Greek Slave* (Gift of Charles F. Bound). Special thanks go to Ruth Janson, the museum's coordinator of rights and reproductions. Thanks go to the Field Museum Library Photo Archives, Chicago, for permission to use *The Women's Building*, as well as to Jerice Barrios, rights and reproductions coordinator at the museum. Finally, I would like to thank the Boston Public Library for permission to use the E. E. Bond photograph "Weavers of Speech." Special thanks go to Aaron Schmidt.

I am grateful to Dave Swanson for permission to use his photographs of the Portrait Monument to Lucretia Mott, Elizabeth Cady Stanton, and Susan B. Anthony. Dave and his wife, Penny Sweitzer, were kind enough to make a trip to Washington, D.C., to take photographs of the monument.

Thanks to the staff at the Workingmen's Institute, New Harmony, Indiana; to the staff at the Library of Congress; and, finally, to the Pennsylvania State University Library and the York campus.

I extend thanks to Routledge as part of Taylor and Francis for permission to use portions of my essay "Weaving and Unweaving Public Woman: Contingencies of Oppositional Discourse," published in the *Atlantic Journal of Communication* 14, no. 3 (2006): 141-55 (http://informaworld.com/hajc), and for permission to use portions of my essay "Weaving and Unweaving the Rights of Public Woman: The Case of Telephone Operators at the Turn of the Twentieth Century," in *Oppositional Discourses and Democracies*, edited by Michael Huspek (New York: Routledge, 2010), 118-31.

I am indebted to the generosity of many who have been my trail angels. It is a bit of hiking lore on the Appalachian Trail that at the right time a person will appear and provide the weary hiker with food or drink to sustain the physical body or a poem and a song to sustain the spirit over the rough ground. There are occasions, too, on the trail when the angel morphs into nature, like the moon and the evening star, to lighten the load across the miles. If you've been out there, you know what I mean. My trail angels include Michelle Ballif, Barbara A. Biesecker, Isaac Catt, Celeste Condit, Deborah Eicher-Catt, Diane Davis, Lisa Ede, Eric Erickso, Robert Gaines, Cheryl Glenn, Cecilia Heydl-Cortinez, Nancy (Sutton) Holzworth, Jack Kearns for his beautiful stone work, John Lucaites, Andrea Lunsford, Robert McCann, John Poulakos, Takis Poulakos, Janice Hocker Rushing, Victor J. Vitanza, Carole Wagner, Kathleen Welch, Valerie White, and Myrt Whiteley, as well as my good Shepherd "Bones."

My heartfelt gratitude goes to the anonymous reviewers of the manuscript and to The University of Alabama Press.

I extend appreciation to Nkanyiso Mpofu for countless conversations.

I am especially grateful to Mari Lee Mifsud for our collaborations.

And to Thomas S. Frentz, who has been a great teacher, mentor, and friend for over thirty years.

Finally, to my husband, Jerry Caslow, for his encouragement, always at the right time.

For all this and more, I am blessed.

Introduction

Scraping the Roof

I thank God with never-ending gratitude that young women of today do not and can never know at what price their right to speak in public at all has been earned.

—Lucy Stone, "The Condition of Women"

It was around noon on March 13, 2009. I was driving north on I-95 going over in my mind the recent revisions I had made to this book and sent to the press when, on the radio, I heard an NPR announcer say that President Barack Obama would be giving a speech shortly. "Now let's go to the East Room," said the voice over the radio. The occasion was his signing of an executive order creating a White House Council on Women and Girls. What I heard surprised and delighted me.

What is needed now, he said, is to prepare the way for future women "to sit in the high seats"—those symbolic chairs of leadership and authority. He was quick to point out how far women have come and cited not only his grandmother and mother as examples but also Frances Perkins, President Franklin Roosevelt's secretary of labor and the first woman to serve in the Cabinet. "But," he added, "when women are more than half of our population, but just 17 percent of our Congress; when women are 49 percent of the workforce, but only 3 percent of Fortune 500 CEOs—when these inequalities stubbornly persist in this country, in this century, then I think we need to ask ourselves some hard questions."[1]

The question of women in the "high seats" is not unlike the question that prompted me to write this book. I take the coincidence of central ideas as a sign that the time is ripe for taking a fresh look at American women and the question of authority. While President Obama situated his message in a house—the White House—and used various houses—for example, the House of Representatives—for displaying inequalities in the culture writ large, I, too, situate my message in a "house."

When we wish to assemble and speak up, we do so in houses: the courthouse, the House of Representatives, the schoolhouse, the House of God, the meeting house, and so on. The English word *house* suggests there is a house made of rhetoric—a structural site that informs, contains, and shapes public life through speech with the process of decision making. I present rhetoric as a house—a structure where the business of deliberation and decision making is transacted. Although the house of rhetoric is imaginary, it is nevertheless a space of and for public life that functions through oral, written, and visual persuasion for the sake of decision making. What makes this space peculiar is that it is embodied; in the course of making decisions, bodies speak and enact rhetoric, conveying from one human to another values and arguments when the ways of solving problems are many.[2] Built out of its (embodied) process, the house of rhetoric is more mortal and organic than it is a building. So a study of this house structure is not exactly a venture into architecture, although it is related and at times useful. Looking carefully at the house of rhetoric involves an "archi-techne."[3] For the time being, let it suffice to note that this neologism has the sole advantage of considering rhetoric as a whole—not in the canonical sense but in the sense of its unique theory, tropical resources, and real sense of the body fused with production. A holistic perspective is crucial for the kind of systemic change I am seeking.

Analogically, I envision the relationship between women and rhetoric as a house, a structure erected upon principles and design concepts employed in ancient Greece and how, historically, that structure has allowed women to enter but has, at the same time, denied them the authority to speak from inside. This is evident by the fact that, despite their rising circumstances in the United States, women for the better part of two centuries are absent from the high seats. That this book coheres around the idea that rhetoric is a house is not original. As far back as the ancient Greeks, rhetoric is described as an *oikodomēmatōn*, namely a house in the building process.[4] Throughout history, others have compared rhetoric to an edifice.[5] But what I am going to do with this old-fashioned metaphor is more than superficially look at the exterior construction, noting the sequential relation between words and stone for erecting a beautiful speech and building.[6] I am going to examine the house in terms of its original blueprints. As I develop the house metaphor interiorly from its blueprints, I am forced to look at angles, planes, and staircases to determine how they facilitate and inhibit those who speak and live in the house.

Broadly speaking, I divide the book into two sections. The first is devoted to theoretical and methodological considerations. I develop an archaeological-tropological method for deciphering how the house is engineered and what this means for women's status as decision makers and what it says about their prospects for sitting in the high seats. The second section involves three case studies set as decisive turns where women were able to increase their rhetorical access but were not able to achieve full authority: the work of Frances Wright and Lucy Stone as well as suffragists Lucretia Mott, Susan B. Anthony, and Elizabeth Cady Stanton; a visit to the World's Columbian Exposition in Chicago (1893), where the busts that became the Portrait Monument were put on display in the Woman's Building, a sideshow in essence; and a study of working-class women employed as telephone operators.

Just as President Obama says we must prepare the high seats so that women can occupy them, so too I resolve the problem of women's authority with a spatial intervention. To follow the arc of my venture through the halls of the house all the way to the end, I offer in the last chapter a new way of doing rhetorical historiography, investing in its capital strength of being "a people art."[7] The spatializing quality of the method refers not to an expansion by the insertion of women in rhetoric but rather to the insertion of a major change in rhetoric's structure, thereby altering the house so that women are regarded as leaders without prejudice against their nature. Put differently, making a path for women to sit in the high seats means scraping the roof of the house, letting in the elements—new perspectives on construction.

House metaphor and organization aside for a moment, rhetoric is nothing less than a prominent and contemporary feature on a multidisciplinary landscape in the liberal arts. It has been the background for a debate, especially propitious for the past fifty years, over the issue of women's agency and the celebration of the exceptional woman.[8] One prevailing tendency is to approach rhetoric as the art of the possible, which in turn invokes considerations of it as a people art, empowering and granting gravitas to those in democracy.[9] This is a practical view of rhetoric and has gained powerful expression inside the academy. There are many voices to choose from,[10] but I think Henry James's message to the graduates of Bryn Mawr College, Pennsylvania, on June 8, 1905, summarizes it best. We live in a world, James said, "made possible" and "verily constituted, by our speech [rhetoric]." Within this world, success can be measured only in "proportion" to "our speech."[11] In light of this commencement address, rhetoric constitutes the world, rendering it vital to the strength and health of the sociopolitical realm, perhaps even as vital as the economy itself. If this seems a bit far-fetched, consider that rhetoric emphasizes agency and engagement through civic discourse. It offers a solution, modeled in a process of rational decision making, to disenfranchisement, real or felt, as well as to various forms of sociopolitical malaise. All of this is what makes rhetoric unique as well as indispensable to feminists and the entire world of political decision making.[12] So the word *rhetoric* calls forth our best intellectual capacities for integrating thoughts, words, and actions.

Given the importance of rhetoric as a sociopolitical practice, *The House of My Sojourn* goes back and forth between houses—an actual structure and a metaphoric one. The actual house is concrete, rendering the context of deliberation visible and, architecturally speaking, comes in a variety of styles, such as a meeting house, a House of Representatives, or the U.S. Capitol. The metaphoric one is invisible, like the atmosphere, and is so large it might as well be a polis or even a sociopolitical sphere. It caps all the small houses. I use an actual house—for example, the Capitol—to ground what I see happening in the metaphoric house—the model rhetoric possesses about its context and itself. By framing the house in these two ways, I am able to stop over in actual houses where rhetoric is practiced as well as in the imaginary one that encircles and lords over the decision-making process.

On the surface, the effort required to follow a house's imaginary contours, much less to stop to figure out how it is engineered, may sound too academic for coming to terms with women's authority and their absence from the high seats. A theoretical venture in a house seems all the more turgid when set against the White House Council on Women and Girls' committee meetings bent on resolving the problem of women's authority. So it might be good to pause to remember that the ancient Greeks built a house of rhetoric. They engineered, designed, and then erected a structure to suit their needs and circumstances. Understanding the actual houses of rhetoric today presupposes knowledge of the ancient blueprints from which their prototype was constructed. What sort of edifice are we speaking in exactly? What kind of activity does it urge us to undertake so as to compose ourselves democratically, as James would ask? I am not the first to make the point that rhetoric needs work.

Working intellectually on rhetoric is a point Friedrich Nietzsche makes in his lectures: "No one should believe that an art [rhetoric] falls from the heavens; the Greeks *worked* it more than any other people and more than at any other thing."[13] If we look closely at rhetoric's ancient architectural contours, we can see that this old house contains ancient Greek values, desires, dreams, and beliefs. In various ways the house of rhetoric is "always already"[14] evoking these values, dreams, and beliefs in its foundation because it is fashioned out of all sorts of material—ancient myth and poetry, ideas about animals, women, and history. In terms of décor, this old house has hanging on its walls scenes of a Greek political culture, architecture, and their understanding of the universe.[15] While the walls are interesting, much of what I see is outdated. So every time I read Nietzsche's lecture on rhetoric, I am reminded of the need to take a look at rhetoric—the house we speak in—and never to deny the enduring influence of its original builders and always examine scrupulously "the unfathomable intentionality" of rhetoric's ancient formation "down to every detail."[16]

Any charge of excess, which theoretical inclinations can evoke, vanished in my mind when I found the "Portrait Monument to Lucretia Mott, Elizabeth Cady Stanton, and Susan B. Anthony" (hereafter "Portrait Monument") in the Capitol's crypt. From the moment I put my foot on the stairs leading to the basement, I *knew* firsthand that getting in the house and having public authority once inside were not the same thing. This firsthand experience—the path that led to the basement and my new point of contact with women in rhetoric—is how I came to understand that the question of women and authority points not to an excess of theory but to a lack of it. If the early Greeks depicted theory literally as a way of seeing or taking a look at something, then I would argue that rhetoric has not used its resources to take a look at what is happening *within* its own realm that it claims for the world. If the early Greeks also envisioned the process of making change, the kind that deliberation entails, as "making a path,"[17] then I would justify scraping the roof to make an escape route. This entails my going to the basement where I make my discovery, climbing the stairs to reveal the results of my discovery and observation, and using this knowledge to find a way to make any high seat available to women. So my experience brings me back to theory as it can illuminate what is happening and explain how access is not equivalent to authority. Given my manner of going from house to house—from an actual to an imaginary one—coupled with the role that my experience plays in proceeding this way, I start with the day I walked in the U.S. Capitol before making my way over to rhetoric.

It was raining that day. To set the scene, I had been there once before, in 1983, as a doctoral student at the University of Colorado in Boulder. After presenting a paper at the annual National Communication Association[18] convention in Washington, D.C., Tom Frentz, Janice Rushing, Mary Hale (a doctoral student Tom called Hale Mary), and I went on a walking tour of the city. When it began to drizzle, Tom, Jan, and Hale Mary thought we should head back to the convention hotel. I wanted to stay, but since I was outnumbered, we headed back. But even though the drizzle turned into a downpour, I went back out and slipped into the nearest building, the U.S. Capitol. As I passed Frances Willard in Statuary Hall, I found myself thinking about something I had heard at the convention about the rhetoric of Elizabeth Cady Stanton. I knew she was here . . . somewhere.

Then I spotted a guard in the Rotunda who was standing beneath John Vanderlyn's *Landing of Columbus* (1847).

"Hello, I am looking for a monument with the stone figure of Elizabeth Cady Stanton."

"That would be the Portrait Monument to Lucretia Mott, Elizabeth Cady Stanton, and Susan B. Anthony," he explained.

"That sounds right," I said. "Could you point me in the right direction?"

"Down the stairs," he said as he pointed his finger.

"Excuse me?" I asked, wondering if I had heard correctly.

I had heard him right. "The Portrait Monument is down there; it's not in the Rotunda," he said.

"Down there" is the Capitol crypt, as the basement is now called after being remodeled in 1963.[19] Congress authorized the Portrait Monument, this gift from the women of the United States, to be placed in the crypt. The Portrait Monument was presented by the National Woman's Party to the people of the United States on February 10, 1921, at which time the Joint Committee on the Library authorized the installation of the monument in the basement of the Capitol. "The monument was stashed next to buckets and brooms, unseen, until 1963 when the [basement], renamed the Crypt, was renovated for public access."[20] So the crypt is where I found the Portrait monument on public display.

So I went down to see it. Adelaide Johnson (1859–1955) sculpted the marble statue in 1920. Each portrait replicates the individual busts—Mott, Anthony, and Stanton—that Johnson had carved for the Woman's Building at the World's Columbian Exposition or the Chicago World's Fair of 1893. The monument consists of three parts: the fourteen-thousand-pound sculpture itself and two rectangular stone base slabs. One slab is made of black Belgian marble and the other is of white Carrara marble. Including the two bases, the total weight of the monument is estimated to be twenty-six thousand pounds. In the moment of finding the stone women, I also found a staircase.

In 1983, when I first entered the U.S. Capitol, just a day after hearing some talk among participants about the significance of women and rhetoric at our national convention, I was directed to the stairs down to the crypt. This going down was puzzling. Just a few weeks earlier in a graduate seminar I'd read the literature about women and rhetoric and was confident, based on what was in the air at the time, that soon their exclusion would be put to rest.[21] Now I entered the Rotunda only to be sent to the basement.

Dare I say it felt like I was in the basement of the house of rhetoric that Aristotle built—where women were denied authority on biological, political, and rhetorical grounds?[22] At any rate, I was taken aback. While I knew that women had endured much as a result of their speaking in public, I did not think for one minute—nay, for one second—that during my studies about women in rhetoric,

I would have to go to the basement to see Elizabeth Cady Stanton. Later, however, I recalled reading that Robert T. Oliver observed that the Portrait Monument stood in the basement.[23] So I shouldn't have been too surprised.[24] But it still distressed me to think that the monument had been housed in the basement for almost seventy-five years, ever since my mother, Amelia, was born in the early part of the second decade of the twentieth century. Seeing the Portrait Monument in 1983 and remembering too that in 1983 Geraldine Ferraro was less than a year away from being nominated as the vice presidential candidate prompted me to study the relation between women and rhetoric and to discover why men and women stood on uneven ground.[25]

The House of My Sojourn takes up the inequalities—to which Obama refers and which I felt in that basement—that stubbornly persist in our country.[26] It asks hard questions by exploring rhetoric's theoretical dimensions in relation to women's rhetorical practices. Toward that end, I consider the following questions: Who can speak? Who can embody deliberation? How does rhetoric determine who has authority to speak? How does this house proscribe women's status in the deliberative process? Can women today supplement a structure designed to exclude them? If so, what form would the supplement take? To address these questions, I examine the history of women's attempts to enter this most inhospitable place.

These are the questions that inaugurated my journey, one that began more than two decades ago. Although now I state my central idea—namely, that all the attempts to include women in rhetoric exclude them in due course and this exclusion is built into the foundation of the house of rhetoric—it was not easy to reach this point for one primary reason: With all the undeniable success of late, it appears—and women in the academy might make it so appear—that women are populating the house as never before. But there is—I know—another story to tell. The following description of Hillary Clinton's ill-fated attempt to secure the Democratic nomination for president offers a poignant example of the need to journey in the house. As Clinton's access to the political forum gained momentum, her potential authority was questioned or dismissed in a number of ways.[27]

Even before Hillary Clinton announced her candidacy, she was subject to campaign innuendo. In August 2005, Clinton was photographed with her teeth clenched around a hotdog. Her bite gives notice of a logic that goes like this: "If Bill had great interns, then Hillary . . ." The ellipsis signifies her sin of omission, which is castration (while Bill's tropical sin is conjugal fidelity).[28] Besides picturing her teeth as castrating, there were other debasing images. Within the first few weeks of Clinton's announcement of her presidential bid, she was immediately cast as a witch—"I'll get you, my pretty"[29]—and referred to as "the vampire of politics—a creature who simply refuses to die."[30] Eventually, the word *bitch* replaced *witch*, only to be widely circulated in the public forum and used to question and dismiss Clinton's potential for authority.[31] If the expression "I'll get you, my pretty" is meant to evoke the Wicked Witch of the West's threat against Dorothy in *The Wizard of Oz*, it is a thinly veiled allusion to the history of witchcraft where women—like Anne Hutchinson—could stand accused of a crime, namely, speaking in public.[32] For this crime, many women were burned and some were suspended against a wall with the "Witches' Bridle," an instrument with four prongs. One "pressed down the tongue, one touched the palate, the other two doing their barbarous work upon the inner sides of the cheeks."[33] In this way, the label *bitch* can be a form of the Witches' Bridle meant to expose, silence, and punish Clinton for daring to scrape the roof—the house of rhetoric's boundary of authority. For example, along with the infamous question asked by a woman—"How do we beat the bitch?"[34]—there was "the fantasy of silencing Hillary [Clinton] in many American cartoons" picturing a restrained and silenced Hillary—muzzled, a zipper for lips.[35] The modernized images of the "unquiet woman"[36] from witch and bitch to her mouth gagged with a prong-like zipper across her teeth[37] was not the extent of the shamelessly posted objections to her authority.

Clinton was also sexually vilified for using her authority in the public forum. Addressing the presidential candidacy of Hillary Clinton, Kathleen Hall Jamieson told Bill Moyers in an interview on PBS that graphic sexual images were manufactured and placed on the YouTube/YouChoose 08 Web site to "reduce Hillary Clinton to sexual body parts."[38] Jamieson noted that they "contain such things as graphic representations of what a donkey should do to Hillary Clinton." Moyers pointed out that the sexist vilification of Clinton was not limited to the Internet; it was also set by the mainstream media. He mentioned several examples, including Rush Limbaugh talking about "Clinton's testicle lockbox . . . and MSNBC's Tucker Carlson say[ing] there's just something about her [Clinton] that feels castrating."[39] As Jamieson has contended, "women who [try to] succeed in politics and public life will be scrutinized under a different lens from that applied to successful men, and for longer periods of time,"[40] and this examination ultimately encourages submission.

In fact, near the end of her historic campaign, attempts were made to direct Clinton's potential for public authority toward a private authority, falling under the purview of the feminine.[41] Not only was the media involved in this attempt but at some Clinton rallies, audience members were tacitly affirming the belief that women have no authoritative voice in the public forum as they raised the banner "Iron My Shirts."[42] The banner, if we analyze it architecturally in house terms, calls for her descent from the podium—that concentrated site of public authority. The banner redirects her authority toward the context of a home concerned with domestic matters, not in the house of rhetoric where political matters are forged and ironed out. As Marie Wilson, director of the White House Project, told Suzanne Goldenberg, author of *Madam President: Is America Ready to Send Hillary Clinton to the White House?*, Americans continue to associate femininity with subservience.[43] In summary, Goldenberg said, "until Clinton, America had still not had a [major party] female contender for president. That's nearly half a century after Sri Lanka delivered the world's first woman prime minister in Sirimavo Bandaranaike in 1960. Since then, 41 other countries have gone on to elect women as prime ministers and presidents."[44] Gloria Steinem noted on Emily's List on July 21, 2009, that even though "women are now being elected to positions we were only dreaming of just decades ago. . . . the odds of bumping into a woman in Congress are still just one in six. Altogether, the United States ranks an embarrassing 71st in the world in terms of women's representation in national legislatures or parliaments, out of 188 countries with direct elections."[45]

These brief examples—Clinton's ill-fated bid for the presidency and my lived experience of finding the Portrait Monument in the basement of the Capitol—indicate that the whole story of the relation between women and rhetoric has not been told. They also point to work that needs to be done. My wager is that by using the power of theory to examine the structure of the house while retracing a hall-like path set down with steps worn smooth over many decades in rhetoric by American women, we will be in a good position to assess what is happening in the present. In this way, I am able to offer up a woman's reading.[46] The part I play in writing this book is not to bring my reading of women's path-breaking trails of the past in association with those of the present but rather to offer an altogether different path, an alternative direction.[47] Stressing full and equal authority in the house, I am convinced, this direction entails nothing less than a (re)theorization of rhetoric.[48] In his classic tale of rhetoric, *Zen and the Art of Motorcycle Maintenance*, Robert Pirsig describes why change must come from a study of causes, not effects: "[T]o tear down a factory or to revolt against a government because it is a system is to attack effects rather than causes; and as long as the attack is upon effects only, no change is possible. The true system, the real system, is our present construction of systematic thought itself, rationality itself, and if a factory is torn down but the rationality which produced it is left standing, then that rationality will just produce another factory."[49] Likewise, change in the relation between women and rhetoric must go farther than the house—the *systematization* of rhetoric—permits.

The problem of female authority implicates rhetoric or "speech" (language and action).[50] When scholars address the paucity of women's public authority, they bypass the theory of rhetoric. Nonetheless they use its various resources to examine an unidentified context of deeply held "cultural issues that keep women out of leadership."[51] Typically, they analyze history,[52] Web pages,[53] campaign strategies,[54] media and press coverage,[55] visibility vis-à-vis money,[56] and portrayals of female presidents on the big and little screens.[57] My view is that the prohibitions to women's political agency began with the way the house of rhetoric was first built in classical antiquity. That house has been remodeled numerous times over the centuries, but its patriarchal foundation has never been changed.

I am not the first to be interested in the relationship between women and rhetoric. It occupied the attention of vast numbers of nineteenth-century feminists, as this chapter's epigraph indicates. Almost a decade into the twenty-first century, the relationship remains close to the heart of many feminists working in the field of rhetorical studies. The significance of the topic is evinced in several ways, including books on the history of women speaking in the United States[58] as well as edited collections and journal articles on individual women and their unique accomplishments in general and in the history of rhetoric in particular.[59]

The thrust of the existing research says that, historically, women were denied, lost, or forgotten but have been granted more and more access to the public sphere. Women in the academy—as far back as 1935 with Doris Yoakam's dissertation, "An Historical Survey of the Public Speaking Activities of American Women, 1828–1860"—have been involved arduously to make their inclusion possible. Within the academy, the remainder of the twentieth century can be characterized as a steady drive toward finding and adding women to rhetoric.[60] This effort is not limited to the academy; it also finds expression outside the academy.[61]

As the movement fed the desire to include women in the public forum, it gained strength, especially in 1989 with the publication of Karlyn Kohrs Campbell's two-volume set *Man Cannot Speak for Her*. This was followed by a debate[62] that, in the end, broke the movement into two factions: the additive and critical approaches. Within these genealogies are many articles and books.[63] Of late, they offer unique insights into women's participation in debates[64] and in education.[65] All told, they generate a vision of women as distinctly rhetorical. In the meantime, the split remains and therein stands a thorny *methodological issue* of what either approach can build ultimately if the grounds of inclusion have remained the same. An engineering maxim states why the grounds are so important: "As goes the foundation, so goes the building." Unless we examine the foundation, the inclusion of women in rhetoric goes according to the building—of the house.

But even if the truth of this maxim is acknowledged, there is a sense that time, and perhaps a little legislative arm, will take care of the problem of authority. Women will inevitably occupy the high seats. If we look closely at this way of thinking, we cannot help but notice that it belies the foundation of rhetoric—that its paradigmatic range of possibility is temporal. But if it were truly a matter of time, why hasn't rhetoric—this temporal art devoted to the here and now—been able to change the condition of American women for more than two centuries even in the wake of critical reflexive practices, feminist and otherwise? Following Nietzsche's line of thinking, there is work to do. To no small degree, I think rhetoric needs a new roof. Metaphorically speaking, it needs to scrape off the old paradigm of temporality and put on a paradigm of time and space.[66] The best way I know how to expose rhetoric's theoretical problems in terms of a paradigm shift is to borrow a cosmic analogy offered thirty years ago to articulate a recurrent setback in rhetoric's evolution.

Rhetoric, Barbara Eakins argued, is much like science in that it seeks to maintain its theory by making exceptions fit the theory. Eakins explains that just as Ptolemy and Copernicus "patch[ed] and stretch[ed] the old system [of an earth-centered universe] to force its conformity with observations [of the planets]," so men of rhetoric—for example, Agricola, Thomas Wilson, and Peter Ramus—perpetuate "old theories of discourse" by "patch[ing], modify[ing], and reshuffl[ing] the ancient tenets of rhetoric and dialectic."[67] In this line of thinking, I don't think we can patch and modify rhetoric's roof to make room for women en masse. As it stands, rhetoric is more than willing to admit an exception. This is how patching and modifying reproduce the status quo. Thus, it is imperative that we understand how the roof in the house—that so-called glass ceiling—functions to obstruct women's public authority as they make their path to genuine empowerment. This means not just shattering the glass ceiling into "18 million cracks"[68] but also rebuilding the house of rhetoric on terms of full inclusion.

It would be fair to say that what counts as rhetoric stands between these two feminist factions. The additive model treats rhetoric as a neutral temporal power. When subjects use the power of rhetoric, they are able to change their putative circumstances and in this way, women, like men, can achieve political status.[69] The critical approach treats rhetoric as a temporal power, too, but one less than neutral because the rhetorical tradition is tempered traditionally by a masculine modality—formally cast within patriarchy, the economic relations of production (Marxism), and the subject's gendered identity (spread among various perspectives)[70]—and thus time and time again, women have not been able to gain and maintain inclusion in the canon. Numerous feminists have tried to extend the boundaries of rhetoric with feminine forms of speaking, ways of knowing, historiography, and so on, all of which destabilize the masculine modality and permit women to slip past the constraints.[71] As the debate grew in intensity, it became so emotionally charged that it ended[72] instead of being settled.[73] The non-confrontational approach is evinced today by the fact that some feminists in rhetoric have settled on organizing the questions that drove the debate.[74] No matter what side is taken, what methodological approach used, or what attitudes are adopted toward rhetoric, all acknowledge that women have been granted more and more access to the public realm. We need only look to the present to know this is true.

Now, with the example of Hillary Clinton, there is no mistaking—the question of women's authority remains. Still, many resist the idea of looking back. The pain involved in looking back is likely why Lucy Stone offered the prayer she did in this chapter's epigraph. Why look back at the jeering, bad eggs, and ink stones pelted at women while they stood on the platform giving a speech when you could be looking forward to a future that seems much brighter? I get that. Clinton gets it, too. Even after all her vilification by the media, Clinton was vintage Stone in her "concession" speech. On June 7, 2008, Clinton eats Stone's advice, suggesting that if there is another story, it is not worth telling or it has lost its appeal because women now have "hope and the sure knowledge that the path will be a little easier next time. That has always been the history of progress in America."[75] However, remembering vis-à-vis rhetoric has nothing to do with that progress.

Rhetoric's canon of memory is as much about memorization as it is about making connections to the past.[76] If memory is lost or dropped as a canon, as it has been before, rhetoric's faculty of connecting with the past is severed. But dropping the canon is rarely a cause for concern among rhetoricians, including feminists, because remembering and dwelling in the past are not without risk. First, there is the threat of enveloping the feminist project in pessimism, a kind of brooding over the past which, as Clinton forewarned, could keep us "from moving forward."[77] Second, there is some risk that in remembering the past the present could become consubstantial with failure. As Jamieson explains, in looking back, women may see themselves as "perpetual victims."[78] In fact, Clinton warned young women of the trap of identifying with a victim, telling them "it would break my heart if, in falling short of my goal, I in any way discouraged any of you from pursuing yours."[79]

These feminist voices are not insignificant and it is not easy to ignore them, making it harder to justify looking back. I never embraced the thinking behind this chapter's epigraph partly because of what I felt and partly because memory—by body—is implicated by rhetoric. Women are in the house of rhetoric and never left out. But, they are in its basement. It is vital to remember that location. Quite frankly, I bet Stanton would give up her place in the Portrait Monument for the chance to retrace her steps through the past and figure out how the arc of her work landed her in the basement.

Because the story I tell looks back and retraces the steps of early feminists, it must involve raw and hurtful detail. However, I think it avoids pessimism and victimhood through what the rhetorician Richard Weaver calls "painful remembering," something akin to critical, self-conscious awareness. Optimism—or more accurately what Weaver calls the "tone of the cheerful forgetters"[80]—signals a danger because it may incur blindness, like a virus. Perhaps because it is so difficult to resist,[81] optimism may actually be the mood that enables blindness. The problem with optimism, therefore, is that we may fail to notice the harm done to women who have access to the public forum, namely that their public authority is challenged and muted. I would locate optimism, therefore, in the effort to come to terms with the past fused with rhetorical invention—a way out.

Eventually, I not only listened to my feelings but ended up following the statue out of the basement to Seneca Falls where the stone turned to flesh and then the women told their stories of entering the house.[82] My inclination, as my methodology will reveal, is to go around the additive and critical approaches. This way of proceeding is rhetorical through and through. In her "Introduction: Finding a Home or Making a Path," Janet Atwill writes, "Early Greek conceptions depicted the [art] as a process and act of 'making a path.'"[83] The main story I tell involves making a path by going down the corridors, up the stairs, and through the house of rhetoric, retracing my steps here and there in order to decipher how women's public authority has been attenuated even as they have increasingly gained access to the public forum. The path making I take is not by narrative line but one drawn across a house to show how the structure of rhetoric and the concept of authority interrelate to affect not only the speech of women but also their lived experiences. Because the path cuts across, up, and through the house, it leads to a new destination where I make a new contact and thus offer a new perspective. I end up in Tennessee, making new contact with the Cherokee. My contact with these principal people is not to secure a space but to work with their perspectives on women and leadership and build on that to make a space of rhetoric now that is as much American as it is Greek. Fortunately, there are a variety of earthy myths, particularly that of Nunne-hi or "One Who Goes About," from the Cherokee,[84] and they offer guidance after the path breaks through the roof and spreads outward.

With respect to my house metaphor, here is how I enter rhetoric to study its structural integrity. At the level of gestalt, I show rhetoric as a house using the ideograph <CIVIC>.[85] The angle brackets encasing the word *civic* signify how the action within (the house) transpires. Because an ideograph is an image, the action is figural or tropical. So prefigured, <CIVIC> is a palindrome. Meaning "running back again," a palindrome, as in the case of the word *civic*, denotes the embodied action of decision making within the house. This is evinced by the figural reality that the word entails, namely that of going over and through again until a decision is reached. <CIVIC> is a holophrasis expressing the model rhetoric possesses about its context and itself.

Architecture is partially useful for reading the blueprints and understanding the house's design precisely because it is a figural domicile. This is why I adopt the neologism "archi-techne." To consider each part of the neologism separately, I start with techne. From the *technical* side, the blueprints of the <CIVIC> show a quality of iteration with respect to the palindromic configuration. The house is made and remade repeatedly as people speak—considering speech as a form of doing where people in the house go over and through again the matter at hand until a convincing agreement is reached. In effect, they continually make or build the house on the spot because over and over, the people do the process of making decisions. In the broadest possible sense of "techne," the blueprints show rhetoric always already being produced, being built, or coming into view as the house (qua <CIVIC>) enacts a figural step-by-step process—the "running back again"—that characterizes bodies engaged in decision making and reaching judgment.[86]

Although it does not pertain to architecture strictly speaking, architecture is useful in understanding the "archi" side of the house as a structure that appears stable and fixed. Rhetoric stands as a *system* opposed to chaos and violence all the while magnifying the virtue of freedom that deliberation holds for people in a democracy. The house of rhetoric, therefore, avoids randomness and seeks order and in this way holds people together so they can make up their minds in a peaceful manner, relatively speaking. Insofar as the blueprint is used again and again and from place to place, the "archi" denotes rhetoric's quality of itineration. So the house, as it were, goes from place to place—from ancient Athens to Boston.

Archi-technically, the house displays an iterative quality (that of going over the matter at hand until a convincing agreement is reached) and its itinerant circumstances (that of re-creating the house again and again in historical time). Doubtless, this is why Henry James called upon Bryn Mawr's graduates to disseminate this house of rhetoric in the United States.

I enter the house of rhetoric from this archi-technical perspective. But to study its relation with women vis-à-vis authority, I adopt a tropological approach fused with an archaeology. My double-visional—archaeological and tropological—way of going about studying women and rhetoric provides insights that more traditional ways of going cannot, especially as they fail to take account of the ancient construction of the house as it engineers various overturns of women's authority even as their status is enlarged. Given the complexity of my method, I am forced to divide it and present each part in separate chapters. The archaeological part in chapter 1 is more or less the systematic interpretative principles under which I work with rhetoric. The tropological part saved for chapter 2 details the tropes and procedure I use to illustrate the relation between women and rhetoric. Taken together, these two chapters stand as a field guide, a stand-alone pamphlet that serves the larger aim of understanding and altering the status of women in rhetoric.

In chapter 1, I burrow underneath the house by descending on a vertical slope, as if there were stairs leading to a cellar in this metaphoric house. There I discover the "bottom." I dig in the ground, archaeologically speaking, and unearth a floor plan showing "elements" or "principles" of speech, something displayed like an arrangement of stones—the partial residue of an assembly or such places of deliberation. Although the arrangement is not really made of stone, it is made out of material called "elements" and "principles," which are, as Aristotle says, different from the common term "speech."[87] Archi-technically speaking, this arrangement consists of four planes, each of which when connected entails the house as a trope, namely a palindrome. When described in full, they expose the design of the <CIVIC>.

The four planes are arranged in a stepped-up manner. This feature supports the house, giving it stability. But this arrangement offers more than support to the house; each plane, due to its stepped-up placement, adds elevation, not unlike a staircase in a house. This causes the house to be self-supporting and gives it movement because the staircase creates a rising effect, as in rising to speak, rising to the occasion, or rising to a position of authority. The stairs, therefore, continuously connect the elements and principles of speech from the "bottom" floor to the roof—of the mouth.

It is on the stairs that a body appears in the <CIVIC> for the simple reason that the staircase—the unique arrangement of the planes giving support to the house—is a spine that connects continuously, creating flow, and thus enables expression, the making of speeches—the full articulation of rhetoric as a productive art. So in the process of uncovering the <CIVIC> floor plan, I discover, therefore, not only stones of an ancient structure arranged around me but also organic matter—the bones of the proverbial "body of a speech." This conceptual body refers to the vestigial gestures of a man—the skeletal remains of a warrior-citizen—who embodies more than himself and through his intercommunication among the planes of the house includes the demos or people.

It is not simply the fact that the house was once peopled by the dead and I now exhume their bodies. Rather, I show a body moving within the four planes of the house. Insofar as the house is organic—and not just a building—the body of speech, like the warrior-citizen, has its movement constrained not only by the four planes of the house but also by the planes of movement specific to the human body. In this way the planes of the house and the planes of the body intercommunicate to lend support to each other as well as to act in a self-supporting manner. I come to see that the plane of content is inseparable from a plane of expression. Thus the house is viscous in its organization and connections that give it life—mortality.

In particular, the warrior/citizen/man lays bare the elements and principles of speech, as he rises up and speaks. As he does, his bones—his vertebral column—imitates the stairs in the house and renders support to the planes of content. With this vertebral staircase down his throat, the warrior-citizen takes charge of the model that rhetoric possesses about its context—its house—opening it up and airing it out to a higher degree of order and arrangement. At its apex, the citizen-warrior becomes disembodied as the "body of speech." His movements structure relations and are used in constituting the logics of decision making. In effect, this body-based rhetoric morphs into a character. This "proof"-like concept enables like-minded speakers to achieve their moral purpose in the world. I use the stairs to unify the four planes as well as a way to negotiate space in the house.

One day after my lengthy sojourn in the basement, I tried to go up the stairs but my body would not fit. Speaking like Virginia Woolf, I "put on the body" as myself.[88] What does not fit me are the skeletal remains of a man—a warrior-citizen. On the stairs, the proverbial "body of speech" forms repeatedly from the floor plan to ground expression, namely decision making, within and against the content of common building practices. In a more concrete fashion, this body of speech is the male body of the warrior-citizen. However embodied—organizationally, mythically, or psychologically—the house animates a male authorial model of decision making, and rhetoric itself enacts the model as it articulates technically who can move to and from that elevated archi-technical feature called a podium—the highest apex of authority. As I could not put on this body, this pelvis, of a man, my legs could not move so well, making my going up the stairs very difficult.

Knowing exactly that a woman's skeletal remains are different from those of a man and knowing exactly that her body is not found in the house brings me to an anomaly—namely, that women are not supported as men are supported by the house of rhetoric. This is evident from the fact that women do not sit in the high seats, but nevertheless and at the same time have gained inclusion in the house. Figuring out why this happens is particularly urgent once we remember President Obama's executive order establishing a committee to ask hard questions about why women en masse do not occupy the high seats. And figuring how it happens that women do not occupy the high seats is all the more urgent if we return to something else Henry James noted about "our speech." In his "The Speech of American Women" published in *Harper's Bazaar,* he claims that our speech is "threatened by . . . its female population as they claim political equality with men."[89] In light of James's commemoration of speech, there really seems to be a deep structural barrier within that keeps women's authority down.

Chapter 2 is devoted to explaining the tropological part of my methodology. Set in the house, I use the stairs to explain with tropes what happens as women climb up them in their sustained effort to rise from within and express themselves with authority. Insofar as tropes are linked to the body, they can explain why a pattern of rising action is separate but interrelated to the house. I discuss tropes in general and identify three tropes in particular: antonomasia, hypallage, and paronomasia. Based on that, I explain how and why the house qua <CIVIC> aligns with them to overturn women's authority. Although I discuss the specific changes brought about by antonomasia, hypallage, and paronomasia in sequential fashion, the tropical steps may not take place in an orderly fashion. Each trope illustrates a particular form of the denial of women's authority once women are included in rhetoric.

Given the intricate house metaphor and the archaeological-tropological method I use to traverse its interior, chapters 3, 4, and 5 present case studies of women's exclusion by inclusion. Each of these chapters coheres around a decisive "turn" and this corresponds with a trope. Before I address each chapter's contents, I overview the unity of the three chapters in light of a decisive turn. What is a decisive turn? And how are they recognized?

I define a decisive turn on the stairs where up fuses with down and down with up and is visually marked and, in this case, appears in the form of statues, buildings, photos—some visual testament to women's achievement. Being like cairns on a trail, these "way marks"[90]—statues and things on the stairs in the house— indicate direction. On what basis is a decisive turn selected? All are derivative of the women of the Portrait Monument. In effect, I follow this stone statue as it sets up, organizes, and brings together the rise of women in the United States. As I follow women, I stop at these decisive turns to figure out with tropes how women were able to increase their access but were not able to achieve full authority.

Chapter 3 is set on the porch of the house, with countless women poised at the threshold. The narrative begins with women, such as Frances Wright and Lucy Stone, as well as Lucretia Mott, Susan B. Anthony, and Elizabeth Cady Stanton, entering the house and gaining access to the podium, but not its authority. I use the trope of antonomasia to isolate a view of how women use an authoritative space—like the podium—in the house of rhetoric to contest their exclusion as well as to configure how their authority at the podium is transfigured with epithets.

In chapter 4 I travel back to the 1893 World's Columbian Exposition in Chicago. The fair becomes an architectural analogy for specifying through the trope of hypallage how authority is turned down through a kind of exchange that reasserts male dominance. At first, women procure a place in the house—specifically, a building for their accomplishments. But as hypallage reveals, the use of this space comes with a price. To have a place in rhetoric means there has to be an exchange. In the case of the Chicago World's Fair, women gain unprecedented respect but lose their authority when their building is put at the entrance of the Midway or "Joy Zone," not within the Court of Honor, the fair proper where men's accomplishments are exhibited. Here the size of the Woman's Building, its location, and other aspects fuse into a decisive moment.

In chapter 5, I sketch a picture of working-class women employed as telephone operators in New York in 1919. While their employment in the public sphere increases the status and prestige of women as weavers of speech, at the same time it implements their practice as a form of subordination. This action is specified by the trope of paronomasia, which combines or unites individuals in the house in order to form community. It also alters women's status for the worse, stopping short of turning public women completely into prostitutes ("public women"). While upper-class white women mostly have managed to escape this stereotype by becoming exceptions (something the house model seemingly permits given its putative investment in contingency and the exception), women en masse do not. Thus conceptual change is not achieved as women's authority, in the main, stays below.

Finally in chapter 6 I wonder whither rhetorical women? I am not out to reform rhetoric but to point toward a different structure. This chapter is not exactly a conclusion but rather a coda, the distinction being that a coda is both reflexive as well as projective. The coda begins by returning to the U.S. Capitol after the Portrait Monument has been relocated in the Rotunda in 1997. I climb up on the statue, put my eyes in the stone sockets of one of the stone women, and follow a visual trajectory to a painting hanging opposite the stone monument—the *Baptism of Pocahontas*. That trajectory takes me on a journey, partly imaginary but mostly historical, in which I end up where I started (in chapter 3), that is, with Frances Wright entering the house of rhetoric with a question: Does speech have a sex?[91] This return to the beginning is not all that surprising given the palindromic pathways in the house of rhetoric. But what is surprising is what I found: a Cherokee woman speaking with public authority. Herein transformation is possible. By retracing my steps through the imagery of a Native American woman hanging on a wall in the Capitol to a flesh-and-blood Native American woman speaking with authority, I am able to posit a meeting, with speeches as my guiding agenda, between Frances Wright and the "Pocahontas of the West"—Nanye'hi. After the meeting, I return to the Capitol where I find Rosa Parks.

Based on the meeting between these two women in Tennessee, I try to recapture a vision I think Frances Wright saw of women's public authority among the Cherokee. There is, in the midst of the Cherokee treaty negotiations with the whites, a practice of women's public authority unimagined by the whites. My goal, then, in setting up this meeting is simple: it may offer, albeit a sketch, a future model house, other than one encoded by the ancient Greeks. At least the sketch would provide something of a blueprint for redesigning rhetoric marked by inclusive views of women as leaders, decision makers, or persons-in-charge.

The Portrait Monument not only marks each decisive turn but also determines the length of my journey from 1826 to 1919. Visual appeals, such as a statue or a building, aid the process of finding decisive turns because visual appeals claim for women their inclusion in rhetoric. In addition to observing a unity of place, I observe unity of action. The three case studies—stopping places in rhetoric—pose the same question: What time o' night is it? Spun from something Sojourner Truth said and promised to do, the question, in effect, heuristically generates inquiry, namely an ability to tell the time or to see interacting contexts that allude and refer in the most comprehensive way to women's inclusion by exclusion.

Near the end of her speech *The Women Want Their Rights!* (1853), Truth said that whenever women speak and deliberate for their rights, sons hiss at their mothers like snakes: "I can see them laughin' and pointin' at their mothers up here on this stage." This public response, according to Truth, reveals the spirit of the people: "I'm sittin' among you to watch, and every once in a while I will come out and tell you what time o' night it is."[92] Insofar as the people compose the house of rhetoric, I use Truth's warning to stop and explore to explain how gains women have made are illusions. Toward that end, I switch the phrase from the declarative mode to the interrogative mode and therefore ask, What time o' night is it? Changing the mode is an effort to question present circumstances while drawing attention to the unsettled boundaries of the house and to its danger beneath the surface as women rise in vast numbers—even as Truth witnessed this rise in 1853.

As for my use of Truth to motivate my exploration of the house, there is cultural resonance that I must mention as it is so timely as to be uncanny. At the beginning of this chapter I mentioned that I heard on the radio Obama's executive order to establish a White House Council on Women and Girls. At the end of April 2009, First Lady Michelle Obama, wearing a striped skirt to honor Sojourner Truth, said this at the unveiling ceremony of a statue of Rosa Parks in the U.S. Capitol: "I hope that Sojourner Truth would be proud to see me, a descendant of slaves, serving as the First Lady of the United States of America."[93] There is a coincidence between this book's guiding question at each decisive turn marked visually and that of the dress—the trope—of the First Lady appearing alongside a larger-than-life statue of Rosa Parks. As Truth promised that she would come out from time to time to tell us what time o' night it is so we must wonder if First Lady Michelle Obama is leading us to question what this statue means for women's authority. I would argue that the recent dedication of the Rosa Parks statue marks our decisive moment in the twenty-first century. This is our decisive moment: the First Lady stands in the house as a free woman, but nevertheless and at the same time, she stands there with full awareness that for women en masse it is still yet night. At the end of this book, I make an observation about what the Rosa Parks statue means for women's inclusion in rhetoric.

The House of My Sojourn is by no means a finished journey. It is more or less a proposition to consider. I see it more as a stone cairn that marks a way or a leap out of rhetoric and into another way of theorizing rhetoric that has its roots in a distinct American culture. If you dare leap, that is jump from the ancient Greek roof to the Cherokee one, the leap could possibly make rhetoric our own in the contemporary world. Such a new rhetoric should be able to extend authority and power and thus agency to women.

I hope the book inspires theorists to construct a house of rhetoric where the authority of women is a given. While I work from within rhetoric and communication studies, I wish this book to be useful to anyone—in political institutions, business organizations, nonprofit groups, as well as academics across a number of disciplines who are committed to the advancement of women, in particular their rise as leaders, decision makers, or persons-in-charge.

1

In the Palindrome of the \<CIVIC\>

Architecture is a sort of oratory of power by means of form.

  —Friedrich Nietzsche, *Twilight of the Idols*

The story around the Portrait Monument—its celebration in the Rotunda and its authorization in the basement—alerted me to the existence of another movement, one of women going down at the same time as they are recognized and ostensibly included within the house. My personal experience of seeing the statue in the basement led me to think about the house I am in: it is rhetoric. Yet the Capitol remains part of the complex that offers a vision of rhetoric as a small house where people assemble and use its process for making decisions.

During my first visit as well as subsequent visits to the Capitol, the awareness that women—Mott, Stanton, and Anthony—are *in* the basement is always immediate to me. But then someone would say, "Oh, it's *just* a statue." To this, some part of me would agree. But as I began to connect my perception of being in the basement with my imagination of seeing the Capitol as the house of rhetoric, I discovered another staircase. Besides the one in the Capitol, there is one housed in the scholarship. So, it isn't *just* a statue; rather, the statue is emblematic of women as they are written down in rhetoric.

I begin again on a staircase, but this time I focus on an imaginary one. To bring it into view, I give an extended example, consisting of a brief summary of the academic climb up and down of women in rhetoric during seventy years of scholarship. Let the stairs begin with the 1930s and end at the top with the 2000s.

In the 1930s, the question of women in public life compelled Doris G. Yoakam to write a dissertation surveying the public-speaking activities of more than fifty women and then to argue that they had made a significant contribution to the field of speech.[1] Yoakam hoped her findings would help provide future students, including "thousands of girls in universities and colleges . . . who are studying speech," with texts that more accurately reflected the past.[2] Also produced during the 1930s were two major textbooks on public speaking for women.[3] Both establish a need for women to study public speaking on the grounds that change and great reforms are the fruits of women speaking in the public forum.[4] Similarly, Eudora Ramsay Richardson's text justifies the teaching of public speaking to women, stating, "Women in our country stand the chance of losing all that has been gained."[5] There is reason to believe the ground "that seemed so solid" is slipping "under our feet," Richardson said.[6] She counts the number of women in state legislatures and in political organizations and finds nineteen fewer women in 1935 than in 1931. She contributes some of the decline to section 213A of the National Economy Act: "School boards and businesses, as well as governmental and state departments, were ruling out married women and giving preference to men, particularly in executive and administrative appointments."[7]

After Richardson came J. V. Garland's *Public Speaking for Women*, arguably one of the best collections of speeches by women in the early part of the twentieth century. When this text was published in 1938, it had the full support and backing of over two dozen women's organizations. A majority of the speeches in Garland's collection display women in politics, business, and education. For example, Ruth de Young, women's editor of the *Chicago Tribune*, wrote a speech in which she underscores the work of "12,000,000 business and professional women" on the American landscape as well as "30,000 women in the United States with the power of the vote."[8] And there is a speech by C. Ormond Williams, honorary president of the National Federation of Business and Professional Women's Clubs. In her radio address, Williams imagines the political power of women through their work in the service industry, especially as telephone operators, propelling women into positions of authority. Given these inroads, Richardson's warning that the grounds of women's inclusion were slipping under their feet seemed pessimistic at worst and exaggerated at best.

In the 1940s, Jessie Haven Butler wrote a public-speaking text for women in response to the decline in the number of women studying public speaking. She emphasized the importance of mingling women's talk with men's talk, for "democracy is government by talk."[9] In this vein, Butler said, "women should not let men write their speeches."[10] At Butler's class on public speaking (held at Pierce Hall, Washington, D.C.) on January 9, 1941, Mrs. Franklin D. Roosevelt (as Butler referred to the First Lady) addressed the importance of speech training by saying that women should augment their voting and the work they were doing in their parties with speech training in an effort to "enter into debate." From Roosevelt's talk, Butler concluded, "when these facts [the relation of public speaking to women's development] become more widely known to women, they will not hesitate to mount the public platform."[11]

In the 1950s, the question of women and public life compelled Lillian O'Conner to gather material on twenty-seven women and their speeches from over forty libraries.[12] Winner of the National Award of Pi Lambda Theta for research concerning the advancement of women, O'Conner's book evaluates the speeches on traditional principles. Her judgment of them is, she argued, based on Aristotle's *Rhetoric* because in the United States, it remains "the best known and most universally respected work on rhetorical theory."[13] O'Conner observed that because John Quincy Adams himself declared Aristotle the best, she saw no reason for departing from his ideas.[14]

Paralleling O'Conner's book on women orators was Elsie E. Egermeier's children's book on the accomplishments and public activities of eighteen women, some of whom were orators, specifically Lucretia Coffin [Mott], Frances Willard, Mary Lyon, and Susan B. Anthony.[15] In her preface, Egermeier recounts stories of women as counselors or mentors to their young "sisters" because, even though the world is now "more friendly toward [women] than it was toward your grandmother," it is not friendly enough.[16] The idea of mentoring apparently has had great staying power; in the 2000s, the concept of mentor or counselor is once again being articulated as a solution to the absence or neglect of women in the realms of public spaces.[17]

In the 1960s Robert J. Brake examined anthologies and critical essays in speech communication and reported that few had given much attention to women orators in the United States.[18] By the decade's end, Brake's exclusionary sentiment reared its ugly head again. It is clearly evident in a book on the history of public speaking in the United States. Primarily devoted to the years 1761–1914, it includes eight women; however, the chapter "The Great Debates That Shaped Our Nation" does not mention any women. Notably absent was Frances Wright's "Fourth of July Oration, 1828," in which she points to "Negro Slavery and the degradation of our colored citizens" as the one evil not touched by the Constitution.[19] This early speech against slavery anticipates one of the great debates that shaped the nation. The women in this text are located in the section on the professional lecturer. Susan B. Anthony and seven others are presented as speakers in the context of temperance, Chautauqua, James T. Pond, and the rise of the lecture bureau. In all, women account for twelve out of the text's 566 pages. In the conclusion of the twelve-page section on women, the author notes that the contributions of women in rhetoric must be seen as passionate advocates and agitators rather than as outstanding individual accomplishments. He closes, "After centuries in training in submission, and from the midst of a social situation that took their subordination for granted, it was too much to expect that they [women] could quickly produce eloquent orators equal to the best of men."[20]

In 1977 Carla Brown, concerned about women, rhetoric, and public life, wrote a text for women and public speaking (reissued in the 1990s) because "we watch women in public life . . . struggle to project authority and power."[21] Keeping in mind individual contributions to rhetoric are details that I wash over in my effort to bring to the fore a staircase in rhetoric, I quickly go to the next decade.

In the 1980s, concerns about women and public life motivated Karlyn Kohrs Campbell to show the exclusion of women from a number of anthologies, including *Famous American Speeches, Contemporary Forms of American Speeches,* and *Twentieth Century Issues,*[22] and to make available a critical study of early feminist rhetoric as well as twenty-six of their speeches.[23]

Leaping to the mid-1990s, Janet Stone and Jane Bachner produced a public-speaking textbook for women but posted this warning: "Don't underestimate how growing up without a view of women in public inhibits the ability of women to speak."[24] Here is how one poet put the problem regarding the habit of speech: "The habit of speech / is not like riding a bicycle, / something you never forget; / it dries up like the habit of tears."[25] So Stone and Bachner's book means to preserve the habit of speech for women through pedagogical practices. As long as the habit of speech goes unpracticed or undeveloped by women, it does not go dormant and lie in wait for the right time to appear; it dies, killing their voices.

Similar concerns obligated Kristin Vonnegut to quantify the absence of women's speeches from the American public address classroom. Vonnegut noted that over four semesters of public address courses, students at one prestigious midwestern university read one hundred speeches of which only six were by women. At another university, no speeches by women were studied, although names of women were mentioned.[26]

All in all, despite exhaustive reviews of literature (Yoakam's dissertation), nice critiques of that literature (O'Conner's award-winning research), and various rational arguments for the inclusion of women (Campbell's lifelong scholarship), this way of going about studying the relation between women and rhetoric is a return to my lived experience of graduate work, particularly studying about women in rhetoric, attending a convention, and going to the Capitol, mainly going down to the crypt to see where the women of rhetoric were kept. The statue is not just a statue. It marks the structure of recurrence—inclusion by exclusion—that troubles the relation of transformational activity between women and rhetoric. This recurrence is where the hall breaks open, existentially speaking, and where my sojourn begins. As I walk this hall-like pathway marked by a statue, the concrete space of the Capitol crypt all but disappears as I enter the ancient house of rhetoric.[27]

HOUSE

The ancient Greeks imagined rhetoric as a house. There is a trace of this imagery in the idea of cosmos or order because the house is, as Gaston Bachelard writes, "our first universe, a real cosmos in every sense of the word."[28] In that cosmic sense, the Greek house of rhetoric is more like a hut, in space, something like a baking cover of air (atmo*sphere*) as the ancient rhetorician Hyperides (322 BCE) suggests. Rhetoric covers an inhabited region (*oikoum[enē]n*).[29] Like a house, rhetoric is a form of protection and a shelter. It aims to protect humans from settling difference with violence. It gives shelter to what is said, which means that it provides order or a system for doing so. Finally this baking cover of air gives humans a central hearth for gathering. In effect, the link that makes the fire equal to a hearth (for warming and cooking) is the imaginary stuff of the poet that dreams up a hearth in a house for gathering. By the *Rhetorica Ad Alexandrum*, the idea of house is less of a poet's fantasy than it is a carpenter's reality. Rhetoric is described as an *oikodomēmatōn*, namely a house in the building process.[30]

All the intellectual materials—terminology, images, speeches—that are stacked up and piled around do not make a house in which humans can gather and use its resources.[31] Rather it is form, the house, that fulfills the potency of the material heap—the stuff lying around rhetoric. The house or form makes rhetoric real—like a gathering place. In another sense, the house is nowhere. It is a metaphor. Such a composite form, whether rendered as a cosmos,[32] an atmosphere,[33] or a building, draws attention to the architecture and to its existential status of order, arrangement, or *disposition*. The latter, in particular, implicates the body because it is through the body, the mouth/voice and hands/gestures, that another body is likely to experience something, including that of being put in place, as the Portrait Monument was *disposed* in the hands of Congress. It is through the literal body that outcomes are settled in courthouses, meeting places, or other various structures. Insight into the house of rhetoric can be had by deciphering its structure, which manifests what people do within it. Throughout this chapter, the house image articulates the parameter of two structures—ancient and contemporary—as well as two boundaries—building as house and body in house—to define the course of my journey.

As I begin my descent on the stairs through the years 1930–2000, I stumble on the last step over what appears to be a small cellar door. I open it and see that the little door opens into a subterranean vault. I enter it and immediately am aware that massive structural principles support everything above me. It is daunting to be here—down below. But soon it feels less intimidating as I become more irritated about a negative I spiraled through over the course of the last seventy years only to have the high point spiral be the basement. I linger in this dark, cold interior tomb with my frustration.

Turns out, I stayed for a decade. During that time, I dug in the ground and scraped at the foundation. I found bits and pieces of vocabulary, terminology, categories, all the intellectual weight-bearing things that supported the house above—that complex archi-technical system of rules, methods, and procedures used to tailor the body of speech, ensuring good reason, right action, moral choice, and authority for the execution of rhetoric's values. Many questions ran through my mind as I sifted through these ancient shards of the past. How is the house of speech built? How do sex and gender figure in the experience of being in this house? How do they constrain women as speakers? Could it be that there are principles of power written in the architectural script creating a boundary of authority, something that prefigures the notorious glass ceiling? If so, how does the boundary act as a constraint girding and inducing women to speak and act in places under the glass ceiling?[34] Finally, could the design of the house induce a performance of its public authority in ways that are knowable? If women like Elizabeth Cady Stanton had understood the structure through and through, could they have foreseen how it would turn out for them—standing for a lifetime in the basement? What possibilities does the house hold for seeing any woman as a leader, person-in-charge, or decision maker? These are some questions that I carried around with me as I toured the parameter and tried to take it all in.

I discovered the foundation has four layers—actually planes—and for the sake of convenience, I have drawn up a blueprint to organize and present my findings. Figure 1.1 is a drawing of the model (house) that rhetoric possesses about its context or, actually, space.[35] It shows four planes—topical plane, structural plane, plane of characterization, and tropological plane—with each connected to a motif: from "escape" to "civic discourse."

Figure 1.1 is the basis of this chapter's organization. As such, it is "escape," "political animals," "defeat tyranny," and "civic discourse." Each motif is a pattern, composed in staircase fashion from temporal to mythic to spatial orientation and thus the chapter is organized as a tetralogy. To read the first plane, the motif is escape and the pattern reveals rhetoric in its temporality, namely the need to escape violence as a frame of mind for civic engagement. From there, the buildup features escape as a turn from speaking and doing "just whatever"

Figure 1.1. The planes of the house of rhetoric.

Topical Plane

"Escape"

- 1 from the life and lair of wild beast and freedom

- 2 from artless and unstudied performance

- 3 from architecture/column to body planting post

Structural Plane

"Political Animals"

- manger-fellows/agora (escape 1)

- boustrophedon–"speaking in the middle" (escape 2)

- podium (escape 3)

Plane of Characterization

"Defeat Tyranny"

- ethos/ēthos (manger-fellows/agora + escape 1)

- antistrophe and subset katastrophe (boustrophedon + escape 2)

- ekklēsia and epithet of authority (podium + escape 3)

Tropological Plane

"Civic Discourse"

- character (ethos/ēthos + manger-fellows/agora + escape 1)

- disposition (antistrophe and subset katastrophe + boustrophedon + escape 2)

- palindrome (ekklēsia and epithet of authority + podium + escape 3)

in a situation without a system. Ultimately the escape yields to a podium, acting as an architectural sign that order has erupted in the house.

In an effort to draw attention to the process as embodied, I use the word *plane*, not level, to delineate the structure. Plane has two advantages. First, it acknowledges the stable board and plank imagery associated with the house. This is important because I want my sketch of the house to invoke the arrangement and order peculiar to it. By using plane rather than a synonym, I hope to avoid the suggestion that the house is filled with psychological repressions as one might imagine if the house had levels, like a basement. In addition, I want to display speech as embodied action, particularly as a form animated through the vivacity of speech. By being an anatomical term, *plane* brings the body of speech to the surface and refers to articulations of how the body moves via a traverse plane, frontal plane, and sagittal plane. So the word *plane* means to render the body of speech beyond body parts. Just as physiologists talk about the body and its movement in terms of planes—for example, sagittal plane—so I use four planes to describe the house of rhetoric and then apply them to what is going on in the house of rhetoric, specifically the process of going back over/through something until a convincing agreement is reached as well as how this iterative quality implicates voice/ethos, moral quality, and social rank in a gendered way. The body brings to the fore the kinds of movement that the house (both a temporal and plastic art) permits.

Before I move into the four planes, delineate them, and specify the design of the house of rhetoric, I make two general observations about the method I use. As the archaeological part of my method led to my uncovering these planes, the fourth one leads to the archaeological part blending with a tropological one. The next chapter specifies the logic of tropes. Suffice it to say that by the fourth plane the house appears large perched atop a palindrome called <CIVIC>. This means the palindrome is the source of the rhetorical activity of the house. What is this activity? In the introduction, I said that a palindrome refers to a word that is spelled the same way forward as it is backward, and this movement accurately specifies what rhetoric *itself* does (qua techne) in the context of civic engagement and democracy. So the activity is this: rhetoric is the process of going over/through again and applying what is said to what was said previously until a convincing agreement is reached. How does the notion of house figure in? The trope secures the building of rhetoric over and back again in time. What is the source of the building? The house emerges from said activity—the archi-techne—in the font of a palindrome.

From within the house, therefore, there is a peculiar kind of participation that subjects can reasonably do and status they can obtain.[36] Specifically, it is proportional participation specified in terms of emotion and reason. When it comes to sex, gender, class, and race, there is an exact amount of reason needed to participate. This exactness—because it construes a logical hierarchy during the process of decision making—is intensely related to authority. Involved in making judgments or decisions, authority (*kurios*) is limited to the role of (Greek citizen) men in the house.[37] So the house of rhetoric is not a neutral order or arrangement, as a container image would have us believe.[38]

The second observation I want to make about the method is related to the body register of the house metaphor. During the dig, I found vestiges of a body. It could be the bones of the warrior-citizen who actually spoke. It could be evidence of a body of speech that refers to speech arrangement or disposition. But either way, the body, if articulated joint by joint, displays the movement of tropes (which were bodies once). Tropes performs "turns"—such as turning toward, turning away, turning into, and so on—and they compose rhetoric's space and its performances. I therefore credit space with an equal status to that of the body in making rhetoric—that process of making decisions. Now by the time I reached the uppermost plane, something like a concrete slab on which the house is built, I shift to a tropological approach. On the fourth plane the house becomes both a trope and a body.

Using the palindrome of the <CIVIC> to designate the house as both structure and the "body of the speech," I map the way of my archaeological dig with figure 1.1. I move through the four planes: the topical plane, the structural plane, the plane of characterization, and the tropological plane. Within each lies something of the warrior-citizen's skeletal remains. To articulate his bones—the "body of speech"—I use the subsets, labeled as 1, 2, and 3, alongside the motifs. In an effort to keep the body intact, I do not divide and separate it as I do the house for analytical purposes. I make every attempt to bring to the surface a coherent outline of the body as it individuates the process of decision making across each plane of the house as it takes on a distinctive spatial orientation. All the subsets within each plane (on figure 1.1) refer not to body parts but to the connections I make between the house and the body of speech.

Although I present my findings in a linear manner, my archaeological dig goes in a circuitous path. I move across the vertical slope as the house rises to its apex by using switchbacks that go from myth to conceptualization. As I go, it may appear that I reverse direction, as sometimes occurs with hiking trails that cut across a vertical slope. By cutting across the house, I am able to gain a unique vantage point on the *technical* means rhetoric employs in its own practice as well as on the activity of men engaged in the process of exchanging opinion and making decisions. Specifically, in this chapter, I "turn" the archaeological ashes of the hearth over, unearth some bones, presumably bones from the proverbial body of speech, and explore the body's innate power and authority through the repeated action of going to and from the podium. This repeated action draws attention to not only the body as male but also to the key trope on which rhetoric's foundation is established. It is here that I bring the kinds of movements the house permits into association with its predicative base.

Design of the House

Figure 1.1, as I mentioned earlier, is a blueprint of the foundation, displaying the house through four planes.

Topical Plane

In the tradition of rhetoric, the notion of finding something is very similar to archaeological work. Just as archaeologists go to a site to unearth things such as bones and tools, a rhetorician goes to a site called a topic (*topos*). For purposes of analysis, it has a physical component. Early rhetoricians such as Aristotle and Cicero frequently characterized a topic as a place, a commonplace, a region, a haunt. What rhetoricians find when they go to a topic is an image or an idea. I, too, hope to find an idea and an image.

A topical place in rhetoric represents the storage of "sayables," that is, an argument. In rhetoric, topics are images and ideas deposited (by whom?) that signify commonplaces "to go to" in order to find or discover or create *something to say*. There are many such places for a speaker to go. An example of a topic (*topos*) is the "more or less." For example, a speaker can go to the place of the "more or less" and find an argument. By going to the "more or less," a speaker finds something to say, whether in the law court (e.g., if a crime could be seen by the light of the moon, more so by the light of the sun) or in politics (e.g., if a common citizen should be law-abiding, so much the more for elected officials).

The topical plane of the house of rhetoric is located in myth, proverb, or fable.[39] They are topical because everyone stores ideas and images and thus can be found and used as a "strategy for dealing with a situation."[40] When it comes to the beginnings of rhetoric, myths are rich topical deposits for finding something to say about the structure of the house. In fact, Ludwig Wittgenstein says, "Our speech is an incarnation of ancient myths."[41] Following Kenneth Burke and Wittgenstein, it would be fair to say that myths are not inert deposits but rather animate dramas that contain and carry information about why and how the house was built. Topically speaking, myths store ideas and images in the form of words. In myths I find shards of how speech was conceived and then reconstruct those fragments so as to sketch an early model of the house.

I present two myths that enable rhetoric to form—the myth of Protagoras and the myth of Corax.[42] Of the many myths about the beginnings of rhetoric, these two are significant for a number of reasons, not least of which is that classical and contemporary rhetoricians articulate these particular ones as the founding package of rhetoric.[43] Most recently, scholarly and pedagogical texts attend to these myths to detail the significance of rhetoric in relation to democracy.[44]

Myth of Protagoras

Here is the myth of Protagoras with emphasis added.

> Having stolen the fiery art of Hephaestus along with Athena's art, [Prometheus] gave them to man. . . . Then too, he devised, through his skill, articulate speech and names for things, and invented houses and clothing and footwear and beds and nourishment from the earth. Thus provided, *men, at first lived scattered,* and there were *no cities.* As a result, *they were being destroyed by the wild beasts,* because they were in every respect weaker than these. Their skill as craftsmen was sufficient to help them get food, but it failed them in their warfare against the beasts; for *they did not yet possess the political art [rhetoric],* of which the art of war is a part. So they *sought safety in numbers by founding cities.* Now *whenever they formed communities they would wrong one another, lacking as they did the political art [rhetoric], with the consequence that they would disperse again and be destroyed.* Zeus, therefore, fearing that our race might be destroyed altogether, sent *Hermes* [god of rhetoric] to bring to men reverence and justice, in order that there might be *governments* for the cities and *bonds to join men in friendship.* Now Hermes asked Zeus how he should go about giving justice and reverence to men. "Shall I distribute these in the same way that the arts have been distributed? For example, one physician is enough to treat many laymen, and it is the same for the other craftsmen. Shall I place justice and reverence among men in the same fashion, or shall I distribute them to everyone?" *"To everyone,"* said Zeus, "and *let everyone have a share in them, for cities would not come into being if only a few shared in these as they do in the other arts.* And lay down this law by my order: let them put to death as a plague on the city the man who cannot share in reverence and justice."[45]

Myth of Corax

The second myth takes place in Syracuse, a place ruled by two savage tyrants named Gelon and Hieron. In the myth of Corax,

> it is said that the tyrants indulged their savagery to the extent of *forbidding the Syracusans to utter any sound at all, but to signify what was appropriate by*

means of their feet, hands, and eyes whenever one of them was in need. It was in this way, they say, that *dance*-pantomime [*orchēstikē*] had its beginnings. But the Syracusans had been *cut off from speech [logou]; they contrived to explain their business with gestures* [or figures, *schēmansi*]. . . . Then, since the citizenry [*dēmos*] among the Syracusans feared that they might in some way fall upon a similar tyrant, they no longer entrusted their government to a tyrant. The people [*dēmos*] themselves wanted to have absolute control over all things. And thereupon *democracy came* once again to the Syracusans. And this man Korax [Corax] came to persuade the crowd and be heard . . . [and] he thought it was *speech by which the course of human events was brought to order.* He then contemplated turning the people toward and away from a course of action through speech. . . . These things he called "introduction," "narration," "argument," "digression," and "epilogue."[46]

Buried deep under the foundation of the house, the myths of Protagoras and Corax are fragments of the house's frame. As such, they provide a vague shape of speech and its unique image of rhetoric as a communal space. These in turn bring urgency to the picture I am sketching of the house. The architectural vision is one in which rhetoric jolts people to act, to bring an end to tyranny, violence, disorder, and chaos. The people's rhetorical action, defined primarily by organizing around a thematic attack on tyranny, whether man or beast, is what enables the city to emerge (or, broadly speaking, civilization, etymologically "citification") in and through the bonds of friendship and democracy.[47] As Emile Benveniste has shown in his study of Indo-European languages, we must understand that demos or people is of Dorian origin and is a territorial and political concept.[48] The word *demos* cultivates a political sense of space rather than a physical sense. It is in this sense of space as polis coupled with another—space as a physical division of land and the "people" who speak—that allows rhetoric to acquire its architectural dimensions and ultimately its scope of authority.

A key architectural image in both myths that seems to support the house's foundation is "escape." The thematic escape in the first myth relates to a need for stability as opposed to wandering and thus promotes the concept of building a house. The second myth extends the escape theme and formalizes its imagery as a house, rendering the escape architecturally as the "pillars" that stabilize the house so that the people inside can organize so as to avoid a tyrant, whether cast as the beast within the human or the tyrant without who rules over the people. Defeating tyranny is thus another key finding in these myths. This topic—"getting around tyranny"—stores within it rhetoric's definitive process of deliberating a course of action in the face of uncertainty.

Putting the myths side by side and in the context of the Portrait Monument, the stone women's arrival in the Rotunda is of mythic proportions, replaying the invention of rhetoric. The women, having escaped from the tyranny of domination by going around the private realm where their influence was confined, gain access to the city's pillars, the Rotunda, where the people are housed in democracy. So the women in seeking authority are going over/through again the topics of rhetoric. However, the original topics forge a foundation that fail to imagine them in rhetoric. So as they use rhetoric to overcome their exclusion, they, at the same time, rebuild the house that always already puts them in the basement.

Now I explore some specifics of the foundation. This topical exploration, starting with the first level "escape" and moving to the third level, means to shed light on the physical and thus lived space of rhetoric rather than a mental conception of it as civic discourse. The word *escape* is a multidimensional complex engaging visual, tactile, and oral dimensions and enfolds three aspects of rhetoric: freedom, art, and architecture. In what follows, I use the word *escape* as a threshold to a crawl space under the floor that gives me access to shift and sift in the dirt among these three aspects: freedom, systematization, and column/upright body.[49] Figure 1.2 stages the theoretical aspects, like a staircase, with "escape 3" being the highest characteristic. As I feature each, I also explain how collectively the three aspects suggest a relationship among themselves to improve communication as well as distinguish a relationship between emotion and reason to effect practical outcomes in rhetoric as a theory and a practice.

Making sense of escape requires contextualizing the word in terms of what it means to be a human-communicator-rhetor. Toward that end, there are two interrelated aspects. First, escape means leaving the wild and going into a house. Second, escape means having freedom to create order in confinement. The first meaning of escape implies that rhetoric is something not yet formed (as a house). In this sense, escape is the navel theme that refers to a need for being together in a house of speech, one conceived as an escape from the wild beast that settles disputes through violence.

To take a closer look, "the escape from the life of the wild beast" as celebrated by Isocrates and Cicero indicates that a human escape is not from captivity.[50] When used as a verb, the word *escape* typically equates freedom with getting out of captivity and returning to the wild. Two examples used in the *Oxford English Dictionary Online* (OED) are a garden plant and a bird. A garden plant that escapes cultivation and grows wild is free. A bird that escapes from captivity is free. However, humans, as the poets and rhetoricians sing the song of speech, are free because they have escaped *from* the wild and *into* domestication. In ef-

Figure 1.2. Topical plane.

escape 1	From the life and lair of wild beast to freedom
escape 2	From artless and unstudied performance to systematization
escape 3	From architecture/column to body planting post

fect, the escape is both a release from having to roam like a free animal and an appeal to staying put like a house and then using the house to create order. The Greek verb form *apēllagēmen*, translated in English as "have escaped," connotes either a release from or an appeal to something. Isocrates, for example, uses the verbal form (*apēllagēmen*) to express escape as an appeal to becoming domesticated. In coming together, building cities, and solving problems through speech rather than through violence, humans have escaped (*apēllagēmen*) and thus are released from the life and lair of the wild beast—becoming domesticated.[51] In its animated role of freedom, "Speech," being a godlike character (Hermes), speaks; that is, the god releases humans from the life of violence or, more accurately, it appeals to humans to exchange their wild lairs and wandering lifestyle with gathering and assembling for the purpose of communication.

Escape as an escape from the wild implies freedom, and freedom stages the first generational support of speech. As such, speech as freedom counts as a major crescendo in the theme song of communication and civilization. Hear its echo in Euripides' *Suppliants* as sung by Theseus: "I praise the god who brought our life out of confusion and beastliness and gave it order through the tongue, word-herald."[52] Standing in the Protagorean myth as the figure of Zeus is Theseus. He makes speech the figurative cause and effect of civilization. Speech is the escape from violence and chaos. The topic of "escape," in effect, animates speech as a tamer of humans; it enables them to create bonds of friendship among strangers.

I would like to think that the category *human* as it is carried in images, myth, stories, and legends is inclusive.[53] In an ordinary way, I can imagine actual bodies of women and men working together to make decisions; as a result, tyranny is overpowered and democracy is invented, along with its use of speech to settle differences. The story of the Portrait Monument tells of this dream. As the three women individually and collectively follow the appeal of Speech and thus aspire to escape the tyranny (of subordination), they enter the house of rhetoric where they mount speaker platforms, organize conventions on women's rights, and lead a fight for the vote.

While both myths hold out the dream that the house of rhetoric *in theory* will be one inclusive of women and men, the actual building, constructing, and legitimizing of the house fell not to the whole society but to men who imagined their political existence in terms of how they fit together equally with other men (of a similar type). As for women, their political and rhetorical status is configured not as agent, leader, or decision maker. In the house of rhetoric where relationships of authority are constructed or legitimized, women are assigned a role on the grounds that they do not have the capacity to make a decision. In this organization, they speak from below. The Portrait Monument's location in the basement is the social residue of this structure. Women's participation—for example, on the speaker's platform—does not change the process of decision making that is constructed to exclude them. In fact, the women's placement in the Capitol—the analogical house of rhetoric—illustrates their role as subordinate even while women respond to their exclusion.

So, while the ancients dreamed of escaping from the wild by building a house of rhetoric, their escape trapped or silenced the dream of full participation. It contained only a limited kind of freedom, one based on hierarchy that establishes (the meaning of) bodily differences. As W. W. Fortenbaugh explains it, these differences are based on the (bodily) virtue of courage. Men have the "courage to command" and women possess the "courage of subordination."[54] In rhetorical terms, men—defined as decision makers or judges—can decide what they will do and whether they will obey.[55] This is not true for women since they are not fit psychologically to be decision makers.

Now I turn to the second use of escape—namely, escaping from an artless and unstudied use of rhetoric. This aspect of the topical plane led to a building site where humans in an abstract conceptual sense gather. So the humans escape into art. As they do, they are ordered in a way that subordinates women's authority through a direct reference to the "relationship between emotion and reason."[56] The role of women is likened to the role of emotion; it accompanies reason. The escape from an artless and unstudied use of rhetoric is achieved by turning wild poetic language into the rational modes of discourse. In the mythic sense, the conceptualization of rhetoric refers to the primal gestures of getting around the tyrants by claiming speech rationally and then taking possession of the claim by staking out a practice of civic discourse.

Historically women have been yoked to this "wild and poetic" use of language.[57] Attached to emotion rather than reason, such use of speech does not deny women the capacity to reason. Nevertheless, it demands a subordinate role or function. If they were to assume a deliberative manner, even one modest by manly standards, it would call them out as "chatterers,"[58] and this chattering reveals the weakness of their capacity for deliberation. Within the yoking of women's voices to emotion lies the semantic force of *idiosis idios*, the English cognate of idiot. [59] The wild and poetic style, because it appears to embrace puerile characteristics, expresses confused propositions. To raise the category of the idiot and put it in the body of women turns their speech into something accidental, abnormal, and unusual. Their wild and poetic use of language in relation to the house means that women's speech cannot meet a determinate end, a requirement of rational discourse qua art. This is so because wild and poetic language is not in the periodic style. Thus it does not have end points—literally periods or stops that typify the determinate end in everyday, rational discourse. [60] While women go into the house (with men), women's speech is not of it.

The poetic manner of speaking reflects the alogical or emotional part of the psychology of women. This deficiency of style does not rob women of their humanity. Rather, it sets up a structure of subordination within the house of rhetoric. Even if women gain access or exude a power to achieve a goal, they remain unfit for making decisions and for leadership because their deliberative capacity remains in service to emotions, not reason. By some accounts, their wild and poetic use of language is formulated as a sign of a corruption, imperfection, a deformity possessed in their bodies, and this is why their speech is accidental, abnormal, and unusual. [61]

On this plane, I find under the direction of Ernesto Grassi [62] shards of examples in which women's speech neither initiates a productive interaction nor properly models the dynamics of rational interaction. [63] In *Agamemnon*, Cassandra speaks like a bird, speech that is hard to grasp, bewildering, and barbarian, wild like the swallow's song. [64] In Euripides, women's actions are compared to animals acting irrationally. [65] In *Bacchae*, the Herdsmen depict them with wings, swooping down upon the herds of cattle. Apparently, such speech is too free and loose inside the polis and dirties the goal or purpose of the civic realm. [66] Speaking like a barbarian or bird that has escaped its cage means that a woman's speech bears little, if any, semantic relation to the voice of a male citizen who speaks in the periodic manner. In the house of rhetoric where the need for forethought comes into play, the female form of cognition tends to manifest itself as chatter in flighty, bird-like ways, while that of the man's voice is endowed with the capacity of decisive leadership because it reaches rational end points. While both men and women share a cognitive capacity, women need guidance when it comes to reason. Although women can perceive reason, they cannot reason. This gender division based on a bipartite psychology has specified the proper role of women in rhetoric for centuries and centuries. [67]

By escaping the wild use of language and embracing the rational modes, the "art" of rhetoric forms a context—or domicile—for public address and evaluation. Having turned speech into a *technology* or studied art, the speaker and the listener are connected by formal principles of speech that are taken as an invisible foundation for a polis, a sociopolitical realm conceived as democratic. Those women—like Elizabeth Cady Stanton—who by speaking against the tyranny of man claim for themselves an escape to rhetoric do so outside the house: that is, where it is wild and bestial. (Is it any wonder they are called pioneer orators?) Because the women claim they are fit for leadership, they threaten the limits and the founding principles of speech. As women gain access to rhetoric's resources, their presence troubles the very way rhetorical existence is imagined. How to reconcile the escape from the wild, poetic use of language that women's cognitive capacity subsumes with the systematization of rhetoric where reasoning is the most effective at discovering the means to achieve a desired goal?

The two first notions of escape (figure 1.2) involve a theory of rhetoric itself as holding down the fort—repeating, reasserting, and implementing its context and itself (something like Congress sending the stone to the basement). Together the two first senses of escape conspire to support the house's mission of deliberative action with reason rooted in authority strictly and properly seated in the souls of men. In this sense, the word *escape* lingers in the social as a form of expansion and innovation. It entails not only getting out of poetic language but also keeping order in the house and using its decision-making process systematically. When women and the question of authority are coupled, they serve as a provocation to integrate women into a traditional male bastion.

Finally, there is the third sense of escape. According to the *OED*, *escape* can also be a noun. Escape has a strong sense of place, loosely as in "Let's make a great escape." Architecturally, the notion of *escape* denotes a column in architecture. The *OED* defines escape as the apophyge (the part of the Corinthian column where it springs out of its base, or joins its capital, usually molded into a concave sweep or cavetto). The third sense of *escape*—the column or vertical structure—has such a strong physical connotation that it envisages speech as a house. This verticality in escape includes not only the column but also implies the upright body speaking, as when people escape tyranny and set up the political realm as their own, not as they are told to do.

As people stake their world and plant their post to signify it, they cast a shadow around them in the form of the civic sphere. As Joseph Rykwert puts it, the escape or column is "an act of taking possession of a ground: every such post implies a circle around itself if only because of the shadow that it casts, whose direction will always be parallel to that cast by my upright body."[68] The setting of a post can be seen in rhetoric as an act of shading in the form of a circular process of decision making—specifically a palindrome. The house designed with escape in mind is set up to be always already parallel to the male speaking body.

This is the body that plants the post and in doing so casts the shadow around which the civic realm is conceived. The escape—from the language of the wild beast and figurative modes of expression to the domesticated man and his rational modes of persuasion—is, in the end, to know the "orthogonality" of the male "body to the ground."[69] The relationship between column and male body is eventually translated in the image of the podium as the post of a decidedly male authority.

To place women in the Capitol Rotunda, therefore, would unsettle the structural integrity, the three aspects of escape—freedom, systematization, and column—on which the house rests.

Structural Plane

The structural plane denotes the action, the way the edifice is put together. So now we're dealing with what the construction workers did on the job site. On this plane, I show how "speaking subjects" become "political animals" and thus related to "manger-fellows." The relationship between "political animals" and "manger-fellows" is referential and built into the agora, with the manger being the visible space of political, social, and economic exchange. To render the agora visible, I picture it as "speaking in the middle."[70] Distinct from the middle voice, speaking in the middle entails making space, namely a circular pattern—a palindrome—cast by the shadow of the male body standing at the podium (figure 1.3).

Insofar as political animals in this structural plane also move within the escape modes of the topical plane, their speaking not only constitutes them as subjects but also satisfies the form of the house in which they speak. These political animals engage in the process of building in three distinct ways: domestication, art, and architecture. Because domesticated animals feed in a manger, unlike animals living in the wild, I'll use this manger metaphor to index moves from domestication to art and from art to architecture. The manger is a key metaphor for retelling the story, myth, and legend of the escape—that of being released from the dangers of finding food. In this sense, the manger becomes a temporary house, a raised mound, where "political animals" would enter and base their appeals. This raised mound, while it may grow at a moment's notice, such as in the case of an emergency, also accrues over time as a stable, regular formation for doing/speaking ordinary business. In time, a manger stresses spatial proxemics as people wallow together. The manger starts as a proximal sign of closeness—like everyone eating in a family or banquet style—and moves to a sign of public distance—like an invited speaker sitting at a table apart from everyone at a ban-

Figure 1.3. Structural plane.

political animals	manger-fellows/agora
political animals	boustrophedon—"speaking in the middle"
political animals	podium

quet. Analogically speaking, as the manger-fellows' relations become more and more formal (political and hierarchical) and less familiar (intimate), they gather in the house according to their roles. As the roles at the manger establish distance among the gatherers and as the house expands its size, not only is a certain inaccessibility of a speaker/man/person (of a certain type) established but also power is entrenched as above or far from the group.

The human manger as an escape shows how speech functions to keep humans intimately in the city and away from living like wild beasts and acting impulsively. The manger of the body (of speech and speaker) is the stomach, located at the midriff; so, too, the manger of rhetoric appears in the "middle" of the city. This is the agora, the marketplace in ancient Greece. Metaphorically speaking, the agora is the city's midriff, the "belly" of the body politic. In this respect, the agora functions as the "umbilicus in the human body . . . and the reason for this analogy is the following: since human nature first takes all its nourishment through the umbilicus, so through the public square all the other places [of the city] are nourished."[71] The city is a body; the body is a house; the agora is the belly of the body and the center of the house. We are now in a position to see why, *as political animals*, humans are free to gather in the agora and to converse and create communal bonds.

In the city's midriff, one speaker appeals to another; and in that process of exchange, people solve problems and make decisions through speech on how to live and what to do in the face of uncertainty. It is no wonder that the "political animals" are, in the language of Aristotle, defined as manger-fellows (*homokapous*).[72] Public speaking is "political animal" food, and to partake of it is to be released from the dangerous impulses and desires of an individual (read: tyrant and women). From stomach to manger to agora, speech is the escape from the wild and the mainstay for holding desire in common. This is good order that moves around the middle. By the social conduct that the movement demands, the distance between speaker and audience grows formal, turning the agora into more of a sacred spot (symbolized by a podium) than a manger.

Marcel Detienne refers to the order and the movement around a sacred spot such as the agora as "speaking in the middle."[73] The phrase collapses the temporal demands of speaking within a definite space as arrangement. "Speaking in the middle" is a gathering in the here and now and refers to men faced with the project of deciding a future. In his study of the secularization of speech, Detienne describes this space as a system in which opinions could be distributed around the hearth of the city. His primary image is that of Greek warriors seated in a circle. This image conveys the idea of equal and similar soldier-citizens engaged in "dialogue-speech." Focusing on political reforms in about 650 B.C., Detienne shows how dialogue-speech develops through the practice of soldier-citizens deliberating over booty. He notes that setting prizes, women, horses, gray iron, and other treasures in the middle of the military assembly enacted a ritual of turning individual property into things that are held in common. As for what is held in common, Demosthenes, for example, speaks of the open prizes of war and re-creates the condition of their distribution as being in the middle.

Only those who had been physically present in the middle of battle could participate in the ritual of going to the center where the loot was brought and engage in a process of exchange. Going to and from the middle meant that the soldier-citizen could obtain a portion of the spoils of war. So while a man may have been under the rule of a commander during the military operation, his subordination is dissolved through the practice of distribution and exchange.[74] Also as platoons of men participate in this ritual, they were each fit to enter the middle, thus symbolically creating their status as ruler, albeit briefly. And so if only those who fought in wars could enter the circle of deliberation, again, women were excluded.[75]

The ritual of setting booty in the middle ushered in the practice of voicing opinions in the middle and treating them as communal affairs.[76] Telemachus, for example, speaks in the middle of the assembly.[77] In effect, his words are like the performance of the warrior setting down booty in the middle. Thus, the ritual of speaking in the middle enacts a pattern of going over/through, which in turn forges a container for holding the affairs of the community together.

Speaking in the middle founds deliberative public speaking. As Detienne points out, "The expression 'to deliberate on the course of behavior to be adopted' is rendered in Greek as 'to set the matter down the middle.'"[78] The notion of "speaking in the middle" denotes a physical space of politics rather than a metaphysical concept.[79] It appears to articulate the manger with the agora. The human act of going back over and through again in the process of exchanging opinion turns rhetoric into a house, much like domesticated animals such as oxen plowing the field.

To amplify the space of speech, I return to the manger and the navel theme of domestication. Oxen are fed at the manger so they are able to plow. Plowing extends the navel theme of manger to escape and reveals how human manger-fellows, like oxen, if attached to the plow, would have the traction needed for overcoming tyranny. Plowing anticipates the nonverbal dimension (expressed in the myth of Corax), in which the people press their point, applying what was said to the opinion of another by means of hands and feet (since the tyrants forbade speaking). The repeated efforts of going to and withdrawing from the middle mark the space of decision making in a distinctive pattern called *boustrophedon*. The boustrophedon pattern is like the successive furrows made by a plow.[80] In ancient Greece, boustrophedon refers to a writing/speaking that goes back and forth, or from left to right and then right to left, as oxen turn when plowing the fields.[81] From the standpoint of the structural plane, boustrophedon refers to a specific *habit* of speaking, a corporeal turning around marked specifically by feet or strophe. This turning articulates a distinct kind of running-back-and-forth movement until a convincing agreement is reached; thus the iterative pattern induces procedures and institutes a particular direction or an end to space. Taking one's opinion to the middle for the purposes of public deliberation favored a spatial design in which this might optimally occur. The speaker entered the middle by stepping onto a raised circular mound called the *bēma*, a place to speak from in a public assembly. To step onto this place is to enter public life (*epi to bēma anabēnai*).

From the standpoint of spatial design, the *bēma* is the material site for the distribution of words—to and from the middle—that preceded human action. We are familiar with this site as the podium, as it constitutes the place from which we engage in public discussion before embarking on a course of action. The podium is also a miniature manger, the umbilicus that nourishes the middle as it grows into a house. Characteristically, the podium—the mound—also denotes the standing of the warrior-citizen who can take his place on the floor. His standing body echoes the column, the architectural escape rhetoric signifies to the world about its context and itself.

Plane of Characterization

So now the concrete foundation is poured and the construction crew has framed the house. Now the carpenters enter it and begin the work on details. These are character/ethos, style, and their propositional relation to authority (figure 1.4). This work reveals the extent to which character stems from the structure of rhetoric; the structure of rhetoric makes claims about character.

If the two myths provide the topical directions for how to build the façade of the house of rhetoric, the following passage serves to summarize the distinctions

Figure 1.4. Plane of characterization.

defeat tyranny	ethos/ēthos
defeat tyranny	antistrophe and subset katastrophe
defeat tyranny	ekklēsia and epithet of authority

I want to make regarding the interior décor: "It may be seen that all the peoples of Greece possessing the best governments *engage in discussion before embarking on action*, well knowing that the consideration of what is expedient by means of discussion is the house [*oikodomēmatōn*] of safety."[82] The house is organic and in the process of building a particular kind of structure, one that keeps humans safe from tyranny and violence. The process involves constructing a system for how to act, live, and function in order to conduct political affairs and do the business of rhetorical deliberation. Specifically, the detail work involves deftly crafting character/ethics, disposition/style/manner, and authority so that the interior décor fits with the façade. For this reason, I go back to the two previous planes to display the articulation between them and the plane of characterization.

Manger-fellows or political animals speaking in the middle of the agora help us see bodies doing the process, whether envisioned as oxen plowing back and forth in a boustrophedonic manner or as citizen-soldiers going to the middle where they enact a boustrophedon effect of speaking by sorting out, exchanging, and distributing booty by going to and from the middle. As the people, not just citizen-soldiers, enact the process they make their first escape by defeating tyranny. In effect, *ēthos*, or character, typifies the body politic going around the tyrant, thus leaving this undemocratic form of interaction behind and then plowing a space through the wilds of speech.

Character does not refer to an individual but to a more general type, like a mask. In this way, character both conceals and reveals the façade of the house. While character speaks of the body politic as escaping en masse a way of settling disputes through violence, character, under the mask of a figure, like Corax, speaks of escape as heroic, as he taught the body politic how to speak or how to get around the violence of tyranny. In this way character begins to enact the role of the head/speaker who addresses the political realm—like at a banquet table within the house—for the benefit of the people.

Character, in the sense of the body politic that houses rhetoric, must be of high moral standing as it goes to and from the middle. As Aristotle explains it, the proper development of character (*ēthos*) comes, etymologically speaking, from the habits of animals (*apo ethous*). In these habits lie the mores of speech.[83]

Ethos, as Charles Chamberlain has shown, refers to the haunts of animals, the places where animals are found because they are accustomed to these places.[84] Feeding warrants the move from *ethos* with animals to *ēthos* or human character. As oxen can be tamed, so the character of speakers can be trained or moored in the city's midriff, the agora. As for the architectural component of escape, the domesticated animal disposed at the manger is the anchor or the post that holds humans to a concept of political animal or "manger-fellows" upon which "character" or *ēthos* emerges in the house of rhetoric. The manger or agora constitutes the column upon which moral character is moored and trained.

Through the training of moral character, citizens are exempt [*apatheis einai*] from some wild forms of emotion.[85] That is the second way tyranny is defeated. Character or *ēthos,* the offspring of speech, suggests an actor above the fray (or at the head of the banquet table). By separating himself from the rest, character acquires aspects of authority. One way to flesh out this authority is to see how it interrelates with habits. Ethical character is, in effect, a performance appropriate to the ritual of going to and from the manger, which is nothing less than the habits of style.[86] While animal habits involve rituals of feeding—regularly going to the manger—habits or customs of a speaking community deal with what is generally true of most people. Good character is revealed in and through appropriate speaking and is recognizable in phrases such as "what is generally the case" or "what is usually true." Using proper habits of style, the speaker invites the hearer to share the view (*doxa*) held in common by the body politic. As Aristotle explains it, a speaker might, for example, say, "Who does not know?" or "Everybody knows." In this manner, the speech of the midriff-agora wards off impulsivity or unnatural or untamed behaviors such as the "fancies of crazy people" that constitute, at best, false reasoning (*paralogos*) and, at worst, silly talk (*paralērēma*).[87] It is the business of rhetoric to speak of what is usually the case or what happens for the most part. The enthymeme, Aristotle's major contribution to rhetoric, is the best example of this. The enthymeme, unlike the syllogism, suppresses its major premise because, since everybody already knows it, there is no reason to state it.[88]

Habits of style constrain impulses of hearers because style is a manner of speaking meant to bring the hearers' opinions to the manger, where they are shared and mulled over with other political animals—or manger-fellows, as Aristotle refers to them. The character of the speaker is contained, if you will, at the manger. As such, the human that once acted like a cyclops through impulses (*hormas*) and desires now has them domesticated at the manger. A speaker's talk resonates with the shared habits, manners, and customs of a community; these habits shape character.[89] The midriff-agora or "common hearth" is the architectural escape/manger for shaping character. By habitually going to and from the site, humans make space that secures a "natural"[90] or habituated site of freedom. In sum, character defeats tyranny not by critical powers but by a deliberative capacity defined by the escape from the wild, the structuring of space, and the attainment of studied performances.

The plane of characterization portrays character and the moral reasoning it must command as growing out of a disposition of corporeal habits—that of going back and forth to the manger/middle. Aristotle intellectualizes the embodied activity of going back and forth as a style and then he defines what rhetoric is, schematizing its primary mode of persuasion as rational. The style is called antistrophic and it is related rationally to dialectic. In fact, Aristotle opens his *Rhetoric* by saying that rhetoric is the counterpart (Gk. *antistrophos*) to dialectic. Many commentators have explored the relationship between rhetoric and dialectic. It is generally accepted that the relationship is best understood in terms of the actions of the chorus in ancient Greek theater. Many see "strophe" as a vestige of the body, namely feet that turn, as in the choral strophe, or turns, in various songs and dances in drama. Along these lines, J. H. Freese (translator) explains *antistrophos* as counterpart: "Not an exact copy, but making a kind of pair with it, and corresponding to it as the antistrophe to the strophe in a choral ode."[91] So understood, the activity of speaking may be likened to the strophe or movement of the choral dance, the returning of the chorus to answer a previous strophe. This dance recapitulates the boustrophedon effect created all the way back by the citizen-soldier going to and from the middle. So the middle is not a grammatical unit as in the middle voice. This middle is a space generated by the warrior-citizen's foot traffic. Following the grooved pattern, the body in motion animates the process of going back over and through again or, conversely, the process is derivative of bodies architecting space. The radical implication of the middle I am suggesting here is that space, not time, precedes change. As for the Greeks, the subject (here rhetoric) emerges in the course of architecting a space of rhetoric that previously did not cohere (arch-technically) as a system of coping with change and the demands of temporality.

Now the pairing of the character's movement in rhetoric with dialectic prolongs the rational mode into dispositions of power and authority through the antistrophic style of speaking. To trace the relationship among *ēthos*, authority, and style, I turn to the way Aristotle articulates rhetoric in relation to dialectic as antistrophic and as "catastrophe," a subset of antistrophe and the strophe that "turns down." The tradition of speech, as Mari Lee Mifsud and I have put it, "is most familiar with catastrophe through Aristotle's *lexis katestrammenē* (a participle of *katastrephō*, the verbal form *katastrophē*)." *Katestrammenē* is Aristotle's word for "periodic style," one that brings an audience "to a pleasant end or rest."[92] Spatially, speech is encumbered with "turning down" steps, and this characteristic manner of moving to an end marks the deliberative style of speaking. Rhetoric is recognizable as an iterate space insofar as it uses a periodic style of going back and forth as opposed to the paratactic style of wild poetic discourse that goes on and on in the manner of the running style or *lexis eiromene*. To speak in the periodic style is to command *ēthos* and to exude authority.

The structure of rhetoric constrains how it can be practiced. As a space, rhetoric is a style unsuited primarily for running or wandering, as in getting off the subject. The house characterizes the manner for staying on course, settling arguments by moving back and forth, and thus bringing matters to an end. Buried in this rational structure is the actual body that characterizes the disposition of power and authority. These are the bones of character out of which the structure of rhetoric is animated. I can now unearth and gather the bones of the body and speech and reconstruct it.

On the structural plane, the bones of the body of speech were those of the warrior-citizen. They were strewn around the middle, where people came together, talked about possibilities, debated them, and then set their future courses of action. Now set in the system of deliberation, the bones signify a body type, and this type of speaker assumes the quality of authority. The sex of the body type of speech is male. Sex in speech is distinguished biologically. This is not by sex organs but by the organ of the heart. The heart of the male (not male slaves) possesses authority (*kuron*), while the female heart lacks the capacity to make decisions.[93] The female speaker is without authority (*akuron*). The house of rhetoric, as a site of freedom, agency, and contingency, admits exceptions, and Aristotle is the first to acknowledge the possibility that some women could possess a heart capable of evolving to a higher level. However, for the most part, women when compared to men are "more false of speech"[94] and thus the sex of the body of speech is marked male. Now that the body of speech has been resurrected, I go to the fourth plane—the tropological.

The Tropological Plane

The tropological plane is the integration of the other planes into an inseparable whole—as context and as itself (figure 1.5). The context of rhetoric is now realized as the palindrome of <CIVIC>, and this implicates rhetoric itself as a character that typifies the process of decision making. In terms of analysis, <CIVIC> is the theme of rhetoric. All the planes specify the house by exerting an influence on it. They hold and contain the diverse and contingent activity of speaking. Without

Figure 1.5. Tropological plane.

civic discourse	disposition
civic discourse	body-character
civic discourse	palindrome

these planes and the categories, the house could not be identified or schematized as rhetoric. It is precisely these planes that determine the role of civic discourse and the structure of relations within it. Finally, the tropological plane transforms the body of speech into tropes. Tropes are vestiges of the body.

I connected the body of speech with the actions of the body of the male warrior-citizen. Specifically, the details and particularity of the house as structure were used to picture the (tropical) movement of the male body doing rhetoric, which entails a process of going over/through again matters until a convincing agreement is reached. On this basis, I then posited this male body within the practice and theory of rhetoric. The male body-head of household, as it were, founds the enduring principle of character (ēthos, ethics), which remains to this day crucial in judging a person's speech. This is so because the heart in the male body, not the female one, houses practical wisdom.

Now as I move through the tropological plane, I see tropes in the place of the male body. Here tropes denote the figural forms of his authority and performances of it. The remainder of this chapter details the figural form of the male body, noting in particular how the form is implicated in the structure of the house. In the next chapter I offer a discussion of how the tropes are involved in setting up and analyzing character as an embodied practice of authority. Also, insofar as the tropes oversee the dynamics of change that women seek within the house, I detail how tropes are themselves *performances* of character, enacting the linguistic structure of the trope itself.[95] In this way they do the work of denying women their status as leaders.

The trope that the house possesses about its figural form (of the male body) is affixed to the *Ekklēsia* or public assembly. As the actual building, it bears the epithet (which is a trope) of "authority" or *kuron*.[96] *Kuria Ekklēsia* denotes an assembly that is appointed or approved as a gathering place that can rise (or be built up as such) in ordinary circumstances. This rising up over time becomes the house of rhetoric qua house upholding rhetoric as a fixed and regular system of decision making. Moreover, this secondary tropological application of *Kuron* turns the space into who has "the best right" to be there.[97] Those who have the best right are (free) men because they alone possess the capacity for deliberation. The epithet of *kuron* or trope of authority on the side of the building (*Kuria Ekklēsia*) signifies the primal post—the architectural escape column—that established the foundation of the house of rhetoric. In effect, the epithet pretends to be the house's columns because in rhetoric the concept authority is a stock theoretical form used to hold up and display good character in the house of rhetoric. The epithet says who can speak and where within its domicile. The trope—epithet—of authority determines who has the prerequisite to step onto the platform and sit in the high seats.

Women do not meet the prerequisite. The want of their deliberative capacity of authority is the heart. For Aristotle, the heart is the organ of the soul. *Kardia*, "heart," is the organ and organizing principle of the space of deliberation. The heart is the countenance of rhetoric. Specifically, in discussions of moral choice (*phronesis*), the Heart (*kardia*) was considered the seat of deliberation.[98] Heart, rather than mind, suffuses the speaker with authority. The union of these two—moral choice and heart—is not only critical to the soundness and the goodness of decision making but, as the epithet (*kurios*) reveals, heart (i.e., authority) constitutes the body part or the prerequisite for entering into the building site of deliberation. This union of heart and authority resounds in the enduring principle of character (*ēthos*).

In fact, women's lack of authority in the city-state is the kind of sociopolitical world recommended by Aristotle.[99] It keeps women in their place—in the basement of the house of rhetoric—since women alone have the power of using speech in false ways. Aristotle's opinion of women as being more false of speech than men becomes all the more significant when linguistic evidence is taken into account. Emile Benveniste in his study of Indo-European language observes that the linguistic tissue of rhetoric for women's speech generally denotes "what is nothing but words, what has no basis in reality."[100] When women speak deliberatively and, therefore, fraudulently, their speaking, Aristotle tells us in the *Rhetoric*,[101] can be declared void like a legal contract. For Congress to authorize the public display of Elizabeth Cady Stanton, Lucretia Mott, and Susan B. Anthony in the basement declares their speech *akuron*, turns it down as fraudulent and thus, in effect, voids it. What is voided is the political status of women as voters/citizens/speakers.

So the structure of rhetoric weakens women's right to speak even as they move into places of power and authority. The house may beckon toward their inclusion, but their character/voice/ethos/heart is designated without authority. Women who do make oral contact with the public realm are inscribed as images in terms of bestiality and unrestraint. Thus the inclusion of women in rhetoric always already turns into exclusion as their speech is marked as having no place at the helm of the politic.[102]

The trope of authority set in stone on the ancient assembly casts women out of the house. As such the epithet (*kurios*), insofar as it denotes authority, is not redundant (as some might claim of an epithet) but is meant to add something to the meaning and thereby develop the *ekklēsia* or public assembly accordingly.[103] *Kurios*, therefore, is not some little tack on or mere accessory to the space of the assembly but rather a significant factor that makes it possible to see how the space is magnetized in a figural way. In effect, the epithet engenders a space called <CIVIC> discourse.

The body of speech is character and character is housed in practical wisdom, and this house is the heart and the heart comprises the principal *organization* of the house of rhetoric. As the pillar of influence and right action, the male body prefigures the space of speech as a mode of order instilling freedom and agency. This order is engendered by a kind of speaking called speaking in the middle. This pattern is a trope called a palindrome ("running back again"). Insofar as a palindrome such as *civic* can be read the same forward and backward, rhetoric, speaking architecturally, may very well have a domed-shaped roof. The forward and backward movement within the palindrome of the *civic* grammatically is the interaction figured as a style called *periodos*, which is a path "around," sometimes pictured as a cupola. The structure in which the palindrome is enacted is the stairs—the separate and interrelated movements—in the house. The stairs indicate the kind of participation in rhetoric appropriate to the male and female. The male because he inhabits the body of the male citizen-warrior has authority to go up the stairs to command or lead and the female who gains access in the house goes down the stairs, an enactive gesture denoting her courage of subordination.

From the bottom of the stairs, I open the cellar door and, grasping its four planes, I crawl up the palindrome's steep grade from myth to the space it makes. As I do, I stop, turn, and look down, taking in the view—how the house floor is laid out aesthetically and systematically in a dominant tropical mode of a palindrome. The palindrome of the <CIVIC> refers, then, to an architectural model that rhetoric possesses about its context and itself, defined in the house as good moral character/ethos. As for the context it possesses, rhetoric finds in its beginning a form of freedom and agency related to speaking.[104] The form entails a process of making a decision about a future course of action. This, too, is an upward movement, characterized by the vigorous activity of forward thinking.

From the top of the stairs, I look back to see the body of the male warrior-citizen in the act of going to and from the middle. As he speaks, he morphs into the body of speech—the schema of thought about speech as well as its practice. From this body of speech emerges rhetoric itself.

The self, distinguished compositionally and performatively, and psychologically, stands as "the body of speech." This body has two reference points. First, it refers to someone—a human body—speaking/doing/delivering/embodying rhetoric. The human body—actually the male form—doing rhetoric is largely covered over by the systematization of rhetoric.[105] The second point to which the body of speech refers is of rhetoric acquiring an ability, quality, or characteristic to do civic discourse—the very house work of rhetoric. The body of speech is a practice that enables rhetoric itself to take charge of its theoretical house and thus assert unity and stability on which the world could stake its claim against tyranny. As a model invested in a high sense of freedom and agency, rhetoric's model house is, therefore, open to change, but nevertheless, it restricts access within its house with tropes. Now with one eye on rhetoric's context and one eye on rhetoric's self, I take one last step and go to the next chapter to explain what happens when women are added to the house of rhetoric.

As I do, I note a seam between houses—the lower (palindrome of the <CIVIC>) and upper (archi-technical frame) melding the received tradition of Athens with America. The house extends beyond Athens into America. Two examples may be cited to briefly illustrate the projection.[106] Here is the first example, from the nineteenth century. Declaring Aristotle the best of the ancients, Richard Whately's textbook *Elements of Rhetoric* had fifty-one American editions from the years 1828–1929.[107] Each generation was brought up in the house that Aristotle built, creating a sense of the meaning of civic discourse and the role of participants in a democracy. Nowhere is an Athenian American house of rhetoric more vested than in the identity of the graduate—that carrier of its blueprints. George William Curtis's "The Public Duty of Educated Men," delivered at the commencement of Union College on June 27, 1877, is such a speech. From the beginning Curtis makes clear that his thesis is "a lesson of startling cogency and power from the history of Greece for the welfare of America."[108] The lesson is this: rhetoric is a great "temple." And by "swiftly passing from the Athenian agora to the Boston town meeting," rhetoric and its principles found and secure the site of democracy.[109] By conjoining the Athenian agora to Boston, the Bunker Hill of American democracy, the graduate is transformed into a peripatetic citizen. The transformation of the student to a rhetorical subject of democracy enacts the process of building the house of rhetoric. As John Quincy Adams put it, "Let him catch from the relics of ancient oratory those unresisted powers, which mould the mind of man to the will of the speaker, and yield the guidance of the nation to the dominion of the voice."[110]

Here is the second example, from the twentieth century, of the ancient house of rhetoric protruding into the contemporary world. In the last dozen years, the National Communication Association's newsletter, *Spectra*, reported an "explosion of interest in Aristotle's rhetorical theory."[111] Indeed, in departments associated with rhetoric in the United States, the study of Aristotle has been enjoying a renewal of sorts. At the 1996 National Communication Association convention, James Hikins led a seminar titled "The Aristotelian Renaissance in Contemporary Rhetorical Theory." That the field is in the midst of an Aristotelian renaissance is evident not only in programs at the convention but also in several distinguished books and articles published recently on Aristotle. The main authors of this renaissance include Thomas Farrell, Eugene Garver, Gerard Hauser, Jasper Neel, Alan Gross, David Furley, Alexander Nehamas, Amélie Rorty, and Arthur Walzer.[112] Like the previous century, this one also turns toward the ideas of democracy that are presumed to exist behind rhetoric. Hauser and Amy Grim's *Rhetorical Democracy* as well as Robert Ivie's work on democratic deliberation, especially that which draws from Chantal Mouffe, stand out.[113] Past themes of rhetorical democracy expressed in commencement addresses resonate with messages articulated in a variety of contemporary books and articles. The message is clear: the Aristotelian tradition of rhetoric has positive functions from which a political world of inclusion, cooperation, and mutual respect might be provided.[114]

There is, therefore, through the medium of textbooks and graduation speeches, a house of rhetoric as the ancient world projects it in the United States.[115] As these forms illuminate the possibility of speech, they also darken it. This is particularly evident from what Henry James noted about "our speech." In his "The Speech of American Women" published in *Harper's Bazaar*, he claims that our speech is "threatened by . . . its female population as they claim political equality with men."[116] Figuring out how and why rhetoric denies authority to women is particularly urgent once we remember President's Obama executive order establishing a committee to ask hard questions about why women en masse do not occupy the high seats.

So as I leave the basement and go up the stairs, I enter the United States only to enter a time of night.

2

What Time o' Night It Is

Sometimes I was in their house, sometimes I was with them.

—Epicharmus

By the time I reach the top of the stairs, the atmo*sphere* becomes palpable. I enter into the house of rhetoric above ground—that world where rhetoric envelops the contemporary sociopolitical atmo*sphere*, like a frame of a house.[1] As it becomes more and more tangible, the atmo*sphere* actually gathers a material weight as it shifts from a figural dimension to a concrete one. So as I reach the top of the stairs, I exit the deepest ancient region of the house and enter another building, the U.S. Capitol. Analogically speaking, the Capitol stands in concretely for the house of rhetoric whereas before—when I was digging beneath the house— the Capitol stood for the palindrome of the <CIVIC>. The Capitol continues to be my dynamic point of departure for leaping from one house to another and back.

I have been in the basement and haunted for over a decade. I had gone down to see the monument to Lucretia Mott, Elizabeth Cady Stanton, and Susan B. Anthony. Now I see it in the Rotunda. Rising behind the three women like a mountain is a fourteen-thousand-pound mass of stone (figures 2.1 and 2.2). The large blank section of stone should be Sojourner Truth.[2] And then again, it could be no one—just an "uncarved block of rock . . . there to haunt us. We should let it haunt us."[3] Perhaps it is anticipating a fourth figure, yet unknown but in full possession of authority. In fact, she may have already arrived, as some imagine the fourth figure is Rosa Parks.[4] At the very least, the portion not yet hewn could be, as the sculptor Adelaide Johnson declared, the "true spirit"[5] as well as the unfinished business awaiting women in a democracy. The inscription at the base of the monument stenciled on the backside seems to corroborate this interpretation.

Figure 2.1. The Portrait Monument to Lucretia Mott, Elizabeth Cady Stanton, and Susan B. Anthony. Photograph courtesy Dave Swanson.

Figure 2.2. Pioneers for women's suffrage. *From left to right:* Elizabeth Cady Stanton, Susan B. Anthony, Lucretia Mott. Photograph courtesy Dave Swanson.

I did not see the inscription in 1983. Apparently, when the monument arrived in 1921, it *had* a 232-word inscription stenciled at its base, a portion of which reads: "WOMAN, FIRST DENIED A SOUL, THEN CALLED MINDLESS, NOW ARISEN DECLARED HERSELF AN ENTITY TO BE RECKONED. SPIRITUALLY THE WOMAN MOVEMENT IS THE ALL-ENFOLDING ONE. IT REPRESENTS THE EMANCIPATION OF WOMANHOOD. THE RELEASE OF THE FEMININE PRINCIPLE IN HUMANITY. THE MORAL INTEGRATION OF HUMAN EVOLUTION COME TO RESCUE TORN AND STRUGGLING HUMANITY FROM ITS SAVAGE SELF."[6] While the Office of the Curator duly records that there *had been* an inscription, I did not know until later what happened to it. In her report on the monument, Susan Brandell writes that after it was first delivered, the "gold-gilt inscription" was "whitewashed" to make it "unreadable."[7] The inscription deemed "pagan"[8] was called "blasphemous,"[9] and at the direction of the Joint Committee on the Library the lettering was removed, a process required "before it was taken into the Rotunda" and then the statue "was veiled in suffrage yellow."[10]

Nevertheless, its arrival marked a day of celebration. The unveiling ceremony was held in the Rotunda on February 15, 1921, for the 101st anniversary of the birth of Susan B. Anthony. The ceremony was attended by representatives of over seventy women's organizations. Members of the National Women's Party referred to the statue as the "Victory Monument"[11] and thought the receiving of it in the Rotunda a breakthrough of the feminist spirit.[12] Pundits, however, responded differently. They called it "Three Ladies in a Bathtub," an epithet that came to signify the presence of women in the Rotunda in the days preceding the congressional judgment of its position in the Capitol.

The ceremony in 1997 was similar. The *Chicago Tribune* reported, "More than 600 women's rights activists, tourists, members of Congress, government officials, and teenage girls in modern-day, mini-skirted white suffragette costumes jammed the Rotunda for the reinstallation, which replicated the first and very brief placement of the statue there 76 years ago."[13] Pundits said the statue was "too ugly,"[14] a complaint echoing the epitaph "Three Ladies in a Bathtub"[15] applied decades earlier to mark the statue's ugliness. The symmetry of language used then and now to warrant the statue's exclusion from the house is too striking to ignore. In 1921 and in 1997, the appearance of the sculpted women is rendered inappropriate for the public sphere.

I have been up and down the steps of the Capitol in search of the Portrait Monument. The Capitol is where I was able to trace my feelings. Now I leave the Capitol and go to the house of rhetoric. It is one thing to trace its story but quite another to craft a method for analyzing how it could be possible that it would end up in a basement. That is what I am up to in this chapter—to set forth my tropological method. My method connects my feelings to my intellect, and it does this by using the resources—tropes, actually—inside the house of rhetoric.

To introduce my method, I start where I left off, which is in the Capitol. Each time I crossed a threshold—going from an actual house, like the Capitol, to the house of rhetoric—I knew, as attested by rhetoric, culture, and society, that women's authority was not fully present. But I couldn't explain how women's contemporary rhetorical experiences in the United States were entangled with the conception of rhetoric imagined thousands of years ago. In effect, I couldn't say how rhetoric is both a woman's liberty and her captivity. More important, I couldn't articulate how the house of rhetoric was influencing actual houses, like the House of Representatives and its association with the genre of political deliberation.

Then one day while taking leave of one house and going to the other, I met Sojourner Truth. What she said embodied a kind of ordinary rationality that led to my ability to relate women's authority to the process of deliberation and imagine how every level of the house is influencing women as they influence rhetoric. What Sojourner Truth did was to make a gnomic statement about the night.

Near the end of her speech *The Women Want Their Rights!* Truth said that any time women speak and deliberate for their rights, sons hiss at their mothers like snakes.[16] "I can see them laughin' and pointin' at their mothers up here on this stage. They hiss when an aged woman comes forth." Because sons hiss at their mothers who speak up, "it is good," Truth said, "to speak a mite" and "draw forth the spirit . . . to see what kind of a spirit people are of." She closed with an oracular phrase: "I'm sittin' among you to watch, and every once in a while I will come out and tell you what time o' night it is."[17] In effect, Truth expresses opinions in a concise and clear manner that intuits something having to do with practical matters of women's speaking. What time o' night it is denotes an epigram that may be thought of as a form of deliberation. Recasting her statement in the interrogative mode is my means of pausing and thinking about women's movement on the stairs as they negotiate their arrangement and order. To become aware of the time of night is useful, for it can tell us something precise about the relation between women and rhetoric, namely, that there is movement of inclusion by exclusion on any given stair, so to speak.

I will go so far as to say, therefore, that Truth's common declarative statement puts my method into play. Like any gnomic statement that deals with practical matters, it aims to express what is happening—to characterize the action and event of women's speaking as they go to the high seats. What Truth does is assemble all that is going on—what women are doing, the responses to them, the images, and so on—into a part of the house—the stairs—and then stop the action long enough to expose the problem of authority. Specifically, the action of women speaking in the house of rhetoric can be explained by breaking it down into two separate but interrelated movements. In ordinary speech, one moment happens in the daytime and this is equivalent to inclusion. The other is separate but connected as day is to night. The night refers to exclusion. I look at the movement of inclusion first.

Using the epigram "what time o' night it is," Truth relates a movement of inclusion to the countless women going up the stairs, toward the light. They are speaking and appearing on the platform. To no small degree they are accepted as leaders. In fact, during the years 1830-60—the very time period that Truth came out to tell what time o' night it is—there were over a hundred women who had become public speakers.[18] Of those one hundred women, one-fourth of them delivered over one hundred speeches, suggesting that women's speaking appearances had become weekly events.[19] Indeed, the *Woman's Journal* reported women were appearing "more fully as day by day goes by" and often announced the name of a new woman orator, such as Maria S. Stetson.[20] So all in all, women were gaining momentum. They were in rhetoric, crowding around the edges of its rooms, advancing up the stairs. Truth sees women filling up the house of rhetoric.

However, Truth sees something tripping women up or turning them around almost at the moment they get to the top. Truth witnesses the audience scorning the authority coming from a woman as she speaks from within the house—the stairs signified by the platform.[21] The scorn—the focal gesture—is doing something to influence what happens next. The gesture effectively occults the light at the top of the stairs; the gesture puts women down, causes them to stumble. If they stumble far enough, they end up all the way at the bottom and in the darkness of the basement. So the hissing, the laughing, and pointing that Truth draws attention to is precisely what troubles women's public authority. And the trouble is that the sons are not alone. There are others who behave similarly. As each gesture is added to the next, they accumulate and become a model with which to "forecast" women's exclusion from rhetoric.[22] It is this model that my tropological approach displays.

Here is an overview. I feature women entering the house of rhetoric. Their entry, being a self-proclaimed form of inclusion or insertion in rhetoric, falls under the auspices of metonymy. Why this is so requires a detailed explanation, which I will address later. For now, suffice it to note that women's inclusion in rhetoric implicates metonymy because this trope invents and masters change through what the ancient rhetorician Quintilian labeled addition (and insertion is a kind of addition).[23] This trope tells us how women act and seek access to rhetoric when they are neglected, refused, or denied its spheres. This trope also embodies the motor logic of how women seek entry in the house. They go to the podium; women step up onto the platform; they are inserted into the history of, say, the pulpit and the bar. To put a face to this motor logic of metonymy, there is Hillary Clinton. She entered the field and made a bid for the White House. And there is Doris Yoakam. She inscribed women's speeches in rhetoric. From a metonymical perspective, this work is addition. Clinton enters the house while Yoakam inserts the bodies of women into the house. Either way, metonymy is a way of adding to rhetoric. I envision metonymy as a performance of the body moving up as if on stairs in the house. Because metonymy has a direct appeal to addition, it marks women's agency to constitute their relations with rhetoric and with the world.

Nevertheless and at the same time, the house of rhetoric is not static. It is a house in the building process and thus imposes its conceptual structure on the action and event of women entering the house. Rhetoric's power (against the inclusion of women) is derived from metonymy, too, but this use of metonymy is geared to the palindrome. Inside the house, metonymy is associated with that upward movement associated in particular with the parameters of character constitutive of and by the body of the warrior-citizen that I used to characterize the aspectual structure of the <CIVIC>. Character is engineered to move within a variety of planes, and this movement is the condition of male authority during the process of decision making. Of importance here in understanding my tropological method is how metonymy is embedded in the system of rhetoric and what this schema means for women's uses of metonymy when they enter and continue going up the stairs.

Set in the context of the palindrome, metonymy bears the function of intercommunication, namely, how to figure the relation between rhetoric and women. As we will see, metonymy figures women in rhetoric but without authority, and it accomplishes this figural reality by designating three family members to work out the details of any addition to rhetoric. In each case, the member of the family indicates its tropical structure of the action. Each is engaged with the project of women entering the house. A family member demonstrates its engagement by constituting its own (tropo) logic of turning down the project, and in this way, it induces control over how women's performances are seen. These family members are antonomasia, hypallage, and paronomasia. As offshoots of metonymy they share a common schema, namely that of offsetting women's agency (metonymically accrued) by making changes to their name. Antonomasia accomplishes this change by designating her membership in a class as the woman enters the house. As women continue and defy these assigned memberships, hypallage takes over and switches their speech with that of another. And when women are able to thwart the exchanges and make it to the top and hold a high seat, then paronomasia is called in to call her out in the name of authority. All in all, the three offshoots of metonymy classify the formal ways by which women's authority is repeatedly overturned. With respect to the night, they function in sequential fashion, enacting the repetition of women's exclusion, but they also, and more significantly, "predict," in a deliberative sense, women's rhetorical positioning in the house.

Methodologically speaking, the story of the relation between women and rhetoric is the meeting between particular tropes. During this meeting, women are closely linked to a trope, and then the idea of the trope is put in place of the woman. As the women are added, they are spoken of in terms of tropes. To make sense of this meeting, I use bodily movements on the stairs to capture the action of tropes. Relating body to trope is not an original idea. Later, I borrow from the ancients the idea that tropes are schemes of embodiment. I am saying that tropes behave like bodies. They are movement, and this movement logically constitutes spatial relations. Tropes are significant in two ways. They are fragments of women's progress, fragments of their quest for authority. They are an emblem or an image of rhetoric—that proverbial body of speech—moving against the inclusion. This movement shapes the house as I witnessed it when I found the Portrait Monument in the basement.

Related to the movement of the body, metonymy and its relational tropes can be identified and classified, therefore, by this twofold significance. The pattern tropes make resemble troops—forming their subtle changes (of addition) or embodied rotations of the name of a woman.[24] It is as if she is on the stairs going up but then is sent down via embodied gestures, such as hissing at a woman speaking from the platform. Each trope I identify provides a particular "angle of vision"[25] to what is happening *in* rhetoric—with respect to the model rhetoric possesses about its context, especially debate and deliberation, as it embodies authority. Within this classification, all of the activity—mobilization (of tropes to enter) and countermobilization (to overturn authority)—occurs, therefore, *within* the house of rhetoric. In using my tropological method, I frame women's relational story as a route conceived in spatial terms as an up-and-down grade that I concretize as a staircase. Going up the grade tells of women's access to the house while going down tells how they are denied authority inside the house. So while tropes spirit possibility, they also *can only act as far as the house permits.*

With this broad overview of tropes, I now set up my model with metonymy and explain specifically how and why I use this trope to ground my method in the house of rhetoric. I especially want to note how metonymy functions to enable a separate but interrelated movement. Then I turn to three offshoots of metonymy—antonomasia, hypallage, and paronomasia. I explain how I use each one to grasp more subtle movements on any given stair, so to speak. After I define my sense of metonymy and its three offshoots, I'll illustrate their theoretical import with fairly contemporary examples. Then in the next three chapters, I use these metonymical offshoots to explore the rise of public women beginning in 1826 and ending around 1919. By using contemporary examples to illustrate how a trope works as well as to trace its force in the history of women's public speaking in the United States, I am able to expose how the stairs create the illusion of a rise in any given time. More important, by exposing the rise of women in rhetoric as a site where the question of their authority is performed again and again, I am able with tropes to tell what time o' night it is. Being rhetoric's own resources, tropes are applicable to deliberation and can offer unique insight, and this applies both to seeing what has happened in the past and arguably to what is going to happen in the future.

Metonymy

Metonymy is the side-by-side trope. It is what Roman Jakobson calls contiguity.[26] The trope serves the function of illuminating the two separate but interrelated movements in a side-by-side manner. One side shows women "outside." This is not an actual place but refers to an existential mode of argument whereby women's authority turns down, as if it were going away from the podium or the high seats of power and leadership. This side of metonymy harmonizes with my feeling side as I descended the stairs in the Capitol. The other side shows women "inside," an existential mode referring to a sense of inclusion. This side of metonymy harmonizes with my intellectual life. Put together, metonymy serves the function, say George Lakoff and Mark Johnson, "of understanding,"[27] and in this case, it shows the relationship between women being "in" and "out" of the house. So metonymy brings to the fore the question of authority against a "house" background composed of planes, angles, and stairs that structure the process of deliberation. My method claims at its core that the principles and elements of speech create a house of rhetoric as a result of the way bodies can move.

Using the Portrait Monument and all that it represents for women in the United States, metonymy reveals women's use of rhetoric to gain access to the house/Capitol and its recourses to incur power. As we know from a variety of thinkers from Hélène Cixous to Hayden White and James Fernandez,[28] tropes can undermine and contest arguments (which doubtless accounts for their deviant status in the house of rhetoric as well as women's association with them).

Approaching the house of rhetoric as if it were consciousness, we might apply Jacques Lacan's view of metonymy here. He writes that it is "the most appropriate means used by the unconscious to foil."[29] In effect, metonymy enables women to outmaneuver the practice of censorship that keeps women out of rhetoric—its history and its canon.

As a form of agency, metonymy is a trope that overcomes exclusion. Performed as the act of going up the stairs, the stated mission of metonymy is upward and outward so as "to represent and bring into association a larger context."[30] In fact, metonymy is something like "a weapon of mass creation"[31] and it has, especially in the hands of women, induced radical change in the house. Consistent with adding on and enlarging the house, the metonymical missive enables American women, like Mott, Anthony, and Stanton, to bring themselves as well as countless other women into association with the sociopolitical sphere writ large in a way never seen before in the history of the United States and in the history of rhetoric. Without a doubt, the gift of the Portrait Monument bears witness to the success of the metonymical mission of representing and bringing women into association with the larger context of the house.

But nevertheless and at the same time, metonymy is not a simple foil when it comes to making change. As a form of addition, metonymy makes change by another algebra—one that entails a subtraction. A method devoted to the tropes has to bear in mind that as women's bodies move on the stairs, they integrate with men's bodies and thus are in the house. But women's bodies must also move separately because their pelvis does not fit in (the house that is also a trope called a palindrome). Women's bodies do not fit or add in as does the warrior-citizen, whose pelvis supports and expressly fashions the archi-technical line of authority. It is not simply the fact that there is not enough room on the stairs for men and women. The house can bear the load as the mass of women's inclusion proves. The problem is that the house does not have the capacity to recognize within its own structure the body of a woman speaking with authority. So the mode of metonymy can facilitate a way to see how women's activity occults inclusion, corralling not their agency but their authority as a sign of weakness in the house of rhetoric. In particular, metonymy (because it is engineered to signify integration of bodies within the house) favors women's inclusion but on (house) terms of extrinsicality.

Specifically, when it comes to tropical addition, the metonymical mode is not simple addition as in $1 + 1 = 2$. Rather, it has a peculiar force of subtraction or exclusion that is at once in tune with addition or inclusion. Addition and subtraction are near in time and sequences because they are of the angles of the house of rhetoric. As women enter the house and use its agential resources to add themselves to it, metonymy enables rhetoric, too. What metonymy permits the house to do is systematically retrofit each decisive addition by using it like a device of subtraction. However, subtraction in the house is accomplished neither in perverse or futile ways.[32] Subtraction is not created by an opposite effect, as perversity intimates. And subtraction does not mean that additive work is for naught, as futility suggests. Rather, the use of subtraction attests to a high sense of freedom and agency invested in rhetoric's model house. It is open to change, but nevertheless, the model it possesses about itself—the body of speech animating the male warrior-citizen—conserves rhetoric's commission in any given case and its putative power to construct a character or ethos associated with authority. Subtraction is the language appropriate to the house of rhetoric to call attention to how it installs women (the additive part) to fit its deliberative context in a manner that satisfies the house's high demand of agency (that, after all, permits women to seek inclusion) but yet denies or restricts women's authority. So metonymy specifies changes (of direction)—addition and subtraction or inclusion and exclusion—as they happen in contiguity.

There is a less technical way of describing all of this. To understand how metonymy works change of direction with its peculiar form of addition, I go to the Greek meaning of the word *metonymy*. Metonymy means "change of name,"[33] thus earning the contemporary nickname the "figure of swap."[34] The condition of subtraction resides in the act of swapping one name for another. The names of Lucretia Mott, Susan B. Anthony, and Elizabeth Cady Stanton, for example, were swapped for "Three Ladies in a Bathtub," a misnomer rendering their rhetorical challenges as extrinsic to the house. This quality of extrinsicality (which is how addition functions in relation to subtraction) resembles a troop-like feature. Once women are in the house, metonymy is free to cultivate its rhetorical protocol of extrinsicality and thus change the *meaning* of women's rhetorical actions. In contemporary rhetorical parlance, the change of name changes the agent-act relationship, making the men's resolution to send them to the basement a replication of the model rhetoric possesses about women's status in the house.

Now as metonymy adds the three stone women to the house, it does so not by an act of Congress but by rotating their names, subtracting them from their proper mode by shifting it, putting their name next to something like a basement—the realm of the unclean. So rotated, "The Three Ladies in a Bathtub" are positioned in a place for the ridding of dirt.[35] By coupling the privacy of bathing with their speaking in public, the misnomer—the little addition of a trope called an epithet—countenances women's attempt to associate themselves with the larger context as inappropriate and impolite and thus not of the polis—that sociopolitical realm where the business of decision making occurs. So the trope subtracts the women from rhetoric. "Three Ladies in a Bathtub" qua metonymy enacts the disposition that its linguistic structure contains. By sleight of hand (an in-house gesture articulated with the embodied practices of metonymy), the trope points down, directing women's authority away from the public sphere.

The accumulation of negative gestures has an embodied force. Using the rhetorical tradition as my cue, I now draw from Paul Ricoeur, who notes, "It appears that, originally the word figure [trope] was to be said only of bodies."[36] Negative gestures aimed at a woman's attempt to occupy the high seat enfigure her body without authority. This integrative function of trope and body allows me to chart how women go up and down the stairs to enter and exit the house via the basement, and it will allow me to show how some women are included once they are in the house. Either way, they go without authority.

Conceived as forms of action, tropes embody changes of direction. This is especially acute in the house of rhetoric that rests on a trope called a palindrome. In this house context, the embodied action—the gestures directed at women's speech—enacts or builds (the house of) rhetoric, actualizing its design as a method for articulating women to rhetoric. The constitutive force of tropes manifested in embodied practice is to indicate—to tell—where women are in rhetoric, showing/telling/gesturing how their speaking is off beam, archi-technically speaking. So tropes signify, watching over the meaning making in rhetoric. I saw this tropical movement in the guard's gesture as he motioned his hand, pointing his finger down the stairs inside the Capitol.[37] When abstracted from the body, tropes mete out the measure of the house, activating its planes and composing the civic realm.

So far, I have identified metonymy as the master trope that rules over changes of direction in the house. Based on the simple fact that women have been progressing and have been effectively rising in public, the house permits change unto itself by addition but this addition is connected with subtraction. In an actual house, like the U.S. Capitol, this peculiar relation of addition and subtraction resembles angles of the stairs, rendering a kind of activity of inclusion by exclusion. To gain insight into the subtle movements on any given stair, I turn to metonymy's offshoots and use them to understand what time o' night it is or to speak theoretically about the separate but interrelated movements of inclusion and exclusion.

Metonymy's three offshoots—antonomasia, hypallage, and paronomasia—are related through change of name. Antonomasia and paronomasia start and end the sequence with hypallage serving as the agent of change. I will use them (1) to show movement in the house, a first of sorts in which women are called a new name (antonomasia); (2) to pinpoint changes to women's leadership (hypallage); and (3) to reveal a relationship between being "in" and "out" of the house with slight change of name (paronomasia). Let's look at these three tropes. I'll define each appendage of metonymy and then I'll use the three variants to generate some insights into contemporary examples, showing the tropical activity that I have been describing. I also discuss the three offshoots in sequential fashion. Although the tropical steps may not take place in an orderly fashion, they often follow a sequence. I take note of it, attending to a recurrent pattern extending for over two centuries.

ANTONOMASIA AND EPITHET

Antonomasia (figure 2.3) literally means "naming instead,"[38] and this action grants it strong familial ties to metonymy's action of changing (direction) with its addition architecturally bounded to subtraction. Basically, this trope calls the woman rising up by a new name to designate her membership in a class. In the house where authority is at stake, the new name is a derogatory name. These new names can be forms of common speech or nicknames that usurp a woman's proper name as in the sentence "Bellacosa Bella [Congresswoman Bella Abzug] has no moral right to run against a man."[39] The proper name Congresswoman Bella Abzug is replaced with "Bellacosa Bella." The "naming instead" calls attention to her leadership as improper in the house.

More often than not, antonomasia is associated with common epithets. For example, take the use of the word *bitch*. This specific use of antonomasia adds an improper name to Hillary Clinton's (proper) name. As a gesture of the body of speech, the epithet fingers the proper name of a woman and changes her political status by adding another name to her name, effectively turning down her authority. As for the movement on the stairs, it calibrates her rhetorical actions, regulating her access—her addition to the White House—as improper. The addition (of bitch) to the addition (of a woman near the house's apex of authority) changes the direction of her rise and sends her down the stairs, obfuscating Clinton's authority and thus making her rise that much more difficult.

As for the development of the classification system, antonomasia and epithet seem to surface *first*, rendering the woman's rhetorical action as a discontinuity. For example, almost two hundred years ago, when a woman gave a speech in public for the first time, the shout was "Put her out! Put the old bitch out!"[40] Fast forward to today and antonomasia is apparent when, for the first time, a woman sought the nomination for president of the United States on a major party ticket. Let's go to Hillary Clinton and observe her moving up the stairs in the American house of rhetoric in ways never witnessed before and take a look at how the

Figure 2.3. Antonomasia.

Antonomasia (an to no MA si a; G. "naming instead")	
The term designates the use of an epithet or patronymic, instead of a proper name, or the reverse.	
Distinguished as description:	An epithet or appellative
	A "type" applied to a particular individual
	A replacement or the removal of an individual
	Used to describe or embellish the acts of an individual
Example:	Bellacosa Bella for Congresswoman Bella Abzug

tropes of antonomasia and epithet initiate the play of separate but interrelated movements.

During a campaign event in November 2007, an audience member—a woman—referring to Hillary Clinton, asked John McCain, "How do we beat the bitch?"[41] Eventually the sound bites faded after McCain attacked the media for holding him responsible for the use of language in the public sphere. CNN's Rick Sanchez said, Senator McCain "is not apologizing, when someone used it in front of him, seemed to laugh it off. So, now he is still not apologizing, and now attacking me personally and CNN. . . . Our staff has put out several statements, I should say, his staff has put out several statements today. None of them offers an apology to women in general or to Hillary Clinton specifically. No matter what you think of Hillary Clinton, and we know that she can be very polarizing, she is a U.S. senator, the former First Lady of the United States. Should her being called that be turned into a joke by a presidential candidate?"[42] As a first offshoot of metonymy, antonomasia signifies a rising action. Pointing to Senator Clinton and calling her a bitch in public indicate that women do not have the prerequisite for authority to be at the top of the stairs. Now the trope rotates the power of addition and sends the woman down the stairs. All of this is played out in the word *bitch*, which enables the playing out of a dialogue in the house, as in the case of CNN.

So antonomasia brings "to the fore certain aspects of the fact which might otherwise remain in the background of our consciousness."[43] Specifically, the trope brings to the fore the new. This is women doing rhetoric and inscribing themselves in the house. By the same token, it brings to the fore certain aspects of differences; intensifying a woman who acts as a leader as not having the authority to do so. In the end, the trope does something to women.[44] In the case of Clinton, it turns Clinton's step up in the house as inappropriate or improper. In this way, antonomasia can constitute the distinctive designation of women's rhetorical agency in the name of progress and can also in the name of authority obtain the force to turn down her going up the stairs.[45] Thus what is coming—the subordination of a woman's political and social status via antonomasia and epithet—is something that happens or is done continuously or repetitively.

While antonomasia fulfills a function of intensifying or heightening choice in rhetoric, it is a choice set up in a room of the house where the speaker and the audience/viewer interact. In terms of the speaker, the choice evokes the right to contest and speak in public. In terms of the audience, the choice consists of effects expressed as values that, in turn, enact an argument for how and where women should occupy the house. The critical turn that antonomasia exposes is that of the house maintaining its structure and order by dividing the sexes, a division apparent on a concrete slab, a building floor, a city, or wherever public speaking occurs.

HYPALLAGE

Hypallage (figure 2.4) clarifies movement after women have been granted access in the house of rhetoric.[46] It marks an upward progression in at least two ways. Women are recognized and this permits the operations in the house to pause briefly on the possibility of women's authority. A good example of this pause is the recognition of women's accomplishments (via the Portrait Monument), which was held in the Rotunda in 1921. Second, there may be a place provided in the house that calls favorable attention to a woman's accomplishments. Given its capacity for correction, the trope of hypallage ushers in an exchange in which women become present even in seats of leadership but they are not *seen as* the person with authority. In effect, the change to leadership seems to be a change (from the other that antonomasia and its change of name had induced); but hypallage switches a high seat for a low one. The woman sits in the high seat but does not hold the name of authority. Using hypallage can help us pinpoint exactly where women are on the stairs in the house of rhetoric.

Let me illustrate hypallage through an example that consists of two parts linked by the interior décor of the table—that quintessential setting of decision making. The first part involves a set of studies conducted by Virginia Valian on perceptions of women's public authority in social settings, specifically ones apropos to business.[47] Subjects in Valian's study were assigned the task of watching slides

Figure 2.4. Hypallage.

Hypallage (hy PAL la ge; G. "interchange, exchange")	
The term designates the particular device that consists of an exchange within a statement between (1) the epithets assigned to specific nouns or (2) activities associated with certain words or their complements.	
Distinguished as emphasis:	Awkward or humorous changing of application
	A change of relation
	Transferred epithet, an educated turn of the phrase, a more decent way to speak
	Used to emphasize and intensify the transfer
Example:	Example chaste Diana/lustful Venus → lustful Diana/ chaste Venus

of five people sitting around a table with a caption that described them as working on a project. Some slides showed five people of the same sex, and sometimes they displayed both sexes seated randomly. In mixed-sex groups, the subjects identified the man as the leader *even* when a woman sat at the head of the table. These studies (done in 1973 and replicated in 1989) indicate that women in the United States are *less likely* to be perceived and described as leaders, as deliberators, as persons with authority even when they are actually seated in positions of authority. Apparently, a woman's position does not alter perceptions of her as not having power.[48] As Valian rightly notes, the studies during the years 1973 and 1989 say nothing of women's ability to communicate, to lead, to make decisions, or to deliberate in public; they say nothing of her ability to act rhetorically. However, they do demonstrate that successful women managers are "perceived as having less leadership ability" than successful men managers.

The scene is rhetorically significant because it reveals an incongruity over the use of table space, and this incongruity is apparent once we apply hypallage to see the exchange of women's places at the table. What hypallage intensifies is the separate but interrelated movement from and to the other on the stairs. A woman is sitting at the head of the table—that quintessential site of authority— and presumably has been given access to rhetoric, but her authority is exchanged, changing her addition to the table for something less than what the chair means. The woman sitting at the head of the table is a changeling; she is not with authority but we say she is in a position of authority. The change induced by hypallage does something to the body. It causes it to move down as if on the stairs, and this movement is evinced by the fact that no one pays her authorial voice any mind. She effectively disappears as a person with public authority even though she is designated to sit in the place of power.[49]

As hypallage shows a very subtle shift on the stairs, it also instantiates arguments for how and where women should occupy the house, thereby justifying the transfer of authority to men. In effect, this trope exposes the non-obvious ways the house of rhetoric seeks to maintain its structure and order, even rotating or turning authority from the head of the table on its side.

Connected tropically to the studies of women in the business setting is a set of studies conducted by the White House Project (WHP), "a national nonpartisan organization dedicated to enhancing public perceptions of women's capacity to lead and fostering the entry of women into positions of leadership, including the U.S. Presidency."[50] The WHP wanted to see how women are portrayed in the context of mainstream media, in particular on Sunday morning talk shows as these shows are considered to be the weathervane of political decision making. What they found, I think, is the embodied practice of hypallage as it emphasizes and intensifies the transfer of women's authority to men.

Between 2002 and 2005, there was a slight improvement in the number of women who appeared on these agenda-setting shows. Unfortunately, the increase in numbers did not alter how often or when they spoke during the broadcast. Women are "significantly more likely to appear in the later (less important and less watched segments)" of these shows.[51] In fact, since 1999 there has only been a 1 percent increase in the number of women who appear in the most visible segment of the shows, while the number of appearances women have made increased by 3 percent from 2002 to 2005, although after September 11, 2001, "the percentage of guest appearances by American women across all shows *dropped by thirty-nine percent.*"[52]

Using hypallage, the trope clarifies how women are seen but are not regarded as persons with authority. Women are less likely than men to be invited back for repeat appearances, which is another way of exchanging their authorial voices for something exceptional, thereby diminishing the position of women in the house. The WHP's original study (1999) found that "male Senators made 245 repeat appearances while female Senators made only 8."[53] While the follow-up study (2002) found slight improvement in female repeat appearances, this result was attributed primarily to the repeat appearances of the secretary of state, Condoleezza Rice. Repeat appearances are significant because they are linked to not only displaying but possessing public authority. A person's repeat appearances to discuss such topics as war and peace function as a means of designating the speaker's voice as an authority on the subject matter, whether one agrees with the speaker's views or not. Repeat appearances confer ethos or authority because repetition resembles and enacts the process of decision making, namely the quality of going over/through again a discussion until consensus is reached. The dearth of repeat female reappearances indicates how the house of rhetoric discounts their public authority.

The lack of women on Sunday morning talk shows also reveals a gender bias against women's public authority. The bias acquires its definitive power in two ways. The first entails the placement of women, the second, their omission from the shows during significant events. Women appear at the bottom half of the show, a placement communicating a basement. Hypallage indicates an angle to the stairs, indicating women as subordinate to men. Like the high seat or the head of the table, it is the head of household who is expected to guide the process in making decisions. It should come as no surprise that several women with authority were omitted from voicing their political views in the months following September 11. Excluded from talking were Senator Kay Bailey Hutchison (R-TX), ranking member on the Commerce Subcommittee on Aviation, and Representative Nancy Pelosi, the ranking Democrat on the House Intelligence Committee. As the WHP reported, "Also excluded were women who chaired the three principal Senate subcommittees on terrorism."[54] To be excluded is especially problematic when a woman with public authority holds a position that would otherwise demand that a man be cast as part of decision making. So while she is in rhetoric, she is not of it, as this trope displays. She may hold the position of authority, like a woman seated at the head of a table, but she is not regarded as the head or the leader with an authorial voice. Her inferior placement demeans her opinion, if it is heard at all, as well as her status as decision maker or leader. Most important, the dramatic drop of female appearances on Sunday morning talk shows after September 11 only strengthens the idea that women's public authority is not appropriate during exigencies or events requiring the full measure of political deliberation. Another factor here is war—September 11 was an act of war against the United States, and men, just as the warrior-citizen entails authority in rhetoric, deal with war; women do not.

So hypallage makes non-obvious points about presence. By presence I do not mean being visible in the way an evening news anchor or a CEO in the boardroom is visible. Rather the presence I have in mind has to do with women being seen or regarded as a leader or decision maker. Presence consists of being recognized as having authority only to have the authority swapped for a subordinate form, thus denying women full inclusion.

In the twin scenes of women in business and women in politics, there are women who have made it to the high seats. But they are not seen as such. Their authorial presence is exchanged. What happens to their authority? It is transferred by the audience, which recognizes women's accomplishment, but this is followed by an exchange that puts the man's body at the head. The trope of hypallage casts the exchange as so natural that transfer of women's authority goes unnoticed.

As I mentioned before, the trope may follow in a sequential fashion. Now it may be the case that the epithet of "bitch" used to characterize Clinton in her first-of-a-kind step up to a position of authority is over. That no one talks about Sarah Palin as a "bitch" might seduce us into thinking that women are very close to holding a position of authority equivalent to the presidency. But the fact that the word *bitch* (epithet) has fallen out of favor in the metonymical formation signifies a shift of tropes. Based on my model, I would argue that the relation between women and rhetoric has moved to a phase of hypallage. Hypallage is a trope that appears to expand the status of women but turns down their authority in the house of rhetoric. The use of the epithet "bitch" suggests, especially with its deep associations with images of witch and teeth, that the woman seeking power is a demon mother who castrates her offspring. But Palin is the epitome of the male construction of the feminine—flirty, cute, a "winker"[55]—but totally inept with regard to politically important issues. In this vein, the trope of hypallage exchanges Clinton for Palin to recognize that women are moving up to the office of the vice president. But Palin's authority is exchanged and downgraded in the process.

McCain sat next to Palin during one of Katie Couric's interviews with her on CBS.[56] He interrupted and answered the questions for Palin. It has also been said of late that Palin is very good at learning and reading (male-created) cue cards; she is referred to as a "quick study"[57] but can't utter a sentence on her own. In effect, the interruption of speech signifies that women are present, but not with authority. Curiously, Palin's name situates her in the *palin*drome of the <CIVIC>. I am not positing an etymological link between Palin and palindrome; rather I am working the idea that the medium is the message. Palin the form is visually appealing in the sense that she leads as the house—the palindrome—permits. The uncanny link between Palin and palindrome can tell the time of night, if we dare see that her presence shifts the tropical activity on the stairs from epithets to seeming inclusion. But, as Truth would say, there is still a pointin' and a laughin' because the interrupting of her speech by McCain resonates architechnically to suggest Palin's authority is always already being shifted to another domain, like the women in the business setting who are *not* seen as leaders even when they sit at the head of the table or the women on Sunday morning talk shows, especially after September 11, who appear at the end of the show.

PARONOMASIA

Paronomasia (figure 2.5) refers to a kind of playing on the sound and meaning of words.[58]

It is the third move, after hypallage. Eventually, women do occupy a high seat and thus have authority to make decisions. In the third offshoot of metonymy, a woman is both in and out of rhetoric. That is, a woman is able to occupy interior places in the house. In this way, a woman in public amounts to the same thing as a man in public, namely, they both share the component of authority. But, the trope of paronomasia reveals a change whereby a public woman sounds like or resembles a "public woman" (in sotto voce). This change covers (the bodies of) women in the house of rhetoric with a form signifying their political status is subordinate to men's political status. The cover slights her name, making it publicly improper. Following the separate but interrelated movements of going to and from the other, paronomasia plays upon such movement with slight changes of name, thereby returning the name of the woman to where she began as the other seeking inclusion. Because she is other, she must cover her body.

Let me illustrate how the trope of paronomasia works by examining an incident involving Lieutenant Colonel McSally, the highest-ranking female fighter pilot in the U.S. Air Force (at the time of this writing). Lieutenant Colonel McSally is required to wear Muslim-style head-to-toe robes, known as an abaya, when she is off base in Saudi Arabia where she is stationed. This gesture covers her voice with the trope paronomasia, like an abaya. So the dress loses its religious, cultural meaning vis-à-vis Islam and operates tropically as a signifier of her impropriety. Women in public do not lead or have authority. Her male counterparts are not required to wear Muslim garb; in fact, they are forbidden to do so. When Lieutenant Colonel McSally puts an abaya atop her uniform, she may be donning the cultural forms of expression for women in Saudi Arabia, but she is also covering her position of authority, rendering it invisible not only to the Saudis but also and more important to the American soldiers to whom she performs her subordinate repositioning by riding in the back seat of a car, a requirement for women in Saudi Arabia, while the men, even those she outranks, ride in the front. Her cover over her body changes how her role as leader is named. Her authority is improper; therefore, she is covered, this "public woman."

John Whitehead, a lawyer with the Rutherford Institute who represented McSally in the lawsuit she brought against the U.S. military, explains the sexism and how it demotes her public authority: "What it [being required to wear the abaya and sit in the back seat of a car] says . . . is like saying, 'You're equal to us but you

Figure 2.5. Paronomasia.

Paronomasia (pa ro no MA si a; G. "play upon words which sound alike")	
The term designates a kind of playing on the sound and meaning of words. To alter slightly in naming.	
Distinguished as reduplication:	Similar words applied to dissimilar thing
	Names made to resemble
	Repetition of same word, creating a deeper meaning
	Used to create the effect of a relationship
Example:	"public woman" and public woman

can't eat in the same restaurant.'"[59] Fighting to remove the Taliban regime, Lieutenant Colonel McSally faces the incoherence of her own public authority as she watches on television women in Afghanistan throwing off their burkas while she and other American women in the military have to wear an abaya on top of their military uniform on designated occasions while serving the United States.[60]

While this case is a legal issue, it is significant tropically. While it enters the public domain as a high-profile case,[61] it may stand for our substantive public beliefs—"our conceptions of who we are, what kind of community we live [in] and what we should do."[62] It also—perhaps because it is a high-profile case—offers a way to see the relation between women and rhetoric. As a case of paronomasia in particular and as a part of the family of metonymy in general, it tells what happens when women aim for the high seats. American wives of dignitaries did not have to cover their heads. They are not in rhetoric as a leader; the wives are with their husbands and perform their function of subordination. Specifically, paronomasia reveals the deeply grooved ground—the palindrome of the <CIVIC>— and of the warrior-citizen doing rhetoric, specifically going to and from the middle and making decisions under the auspices of authority that the house cedes habitually to him alone. Paronomasia (via McSally) surfaces and seeks a structural change in the treatment and perception of women with public authority. This gives us a glimpse of the house of rhetoric as it could offer authority to women as it offers it to men. Nevertheless, as McSally stands at the top of the stairs, her authority is covered. In the high seat, her name is slighted: this public woman invokes paronomasia for protection. When the door opens, the house of rhetoric remains what it is, namely a palindrome, and now we see it activating paronomasia to preserve its concept of authority. The advantage of the judicial case is that it takes us to the core of rhetoric's judgment and greatest weakness: the doubting, denial, and debunking of women who act as persons with authority.

To consider the notion that tropes often act in sequential fashion, it is worth noting that in the early days of the campaign, Hillary Clinton was once again called a "bitch." This epithet is an indicator that change is happening in the house. After Clinton entered the debates as contender, the trope of antonomasia can tell us about her subtle movement on the stairs. Let's go to the top of the stairs as Clinton stood on the debate platform.

The door latch to the house of rhetoric jams under the pressure of Clinton seeking her party's nomination to run for president of the United States. The *first* question presented to presidential candidate Hillary Clinton allows us a way to capture what is happening on the stairs.

During the YouTube debates hosted by CNN on July 23, 2007, John McAlpin, a member of the U.S. military serving overseas, asked Clinton, "The Arab states, Muslim nations, believe its women [are] second-class citizens. If you're president of the United States, how do you feel that you would even be taken seriously by these states in any kind of talks, negotiations, or any other diplomatic relations? I feel that is a legitimate question."[63]

McAlpin's question, in effect, launches the democratic campaign about the viability of a female U.S. president in the near future. Why select this question? What does it mean to open the debates with this particular question and put it to the very first woman running on a major party ticket for president of the United States? At the very least it indicates that the condition of public authority for women is not yet developed in the United States and by extension neither is the house of rhetoric, where its major living room is dedicated to debate. The existence of Islamic states is used to frame the proper function of women in the context of rhetoric and its model of leadership and authority. In both cases—McSally and Clinton—the question of authority they face hinges on the house of rhetoric offering up a model of women having power in any given case—particularly in the case of Islamic states. While Clinton ably refuted the claim with examples of women from all over the world serving as heads of state and conducting foreign policy with various Islamic states and McSally took legal action, both women contradict the authority as it is embodied in men and accompanies masculinity. This is the dark thing at the top of the stairs as McSally and Clinton stand poised at the threshold where trope/troops guard the door, directing them down the stairs.

Clinton's entry into the political debate sparks paronomasia in two ways. First, her authority is doubted by casting her leadership provisionally in the scene of

Islamic nations. In effect, the first question asked in the debate room is a burka, covering her authority to speak/act as a leader. Second, the question as it frames her in clothing that subordinates her authority evokes a sexuality sealed in the house about women's activity in public. In this way, Clinton moves back to the first stage of development as signified by epithets—bitch, witch, and so forth—used against her. This reversal—the action of shifting authority under and down as specified by the trope of paronomasia—unites the house as it designates women as public speakers while altering their status and prestige but returning them to their presumed capacity—subordination.

Insofar as women seek to be included in rhetoric, I selected the trope of metonymy—the primary strategy of addition according to the received tradition—as a guide to understanding the times—the relation between women and rhetoric—and I used all the major modalities of metonymy to tell what time o' night it is, namely to delineate how the tropes turn women down the stairs.

In each incident, I considered on one side how women seem to climb the stairs or advance as speakers in the house of rhetoric, but how examining this ascension tropologically showed a descent as well in terms of authority. Viewed as action on a staircase, each trope provides unique insight into how the <CIVIC> is *always already built up in* the speaking situation and *how* speaking women are also caught up systematically in an interior system of argumentative values that rotates or puts down the authority of speaking woman, thereby impeding her rise. While knowledge of how the tropes/troops rotate women at the top of the stairs may itself be turned and act as a guide by which public women might move strategically step by step toward the future, the knowledge of them would be served by designing a house of rhetoric hospitable to women's authority and power.

My descent to the interior region of the house of rhetoric where I unearthed the elements and principles of speech revealed that rhetoric obscures the presence of women. The presence one ordinarily associates with visibility, such as the presence of women in government, business, the media, and elsewhere, concentrates on immediacy. The presence I found in the darkest regions is insinuated in the foundation, in that stone formation organized around a prerequisite to authority as well as in the bones of the body of speech, its joints articulating a body *type* of speech that performs the house of rhetoric, bidding the dream of the <CIVIC>.

As I climbed the stairs out of the palindrome, I entered the U.S. Capitol and proceeded to haul out the whole foundation as well as the bones of the body of speech to the surface and then make the house visible. I attempted to show how the house of rhetoric looked aboveground thousands of years later. Then by walking around, I was able to observe women from within. I used my observations to decipher the effects the house has on women's public authority in various ways today.

In the chapters that follow, I detail three critical moments in which women have gained access to the house of rhetoric and for all appearances are included in its decision-making practices. In each case, I bear witness to a strong presence of women as they go to and from the podium. As I mentioned before, I have another presence in mind, that of authority. Authority, and thus the presence of women in rhetoric, is by no means established. The relation between women and rhetoric is put to the test in the crucible—the house where the body of speech—its practice in the world—subjects them to an ordeal of authority that changes their speech into a form of subordination. The palindrome, therefore, is the phenomenon that generates and is generative of tropological activity proper as well as improper to its manifest structure. The <CIVIC> contains the story of women's access, their partial addition to the house of rhetoric, and the turning down of their authority. I decipher the reception of women's authority in the American house of rhetoric as it is built upon the palindromic qualities of repetition—that of going to and from the hearth/podium to participate in decision making.

3

The Path–Then

At length the door in the rear opened and a neat foot was placed upon the platform.

—Elizabeth Oakes Smith

I am in the Capitol, climbing the stairs out of the basement to the Rotunda. Once I enter the Rotunda, I actually cross the threshold of the house of rhetoric. In this house, the Portrait Monument is my cairn. I use it to locate a trailhead and start following the stepping-stones that women set down in the course of their moving toward the Capitol. Eventually, the course they set enabled others to arrive in 1921 to celebrate Susan B. Anthony's birthday.[1] I want to find the porch leading to the house of rhetoric because this will allow me to see where women entered the house and how they were received. The question of how re-verberates back to Sojourner Truth's question—how to tell what time o' night it is. Telling time means deciphering separate but interrelated movements: one of women actively gaining access, the other denying their authority.

So following where the Portrait Monument cairn leads, and taking the dedica-tion page of the first volume of *The History of Woman Suffrage*[2] as my cue, I begin with Frances Wright. This chapter starts with a dedicated name, then goes up the steps and through a rear door where Wright gained entrée into the house and made her way toward the center. As she did, many women followed her, in-cluding Lucy Stone, who forged a new direction after seeing a statue, *The Greek Slave,* a turn that prompted the movement's purpose for the next fifty years.

When Frances ("Fanny") (D'Arusmont) Wright (1792–1852) stepped onto the platform in New Harmony Hall on July 4, 1828, to address a small utopian com-munity in Indiana, she created a new beginning—a "first" of sorts—for women and public speaking in the United States.[3] Years later the notable feminist writer Elizabeth Oakes Smith gives an account of the only time she saw and heard Fanny Wright speak: "It was a cold winter's night. There might have been fifty or more persons present who presently began to shuffle and call. It was so much more gross and noisy than anything I had ever encountered that I grew quite distressed. At length the door in the rear opened and a neat foot was placed upon the platform."[4]

With this description, we observe Frances Wright after she gains access to the house. The movement of her feet on the interior décor of the house—the platform—signifies upward activity. To explain how her authority shifts down, I use the trope antonomasia and epithet that I described in the last chapter. To refresh, antonomasia literally means "naming instead." Very often it is a belittling name, like "Chainsaw Drew," which was used to replace the proper name of Drew Gilpin Faust, the first female president of Harvard in 350 years.[5] Extend antonomasia and it is an epithet—like referring to the Portrait Monument in 1921 as "Three Ladies in a Bathtub" or in 1997 as an "ugly thing." The trope seizes the proper name, rotates it in a deprecating manner, and turns down the woman's authority, marking her entry in the house as out-of-bounds. The selection of epithets specifies how far a woman has moved beyond her function as well as how far her stumble—the correction—down the stairs may go.[6]

A woman speaking in the center of town, on a national holiday, and in front of an audience was unfathomable in American cities such as Philadelphia, but not in New Harmony. In fact, this utopian community invited her to speak on, ironically enough, Independence Day, the Fourth of July. In this way, this very special community opens the door into the house of rhetoric. Perfect, too, because the opening gives Frances Wright immediate access to epideictic oratory, a genre reserved for the greatest rhetoricians, reaching all the way back to Isocrates. Finally, slipping in through the rear door is perfect because Wright is able to speak not just before women, as women before had done, but before men and women—a mixed audience.[7]

On Main Street USA, the front door to the house of rhetoric was slammed shut, locked up good and tight, even ten years after Wright sneaked in through the back of the house. In York, Pennsylvania, Wright was permitted to speak in front of the building, but not inside it. Outside York's courthouse on a Saturday evening in August 1836, Frances Wright gave a speech after being run out of Philadelphia,[8] mostly because the crowd "objected to a woman speaking in public."[9] Before she reached York, Wright spent the night in the town of Locust Grove on the banks of the Susquehanna River where she wrote to her daughter Sylva. In that letter, Wright imagined a better world for Sylva,[10] explaining how traveling and speaking on topics associated with freedom, including the freedom of women to speak in public, would make things easier for women in the future. Three days after she left Locust Grove, she arrived in York, where an attempt was made "in the name of *Morality* and *Religion*" to get a "*mob*" together to prevent her from speaking in public.[11] It failed. The editor of the local newspaper, the *York Gazette*, acknowledged her right to speak by evoking *"freedom of speech"* as a privilege to be enjoyed by "every human being."[12]

There was a good deal of outrage, including public debates circulating in the press under the question, "Is it proper for a woman to address a public assembly?"[13] Many, including Horace Mann, argued against women speaking in public.[14] In a small book with wide circulation in 1838, Hubbard Winslow used the question of women's speaking to address the question of authority and leadership. He wrote, "Man should always sit at the helm, to lead public sentiment and control public movements."[15] All public institutions, he continued, "especially institutions embracing both sexes," should be "headed and controlled" by man.[16]

Ironically, some women even spoke in public to denounce women speaking in public. Anna Gardner cites Tennyson in her description of women wandering around and speaking: "Nature made them blinder motions bounded in a shallower brain."[17] Thus, "women need fixedness—fixedness both in character and place," proclaimed a speaker before a maternal audience.[18] If not linked to promiscuity and/or with a shallow brain indiscriminate in its dealings, women who spoke about women's rights were referred to as a "terrible horrible."[19] The emblem of the terrible horrible is the monster. The very idea of a woman speaking on various topics—women's education, women's rights, and so on—was deemed "an ever-present hideous apparition."[20] By 1859, when many more women had become professional lecturers and were no longer called monsters, they were still not "ladies."[21] But by speaking on the Fourth of July before a mixed audience, Wright announced to the world that women have the authority to stand at the podium.

Wright uses the Fourth of July to exercise her independence and to ask why women are not equal, especially with regard to education, particularly in the instruction of speech.[22] For Wright, women are in chains politically and socially because they are free to speak "only in theory."[23] By the phrase "only in theory," Wright distinguishes a real world from an imaginary one. Only in a utopian place can a woman and a man speak in the house of rhetoric, as Wright demonstrates by speaking on the Fourth of July.

But if Wright has gained access to the house of rhetoric through the back door, she nevertheless gets inside the house. After New Harmony, Wright began her formal career as a public speaker in Cincinnati in 1828. Then, after a brief time in Europe, she resumed her speaking on the platform in front of the courthouse in Cincinnati on May 15, 1836, with "a copy of the Declaration of Independence in her hand."[24] When Frances Wright first began to speak in Cincinnati, New York, Philadelphia, and all the towns in between, she appeared in public spaces that had not been associated with women speaking. If a public space were denied her, she found another site or transformed the existing space so that she could appear. In New York, for example, Wright bought a church, a space that did not permit women to speak,[25] and renamed it the Hall of Science.[26] Once she was inside the house of rhetoric, Wright rearranged the furniture, offering the "Hall as a place for instruction" (to women and men) in "public speaking" and devoted sessions to "public debating both sides of a question."[27]

Lucy Stone (1818–93) was a teenager when Frances Wright was lecturing on women's rights. Although there is no evidence that Stone heard Wright speak, she probably knew of her. The Stone family subscribed to the *Thomas's Massachusetts Spy or Worcester Gazette* and it reported on a "Fanny" Wright lecture.[28] By the time Lucy was in her teens, her family subscribed to the *Liberator* and the *Anti-Slavery Standard*,[29] two newspapers that would certainly have given Stone exposure to the idea of women transgressing the barrier of feminine propriety. For example, in 1832, when Stone was fourteen years old, William Lloyd Garrison—editor of the *Liberator*[30]—depicted a slave woman in chains under the caption, "Am I Not a Woman and a Sister?" and concluded that a "Ladies' Department" in the newspaper "would add greatly to its interest, and give a new impetus to the cause of emancipation."[31] Noting that one million women are enslaved, Garrison urges their white counterparts to act on their behalfs. The image of that woman in chains combined with Wright's idea that women are entitled to an equal education, especially instruction in speech, may have fired Stone's desire to go to college even when no college was open to women: "When her father heard of her wish to go to college, he said to his wife, 'Is the child crazy?'"[32]

In 1843 Lucy Stone enters Oberlin College, the only college in the United States that gave degrees to women that were equivalent to a bachelor's degree. And Stone is the first woman to major in speech and become a public speaker. While at school, she writes to her brother, saying that with an education in speech women will be able to determine what their "appropriate sphere" is.[33] She believes she can secure speech training at Oberlin,[34] even though Oberlin had never previously permitted women to take courses in rhetoric or public speaking. In fact, Professor James H. Fairchild, who calls the women's rights movement "the Rozinante of reform," tells his students "it is a thing positively disagreeable to both sexes to see a woman as a public character."[35] When Abby Kelley lectures at Oberlin, Fairchild describes her as "a shocking specimen of what woman becomes when out of her place."[36]

Oberlin's stance on women and public speaking was typical. Six years before Oberlin had opened its doors to women, the General Association of the Congressional Ministers of Massachusetts issued a "Pastoral Letter" to the churches under their jurisdiction, warning them "against letting women speak in public."[37] In this light, Emma Willard's proposal to the New York Legislature for opening an Academy for Girls in Troy, New York, assures them "that public speaking [would] form no part of female education."[38] And three decades after Lucy Stone graduates from Oberlin, Rev. Dr. Isaac See is censured by the synod of New Jersey and the General Assembly of the Presbyterian Church for allowing two unmarried women to speak from the pulpit.[39]

Lucy Stone is angry and frustrated after learning that the Oberlin faculty has voted to exclude women from *participating* in the speeches and debates in rhetoric classes. She had entered college to learn rhetoric and public speaking only to be told that gender is the deciding factor in the practical application of rhetorical principles. In a letter she wrote to her parents during her first year at Oberlin, she reveals her disappointment: "I was never in a place where women are so rigidly taught that they must not speak in public."[40] She experiences firsthand the degree and severity with which she is set apart from rhetoric while at the same time she is included in it. But Stone can only audit the class taught by Professor James Thome, head of the Rhetoric Department at Oberlin.[41] Once, Professor Thome agreed to a debate between Stone and Antoinette ("Nette") Brown, who became the first female Protestant minister in the United States. However, the girls' debate "drew fire" from college authorities and the Ladies' Board.[42] Eventually, Lucy and Nette organized their own rhetoric group, which met in the woods to practice debate. During the winter months, a woman agreed to let Lucy and Nette debate inside her home. One debate, titled "Resolved: That Women Should Not Study Politics,"[43] suggests that women are actively moving in the house of rhetoric and gaining the use of its powers of decision making but that the display of women's power and authority is sequestered from the main floor of the house.

To prepare for the debate, Stone relies on the two texts from Thome's class that she audits, Porter's *Rhetorical Reader* and Whately's *Logic and Rhetoric*. The "charging records" from the Oberlin College Library also show that Stone checked out Hugh Blair's *Lectures on Rhetoric and Belles-Lettres* on March 4, 1846.[44] Although there is no record of what happened during the debate, the details from this vignette, in particular the secretive schooling, leave behind footprints, showing how women's entrée in the house continues via the back door. Eventually, as Stone practices debate and gains rhetorical skills in college, the corridor-like path extends further in the house. As it widens, women gain increasing access to the interior décor—the public platforms and podiums as Stone breaks more ground at Oberlin, but, at the same time, her authority is denied.

At an Oberlin commencement during the mid-nineteenth century, it was commonplace for essays to be composed and read by the highest-scoring members of the graduating class. For Lucy Stone, a first in her graduation class, it also meant that she would have to remain silent at the spring commencement in 1847 while the rhetoric professor delivered her essay. At this juncture in the house of rhetoric, Stone refuses to submit an essay and then uses her refusal as a comment on the situation of women in the house of rhetoric. In a letter to her parents, Francis and Hannah Stone, she explains why she will not submit an essay. It "would make public acknowledgment of the rectitude of the principle which . . . denies to [women] the privilege of being co-laborers with men in any sphere to which their ability makes them adequate; and that no word or deed of mine should ever look towards the support of such a principle, or even to its toleration."[45] Her family supports her decision not to write. Her brother says in a letter of June 6, "You spoke of not writing for commencement unless you could read your own composition, as you think it would be a sacrifice of principle. We think you do right in not writing."[46] After leaving Oberlin, Stone sets a path straight for the center of the house—the great room reserved for the warrior-citizen.

Although Lucy Stone's family supported her decision not to submit a graduation essay, they were not keen about her going out in the world and speaking in public on women's rights. Her brother, Francis, calls it a "lean" pursuit.[47] Her mother, Hannah, refuses to give consent to her daughter's decision to become a public speaker because she objects to women speaking in public. However, she tells her daughter that she would approve of Lucy going from house to house and shoring up interest in her cause. In response to her mother, Stone writes: "Should I go, as you said from house to house to do it [speak publicly], when I could tell so many more in less time if they should be gathered in one place? You do not object, or think it wrong for a man to plead the cause of the suffering and the outcast, and surely the moral character of an act is not changed if it is done by a woman. I would not be a public speaker if I sought a life of ease."[48]

Striking out from college on an abolitionist path that many women would follow, Stone lectures for the Anti-Slavery Society. In Boston, she goes to the Great Exhibition of 1851 and there sees Hiram Powers's statue *The Greek Slave* (figure 3.1).[49] Considered one of the "lions of the exhibition,"[50] it is located in the American section, where it stands in the middle of the room.

The Boston that Stone arrives in is becoming something of an "Athenian agora,"[51] a miniature "Athens in America."[52] Stone is entering not only a city but also, allegorically speaking, the original house of rhetoric. Based on "the idea of educated gentlemen engaged in civil discussion with a tolerant regard for the differing opinions of others,"[53] Boston embraces "rhetoric" as its "great temple,"[54]

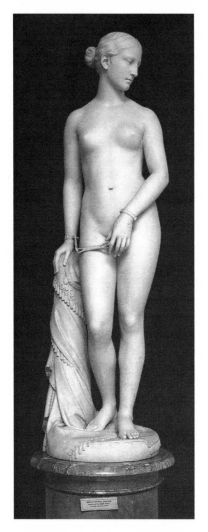

Figure 3.1. *The Greek Slave,* 1869. Hiram S. Powers, American, 1805–73. Marble statue: 65 ½ x 19 ¼ x 18 ¾ in. Height of pedestal: 30 ¼ in. Brooklyn Museum 55.14. Gift of Charles F. Bound.

recuperating the notion of rhetoric as an archi-techne that envelops the contemporary sociopolitical atmo*sphere*, like a frame of a house. Ironically, set in this temple and gathering the material weight of rhetoric's great theme of freedom and escape from tyranny is *The Greek Slave.*

While the stone is used to feature the quest for human rights in the temple of rhetoric, the figure of a woman[55] also elicits public controversy on account of her bare breasts. The rhetorician Edward Everett praises the statue, framing a woman's nudity in terms of the Humility, Modesty, and Restraint that women must show in public.[56] Everett's praise rehashes a familiar line of thought running through the discourse about women in the house of rhetoric. Their presence is tolerated if they plead "the cause of justice and human rights in her sphere"[57]— that is, the sphere of the private. So the nudity of the statue exposes (no pun intended) that women's lives are of the private realm even as they appear in public. In effect, the nude woman is a public expression of the subordinate status of women. The Portrait Monument's nickname, "Three Ladies in a Bathtub," also illustrates women's place. While Mott, Stanton, and Anthony are in the Rotunda, they are bathing and thus nude, and of the private realm not the public realm of speech. It is no wonder they were sent to the basement. For Lucy Stone, Powers's statue was, strictly speaking, a cairn signifying denial.

While Wright had gained an entrée for women in rhetoric through the back door, Stone, by coming to the center of the Boston temple of rhetoric, makes a radical change, one that veers from the project of speaking for women to seeking the authority of women in rhetoric. Stone has been using rhetoric but always under the purview of men and their attack on the institution of slavery. When she veers from her duty, so to speak—that of expanding views of human rights on behalf of the abolitionists to include blacks—many of the abolitionists are conflicted about women expressing "ideas orally in public."[58] In general, there is great support for women to go from home to home and raise money or speak on behalf of the abolitionists' cause.[59] This was, after all, a mother's plea to her daughter. The idea of a woman being a public speaker by going from home to home continually shifted a woman's authority away from the podium—the center of the house of rhetoric—to a private matter—a chat in the kitchen. But when Lucy Stone enters the exhibition in Boston, the cairn in the middle of the room takes hold of her: "There it stood in the silence with fettered hands and half-averted face—emblematic of women."[60] From then on, she proclaims, "I was a woman before I was an abolitionist. I must speak for the women."[61]

To speak for women's human rights marks a significant change in upward direction in the house of rhetoric. In a larger sense, the cairn intensifies activity in the house of rhetoric already begun during the summer of 1848 at Seneca Falls. In a short time, newspapers such as the *Liberator* as well as women's magazines and gift books are "studded" with stories of women speaking in public.[62] One story from 1859 is the novel *Beulah*.[63] Also, on October 17, 1853, Michigan Central College in Spring Arbor reports that two women gave ten-minute speeches on women's rights: "No woman has heretofore been found who dared make this innovation [to speak in public] upon long-established customs."[64] In 1870, the Chicago Board of Education appoints Miss Camilla Leach professor of rhetoric and literature in the high school.[65] In 1871, Frances Willard becomes president of Evanston College for Ladies, which, at that time, has no institutional affilia-tion with Northwestern University.[66] In June 1873, the institution incorporated into Northwestern University and, under conditions largely dictated by her, Wil-lard becomes dean of the Women's College and professor of rhetoric in the Fac-ulty of Liberal Arts, composed entirely of men, "most of whom were educated in European universities."[67] In terms of teaching rhetoric at Northwestern, Willard organizes what amounted to a Senate and House of Representatives of young women in the college. These women deliberate on issues of policy.[68] Now I re-call Willard's inclusion in Statuary Hall.

All in all, between 1830 and 1860 over a hundred women became public speak-ers.[69] In this way, women were adding and inserting themselves into the house of rhetoric. As such, they were using the missive of metonymy—to bring themselves into greater and greater association with the house of rhetoric—strategically.

There is, as I mentioned before, a critical moment in the rise of women, a moment called time o' night. This time happens in the midst of a sea change, a radical turn where women pursue not access as much as their authority. In dra-matic terms, the critical moment irrupts when Stone enters Boston—that temple of rhetoric—sees the stone statue, and proclaims that from then on she would speak for women. In a larger sense, the critical moment can be sensed as women—like Elizabeth Cady Stanton and Susan B. Anthony—organize to change the subject, a change marked by a move from women using speech to speak about slaves' rights to using it to address women's rights. With this shift, women enact authority to be decision makers (or voters). Stone describes women changing the subject of their speeches as an impetus that exposes a time o' night—taboos against women in rhetoric. "She [Angelina Grimké] found foes in the Anti-Slavery household." Her greatest foes, however, are men who harbor a "prejudice against a woman speaking in public," a prejudice so deep that it outweighs their love for the cause of freedom.[70] Elizabeth Cady Stanton notes it is just fine as long as "Sarah and Angelina Grimké and Abby Kelley" were advocating "liberty for the black race," but it is not permissible for women to claim authority for themselves. Stanton says the opponents to women speaking in public are everywhere. The opponents are "found not only in the ranks of the New England clergy but among the most big-oted [and liberal] Abolitionists." In fact, "many a man, who advocated equality most eloquently for a Southern plantation, could not tolerate it at his own fire-side."[71] The prejudice against women's authority in the house of rhetoric is deep and wide.[72]

The core of this objection to women's authority, as one newspaper astutely noted, is that women "lacked the capacity to reason equally with men" in the sociopolitical realm.[73] The attribution of the lack, we must recall, is built into the very decision-making process as a rhetorical practice. The lack of women's authority is visible in the house, theoretically and concretely. Since women lack the capacity to reason as well as men, the theory goes that women are *akuron*: they do not have the prerequisite of authority for deliberation and decision making. This prerequisite is hewn in the place of the public assembly in ancient Greece. In the depths of the house—the palindrome of the <CIVIC>—there is the rattle of bone on the floor—that of the male warrior-citizen going back and forth from the podium to speak about political matters, one who possesses the exclusive power to reason. In this house design, women do not possess the prerequisite of authority to enact the process. Thus, as women make inroads and assert their authority, the ground beneath them is "always already" shifting their path. The palindrome of the <CIVIC> is translating or altering their steps.

The translation in the first instance—first meaning women seeking authority in a way never before imagined—is achieved using a protocol of metonymy—antonomasia (literally "naming instead") and its worker bee "epithet."[74] The trope does what it literally says it does—it uses another name instead of the proper name and the new name diminishes women. In this way, the trope does the duty of shifting women's authority to a realm below that of a man's power. What is crucial to note about the shift is that few observe it; if they do notice, they dismiss it as petty since the focus should be on the actual access a woman or a group of women garners.

What happens to Frances Wright and Lucy Stone (even Hillary Clinton, to some degree) after they enter the house of rhetoric—as ruled by antonomasia—follows a predictable pattern. The trope replaces their proper name with another name. Often this "naming instead" works in conjunction with an epithet that is used to draw attention to the authority a woman claims for herself as accidental or unusual. In this way, the woman can be added because she is the exception, which ultimately (as we will see in the next chapter) sets her up to exchange her authority for something far less than what she bargained for, or, as we will see in the following pages, the accidental functions to retrofit a woman's putative authority with "accidental" traits—that of being weird and monstrous. No body, much less that of a woman, would want to claim these traits for herself. The accidental traits morph a woman's body into something that does not belong in the house proper.[75] In this way, the trope gains its power to oust her authority and justify banishing a woman to the basement. It is also worth noting that before a woman is sent below, she may provide the audience a kind of pleasure, especially for the audience that is inclined to enjoy watching the deviant perform. She becomes a freak in a carnival sideshow.

At the turn of the nineteenth century, one of the most used epithets was "infidel."[76] One of Frances Wright's many epithets was the "High Priestess of Infidelity"[77] or simply "The Infidel."[78] Sometimes, of course, infidelity is another word for atheism and, as such, it refers to the content of a woman's speech. In 1828 in Cincinnati, for example, when Wright said, "I am no Christian, in the sense usually attached to that word. I am neither Jew nor Gentile, Mohammedan or Theist. I am but a member of the human family,"[79] the clergy called her an infidel and attacked her views as heretical.[80] The clergy is not applying the word *infidel* to Frances Wright, but they may have selected the word for its resonances with the epithets associated with her. Epithets gain their power to overturn the addition not by extolling or deprecating the behavior of a particular individual but by designating the named subject's membership in a class of behavior types.[81] The epithet means to show the typical, regular, definitive characteristics common to the subject named. Insofar as the epithet refers to what can be said about a subject and is used symbolically to represent a class or type, it reflects how hearers were *usually* disposed to see the unusual event of a woman speaking publicly for the first time. "The Infidel" signals an impropriety, an accidental loosening of the prerequisites in the house. So typed and identified, the woman's presence is altered and then her authority is undermined.

Frances Wright was also called "The New Aspasia."[82] In ancient Athens, Aspasia was an "intellectual companion" to Pericles.[83] She gained access to the intellectual scene as a *hetairos*, a "courtesan," as opposed to a "common prostitute."[84] With respect to the intellectual and political scene, letters to the editor encouraged listeners and spectators to hear and see the figure of the public-speaking woman in nineteenth-century America as Aspasia. Such letters depict Aspasia as a "prostitute" who gains control of Pericles/leaders and, by implication, Athens/America through assertions of sexuality,[85] whereas popular theology represented women speaking in public in terms of social "pollution"[86] and used the figure of "Jezebel." The epithet of Anne Hutchinson was "American Jezebel."[87] The press and editorials represented women in speech in the context of ancient Athens. They were cast as Aspasia-like, leaning on a would-be leader and exercising undue influence by "sitting in the laps of the highest and lowest" of men.[88] It was a natural next step for the press to label a woman who spoke publicly as a whore; in fact, women who came to hear women speaking in public were also called "whores and harlots."[89] Seen as having no legitimate authority, a woman who displayed power was called a bitch. In New York, a mob shouted out at Frances Wright, "Put her out! Put the old bitch out!"[90] The expression "put her out" brings into sharp focus how the trope functions to swap a woman's proper name in the name of prostitution. It also shows its capacity to grab, hold down, and capture the authority of a woman. In this way the epithet of "bitch" is the main rhetorical trope used to turn women who speak into "beautiful female devils."[91] In effect, the trope is the motor logic that takes them out of (public) office. With respect to the house of speech, a woman who spoke in public had to be "put out" because she was an "incendiary."[92] As the word *incendiary* suggests, women who were speaking in public were so disruptive to the arrangement or disposition of speech—the arrangement of the city, the concrete slab on which the house stands—that any assertion of authority expressed by women was comparable to a moral and political destruction by fire.

A more moderate view, however, held that women either improved or lowered the standards of those they touched. "Civilized society" spends much of its time around females. Time spent with females has an "influence among us." Either females "perpetually" improve "our [male] character" or they "debase it." The *Liberator* reported the problem: Women (potentially) debase the character of men because women disregard what is proper.[93] Their talk is so "debased" that they enter "as a vice of style, rather than a virtue of style. They have made every subject they touch odious."[94] The disregard for the proper is treated as a systemic problem in the house of rhetoric. Aristotle forewarned of this. He explains the "looseness (*anesis*)" and impropriety of women is attributed to their "laxity of manners" and qualities of mind generally associated with "servility," which is typical of the "character and conduct of women."[95]

In addition to the epithets "infidel," "Jezebel," and "Aspasia," the monster, as I mentioned before, is another of its forms by which the presumed authority of a woman speaking publicly is discovered and sent down the stairs. On at least two separate occasions, Lucy Stone described how women who spoke in public were "regarded as something monstrous" and called "monstrous woman."[96] Frances Wright also acquired epithets related to the monster. Added to her name were the epithets of "Beelzebub," "female monster," and "unnatural."[97] The *Louisville Focus* treated the idea of a woman speaking publicly as an animal let loose: "Miss Wright . . . has with ruthless violence, broken loose from the restraints of decorum, which draw a circle around the life of women; and with contemptuous disregard for the rule of society, she has leaped over the boundary of feminine modesty, and laid hold upon the avocations of man, claiming a participation in them for herself and her sex. Miss Wright stands condemned of a violation of the unalterable laws of nature."[98] Wright's speaking in public was represented as a hideous apparition.

The *New York Commercial Advertiser* (October 20, 1836) described Wright as a "bundle of womanhood, somewhere about six feet in longitude, with a face like a Fury, and her hair cropped like a convict." The *New York American* (January 8, 1829) equated a woman speaking in public with vice and imaged it as a monster.

One cartoon, "A Downwright Gabbler or a goose that deserves to be hissed," depicts Frances Wright lecturing with the body of a woman and the head of a goose.[99] Fusing a woman with a bird associates women with an irrational capacity for politics, signaling her lack of authority. One reporter expressed the relation between a woman and birds this way: "But when one . . . shamefully obtrudes herself upon the public waiving alike modesty, gentleness, and every amiable attribute of her sex . . . she ceases to be a woman" and becomes "a female monster."[100]

By 1870 the epithets of "Jezebel," "monster," "Aspasia," and "infidel" fell from common usage. Women who followed the path of Frances Wright are called "Fanny Wrighters." The new epithet continues to fix attention on the referent's lack of fitting behavior—moral and bodily deviations—within the house. But as we will see in the next chapter, the translations of their authority continue, giving the impression that the rules have changed and that women are gaining ground and pushing down the barriers of authority. But the epithets remain, albeit in a shadowy way, keeping the question of a women's propriety with respect to public positions an open one.

For example, when Susan B. Anthony speaks on May 19, 1893, to the Congress of Representative Women, held concurrently with the World's Columbian Exposition, she quotes a preacher who had come up to her after one of her speeches and said, "I would rather see my wife and daughter in their coffins than addressing a public meeting."[101] And in Laramie City, Colorado, where the first panel of women as grand jurors was sworn in, the judge's response to the motion to quash the panel suggests that the epithet of the infidel was still figuring the body of a woman: "There is not the slightest impropriety in any lady occupying this position." It is "eminently proper for women to sit upon the grand juries."[102] The judge's response indicates that while women appear in public as decision makers, what they are seen as assumes their authority to be below that of a man's. The issue is not that the epithets from "infidel" to "bitch" have ceased to figure the body of a woman in public; rather, the issue is that the epithet functions very well.

In this vein, I want to recall that in the 1970s "Bellacosa Bella" was cast as a woman having no "moral" right to run (for political office) against a man. And more than thirty years after she ran for office and as women continue to gain more and more access to leadership opportunities, the epithets are still out there, hunting down the body of a woman. Upon her appointment as Harvard's first female president, Drew Gilpin Faust, as I mentioned at the beginning of this chapter, acquired the epithet "Chainsaw Drew." While the name swap may refer to her cost-cutting measures while at the Radcliffe Institute, the teeth of the chainsaw allude to the scary imagery of the vampire-monster, whose teeth also make cuts. Bitch, witch, and chainsaw: as Hillary Clinton made a first try at assuming authority of the highest kind, the oldest epithets were let loose to hunt it out and turn it down.

While Lucy Stone never wished for women to experience what she had endured, it remains a problem if we do not "[t]hink what it would be like to live perpetually in the midst of scorn and reproach; to [hear], 'This Jezebel [read: this bitch] has come among us.'"[103] Women in positions of leadership are quickly demonized. As Kathleen Hall Jamieson puts it, "women who [try to] succeed in politics and public life will be scrutinized under a different lens from that applied to successful men, and for longer periods of time."[104]

Postscript

The function of this postscript is to display how antonomasia and epithet are used continually in the house to grant access and deny authority to women. Specifically, it is imperative to realize that the epithets that chased down Frances Wright continue to chase women who seek positions of power. For example, let us jump ahead one hundred and fifty years to the late twentieth century and consider a question put to the first woman elected to the House of Representatives from Colorado. When a constituent asked Patricia Schroeder how she, a mother of two small children, could be a legislator at the same time, she responded, "Yes. I have a uterus and a brain, and they both work."[105] That the uterus draws from women's capacity for speech, thus leaving her unfit to lead, can be traced back to a theory of sex set forth in ancient Greek (Aristotelian) thought, specifically that children draw from the mother's capacity for reason or speech.[106] In effect, the constituent's question—designed to undermine Schroeder's authority to lead—reflects the residue of a belief transmitted through educational institutions for several hundred years.

The uterus-trumps-the-brain logic resurfaced on YouTube in the twenty-first century with depictions of Hillary Clinton as a bitch, a uterus metaphor applied to a woman's speech.[107] To refer to a woman as a bitch replicates the view of a woman as a performing dog who in bearing a child has forfeited any chance of delivering a speech with authority, the prerequisite to being a leader. Women do not have the goods to be a leader, decision maker, or president because they (are expected to) give their speech over to their womb for birthing a child.[108] The bitch is also the sign of a female dog, an image that mocks the authority of woman and signals the end of her speaking as such.[109] In the widely quoted words of James Boswell, a woman speaking in public "is like a dog walking on its hind legs."[110]

When I heard Sarah Palin accept the nomination for vice president at the Republican National Convention, I cringed when she compared herself to a dog. Palin used the image of a mother/bulldog with lipstick to refer to her authority to lead. As this mother of five children fuses her image with that of a dog, I can't help but wonder if she has not translated her competence as a leader into old terms that will diminish her.[111]

In fact, there is evidence that the exceptional woman, which Palin may be headed to become, may be called a cynosure. Lest we forget, a cynosure is at once a bright star and a dog's tail (from the Latin *Cynosūra*, Greek *Kynōsoura*, the constellation Ursa Minor, equivalent to *kyn[ōs]*, dog's genitive of [*kyōn* + *ourá*]). The cynosure has been admired and accepted within the rhetorical places. There is a room for this dog with lipstick in the house of rhetoric, but no room for bitch or witch. As the *Rochester Democrat* proclaimed it more than one hundred years ago, "As the *rule*, our prejudice [against women orators] is still very strong, but as the *exception*, as the act of a few women of peculiar gifts, we confess our objections very quietly laid to rest."[112] Or as reported in the *British Anti-Slavery Advocate*, "no one objects to a [singular exceptional] *woman*, the sovereign of England giving a speech from the throne."[113] The distinction I want to make concerning the lipstick, the dog, and the *femme d'exception* is that there is room in the house for one woman or maybe a few women, but not for women en masse.[114]

In fact, eighty years after women entered the house, the case for the exceptional woman was renewed in the first half of the twentieth century just as thousands of women moved into public-speaking positions, such as telephone operators. Professor John Erskine,[115] for example, wrote about the exceptional woman and insisted that "we men" have reason "to be on guard against women."[116] It should come as no surprise, then, that Erskine admires the singular woman in the history of rhetoric, such as Sappho.[117] The last chapter of his *Influence of Women and Its Cure* is devoted to retelling Greek legends, always turning an exceptional woman into an icon of power associated with woman.[118] Because the exceptional woman has long had an honorary place in the United States, her acting rhetorically is not an acceptance of women's authority[119] and, thus, the cynosure is not a threat. This may explain, in part, Palin's popularity among men. Her appeal may derive from the simple fact that she cast her authority as an outsider and thus appears as an exception in the house.

4

The Building—of the Future

The end is not yet in sight, but it cannot be far away.

—Lucy Stone

. . . you pass under a bridge . . . and all of a sudden . . . you are in the Woman's Building . . . and you know that in what seemed like one step you've passed out o' darkness and into the light.

—Clara Burnham

The road before us is shorter than the road behind.

—Lucy Stone

In the last chapter I discovered Frances Wright in the house of rhetoric. I began moving down the halls and eventually came to Lucy Stone. Meeting up with Lucy Stone meant another trip to Washington, D.C. At the Library of Congress, I read some of the speeches and private letters she had written and that were written to her. Using Lucy Stone as a placeholder of women's rise in the house of rhetoric, I left the library around noon for a walk. As luck would have it, the Capitol is close by just as it starts to rain. As I enter the Capitol, I am in another time and place. It is 1893. I am standing in the "White City," a nickname for a group of five white buildings that comprise the main area—the Court of Honor—of the World's Columbian Exposition in Chicago.

What propels me from the Capitol to the "White City" is the imagination of the "Traveler" (William Dean Howells's disguise) who visited the fair and wrote about it. Upon his arrival, the Traveler said, it is as if the Capitol in Washington, D.C., "had set sail" and "landed" on the shore of Lake Michigan.[1] I am not all that surprised, therefore, when the Capitol turns into a sailboat that washes me ashore at the fair's main gate. For the character called the Traveler, the connection between the two places is architectural. The Traveler made the metaphoric leap from the Capitol to the "White City" based on architectural appearances. The Capitol is white and the buildings of the "White City" are white. Thus they connect in time and space through color. But there is a deeper underlying architectural connection between them. This is the architects' conception of civic space based on a model of civic exchange. Therein is the house of rhetoric. Everything— and I do mean everything—is meant to promote a people's experience of the civic realm.[2]

As I set up my stay (actually a stay in two spaces), the fair and the house of rhetoric—I continue to use two kinds of movements—that of going up and down signified by the staircase—to trace the path of women from within. Unlike the Capitol that gave me access to the house of rhetoric before, there is no staircase in the space of the fair proper; rather there is the projection of a hierarchy in the conceived space of the fairgrounds. Arranged by those in power, the buildings create an order as well as order the fairgoers' experience that is akin to walking up and down stairs. As I make the hierarchical projection visible, I stage the two kinds of movements.

Here is how the movement generating women's access in the house of rhetoric looks in the fair proper. Women have for the very first time their own build- ing—the Woman's Building[3]—for the official display of their accomplishments. In fact, it is billed as a major "discovery of women." As one woman put it at the building's dedication ceremony: "Even more important than the discovery of Co- lumbus, which we are gathered together to celebrate, is the fact that the General Government has just discovered women."[4] This new mode of inclusion within the fair represents upward movement—like going up the stairs in the house. As I turn to the Woman's Building and follow a particular tropical movement asso- ciated with metonymical addition, I feature a productive change of relation be- tween women and rhetoric. The indecent epithets used to speak of women's pres- ence as leaders are rotated far out of range to warrant any impact. So how are women turned down the stairs? Using the classification system as key indicators of the development of the denial of women's authority, the next stage features the tropical action called hypallage. To banner it as the changeling is useful be- cause it exposes both sides of the action of exchange and its effects. One side of the action renders women present, and yet on the other side this presence con- ceals the fact that their authority is not present, a denial especially blanketed by the public recognition of women's work and accomplishments.

The second kind of movement that hypallage entails is finding how, where, and to what extent women are separated from the condition of authority even while they are included in the house of rhetoric. Remember from the last chap- ter that epithets act like notices indicating that women have gained access to the house. But they were also the obvious ruts that kept women from being regarded fully and equally as decision makers. As tropes, the epithets overturned women's version of themselves as leaders and in effect stifled their advances. Now as we go to Chicago, where women have their own building, the movement of separation or the going down the stairs is not flagrant because the tropical force of exchange is to make things look equal when they are not.

Here is how I use hypallage[5] to track women's separation from the condition of authority in the house of rhetoric qua the World's Columbian Exposition. I make two visits to the fair. I use each day at the fair to address one part of the tropical exchange. First, I go to the fair and I use the main gate, the most renowned of the three entrances as it invites the fairgoer to interpret his or her experience of being at the fair as tantamount to the civic realm. From that entrance, I'll saunter over to the Woman's Building. My motility gives me unique access to the representation of the civic sphere. As I explore the fairgrounds, I rely on the architects and their conceived notions of how to create space for public use.

The next day, I go to the fair, but this time I use another gate—a third entrance leading directly to the amusement park. Again, I will make my way to the Woman's Building relying on various books. As I go this way, I encounter plenty of excitement, including all kinds of food, amusements, and exhibitions. To decipher what I see and feel in my immediate physical environs, I rely on various books, such as W. Hamilton's *The Time-Saver: A Book Which Names and Locates 5,000 Things at the World's Fair That Visitors Should Not Fail to See*.[6] When I arrive at the Woman's Building on the second day, I have come back to the place I arrived at before. With this return, I am to witness the connection between the gates—that of the main entrance leading to the Court of Honor with the third gate leading to the Midway or amusement park. As the point of connection between the gates induces a (hierarchical) pathway in and through the fairgrounds, it brings about the image of a going up and down. This leads to a mirror image of the staircase. I pass through the Woman's Building. In the reflective bend is where the tropological activity transpires, an exchange happening on two levels. Outside the Woman's Building the stairs figure in the design as the architects approved all that was erected inside the fair. Inside the Woman's Building they are prefigured by the decisions of the fair's architects to conceive the inner space of all buildings as coherent with the exterior order. The buildings—their unity of style, order, and arrangement—should be the "sure index"[7] of what is expressed within.

To review, my two days at the fair bear witness to two realms—one physically represented by the buildings and one serving as a context for rhetoric. The two spaces do not add up; rather, they create a pathway from one gate through the Woman's Building to another gate, an angle of vision where I feature the tropical action of hypallage coming into play. I use the insights I glean from their model—specifically the architects' vision of the buildings as a conceived experience of civic exchange drawn from the ancient Greeks—and link them to the palindrome of the <CIVIC>—the model rhetoric possesses about its context and itself. Drawing from both models, I detail how the Woman's Building marks women's important addition to rhetoric and at the same time how it denies them full exclusion by weakening the conditions of their authority.

Because my visits at the fair culminate each day at the Woman's Building, I begin with a brief overview of the circumstances surrounding the Woman's Building.

Having a Woman's Building was no small feat. It stands at a halfway mark, pointing to the outgrowth of intense and sustained activity in the women's movement. What happened almost twenty years before in the Centennial Exhibition of 1876 in Philadelphia puts this building in perspective. The plan and design of the Centennial failed to include women. Many women were very angry. The president of the National Women Suffrage Association, Matilda Gage, held a meeting in New York City and said it was high time that women embrace the words of Abigail Adams and "foment a rebellion."[8] Following Adams's lead, Gage proclaimed, "We will not hold ourselves bound by laws in which we have no voice or representation."[9] Toward that end, Gage and many others, including Susan B. Anthony and Elizabeth Cady Stanton, protested women's exclusion by going to Philadelphia "to declare freedom."[10] Their plan was to make a Declaration of Rights of Women on the Fourth of July on the fairgrounds, thus marking women's long walk down the hall of rhetoric that Wright began on the Fourth back in 1828. The chairman, however, refused to allow this event. Long story short: Susan B. Anthony eventually read the document at the Centennial Exhibition.

Not to diminish Adams's moment of "foment," but it was no accident that Anthony got away with her act of disobedience without a fine or some other punishment. The planners—the Centennial Board—realized that to have a celebration would actually require the cooperation of women; they needed them especially to attend to the details and generally assist with the organization to ensure the success of the Centennial. In an effort to appease the protests against the exclusion of women and not have Gage and her group create a scene, the board looked the other way when Anthony was speaking. Then it instituted a women's committee of thirteen members, one for each of the original states. Elizabeth Duane Gillespie was invited to head this committee. I know little about her except that she agreed under the condition that women's work would be included in the Main Exhibition Hall. In addition, she agreed not to take pay for her time and energy but asked that the pay she would have received be diverted in a special budget to support the women's exhibition. The board agreed to set up a budget, but the director general did not hold up his end of the deal and eventually denied women the space they had been promised. Despite protests by several women, the director general refused to budge, saying that there was no room for women's work. The space was used up. Not wanting to be derailed, the women on the committee decided to have their own exhibit and their own building. They asked for Gillespie's pay back—the pay that was meant to be used for the women's exhibition. The director general said he had no money "left in the coffers" to support a women's building.[11] In the end, the accomplishments of women, whether related to their public voice or to private work, were not "officially" recognized (i.e., neither publicly funded nor financed by private enterprise) at the Centennial Exhibition in Philadelphia in 1876. There was no women's exhibition in 1876. But in 1893, with the Woman's Building, there was. The Woman's Building was something of a coup d'état.

The story of the Centennial is not yet over and I understand what happens next as crucial for seeing how the "exchange" works, tropically speaking. What happens next is debate among two groups of feminists about how women should be recognized and what role—if any—the Woman's Building should have at the exposition. By going through this debate, we can grasp the staircase running through the building. That is to say, the same two kinds of movements—one that actively adds women and one that separates their addition from authority—can be experienced by the discerning viewer. In effect, the Woman's Building becomes another version of the house of rhetoric but even more insidious than the original, as women internalize it, splintering white women from black women and upper-class women from lower-class women. I do not devote my time in the house to exploring all of the various side rooms that deal with political nuances and ideological factions of the interior struggle among women in the house of rhetoric. Rather, I am interested in what the interior struggle meant for the larger question of authority at the fair as well as in the house when not one woman—in or out, white or black, upper or working class—could meet its condition.

With money raised "through the exertions of women of the United States," the exhibition of 1876 included a Women's Pavilion, a little wooden thing. Under the charge of Miss Emma Allison of Grimsby, Iowa, the Women's Pavilion exhibited paintings, machines, and products invented by women, and embroidery and photographs of institutions established and/or run by women.[12] That the accomplishments of women were not "officially" recognized at the Centennial Exhibition in 1876 was considered by many, including Susan B. Anthony, to be "a great disappointment to all interested in the advancement of women."[13] Elizabeth Cady Stanton felt it was good to exhibit women's work in the Women's Pavilion but said that it was an "afterthought, as theologians claim woman herself to have been."[14] The little wooden building "was not," she added, "a true exhibit of woman's art" because it did not reflect her situation. If it were to be a grand exhibition of her life, it would bear "framed copies of all the laws bearing unjustly on women—those which robbed her of her name, her earnings, her property, her children, her person"—on its walls.[15] There is, in this story of the Centennial, a push for an exhibit of women within the main exhibit that is denied. There is also with the Women's Pavilion a push back from this denial. This push-pull played into a configuration of the Woman's Building as a possibility of women's equal authority in the sociopolitical realm and a throwback to the past where it was possible to deny it.

In 1889, when Susan B. Anthony learned of plans for a great world's fair, she began to work and lobby for the inclusion of women.[16] She got it; however, the question of how and in what capacity women would be included remained unsettled. Toward that end, President Harrison in 1890 established a governing body called the Board of Lady Managers.[17] This governing body paralleled the all-white male National Commission, which selected the Board of Lady Managers and charged them with the task of overseeing the exhibition of women's work throughout the exposition. The "chairwoman" of the board was Bertha Honoré Palmer.

By 1890, the question of whether women should work for a separate exhibit or an integrated one was a hotly contested issue. One side, referred to as the Isabellas because they intended to recognize the queen's role in enabling Columbus's discovery, did not want to segregate women's exhibits. This side was composed of suffragists and professional women. Advancing the cause of suffrage, the Isabellas advocated the integration of women's achievements throughout every building in the fair. As Bertha Palmer explained the Isabellas' position, "the exhibit should not be one of *sex*, but of *merit*, and that the women had reached the point where they could afford to compete side by side with men with a fair chance of success, and that they would not *value* prizes given upon the sentimental basis of sex."[18] The main argument for putting women's exhibits alongside men's went something like this: The work of both men and women, from farm to industry, was important and should be displayed together because in daily operations they were already woven together. Since women's work was not easily separated from men's work, it would be difficult, if not impossible, to recognize women's accomplishments separately.

On the other side of the debate was the group known as the Women's Auxiliary. This side was formed through the male exposition committee and consisted of affluent Chicago women who were members of women's clubs, philanthropic societies, and reform groups. Arguing against the Isabellas' position, they advocated segregation and thus a Woman's Building for the exhibition of women's accomplishments. Using the experience at the Centennial Exhibition in Philadelphia as a precedent, the Auxiliary argued "that the valuable work done by women would not be appreciated or comprehended unless shown in a building separate from the work of men."[19] In fact, they argued, it might not get shown at all.

Eventually, the two groups agreed to work together on the Woman's Building. In the end, whether one was identified as an Isabella or an Auxiliary, the majority agreed that there should be a Woman's Building whatever its function and scope. To the satisfaction of the Isabellas, the referendum on the Woman's Building did not require women to enter their work in it. The building's stated function and scope called for women to compete with men for the display of their work and to have it shown appropriately in any building (i.e., Agriculture, Fine Arts) at the fair.

To the satisfaction of the Women's Auxiliary, the Woman's Building represented the official representation of women's accomplishments in all areas, something denied in Philadelphia. Based on Chairwoman Bertha Honoré Palmer's speech delivered at the dedication ceremony of the Woman's Building on May 1, 1893, the general philosophy that guided the process of placement was fairly clear. Adopting a set of values based not on sex but on exceptional service to humanity, the women were given the freedom to choose where they wanted to enter their work for acceptance and ultimate display.[20] When the Board of Lady Managers deemed an exhibit to have "rare merit and value" for humanity, they "encouraged" the exhibitor to have her exhibit "placed under the special care and custody of the ladies,"[21] not in the main exhibit.

In her address, Palmer described the Woman's Building as a sign of the times—a true inclusion, inscription, and addition of women. Using its neoclassical architecture as a signifier of equality, she noted that the building through its symmetry relayed the message that women are equal to men. And the contents of the building testified to women's power and strength and thus supported the architectural form. Although the building housed only women's accomplishments, Palmer emphasized that the building did not stand for the idea that her abilities were "a matter of sex."[22] Thus she did not "wish [the Woman's Building] to be understood as placing an extravagant or sentimental value upon the work of any woman because of her sex."[23] Rather, the building stood as "the first official utterance of women on behalf of women."[24] Here women could represent their position and status for themselves, rather than have their position and status represented by idealists and political economists who fancied that women's place was in the home and who fervently objected to the competition that would result from women's participation in the workforce.

The Woman's Building testified, therefore, to the reality of women, namely that many women—"perhaps three-fourths of the women in the world"—had to work outside the home.[25] It was, therefore, dedicated to women's work that had "been produced in factories, workshops, and studios under the most adverse conditions and with the most sublime patience and endurance."[26] Visitors to the fair were meant to see, in a single showing, women's status and position through their work and their service to the world. Lucy Stone, in a letter written for the World's Columbian Exposition (which was read by her husband, Henry B. Blackwell, since she was ill and near death), summarized the Woman's Building as an alliance with the future: "The end is not yet in sight, but it cannot be far away. . . . The road before us is shorter than the road behind."[27]

With the historical overview in mind, it is time to go to the fair. Each day I walk to the Woman's Building. On the second day, I take a sojourn and go inside.

Of the many ways to enter the fair, the most spectacular is on an actual steamship that goes to the main gate. Doubtless this is why the fair at first sight conjures up the Traveler's vision that the U.S. Capitol as if by sail has landed on the shores of Lake Michigan. As the steamship approaches the main gate, passes under it, and lands, I participate in a ritual of countless fairgoers and observe how they are prompted to move along. I use this observation to detail the conceived space as a civic order. As I go about my day, I follow the steps of tropical movement (I just described as hypallage) and trace the exchange made in procuring the Woman's Building.

From the steamship, I catch a glimpse of the gate. It is a peristyle, which is a series of columns placed strategically to surround and balance the grouping of exhibition buildings to the north and south of the basin. As I pass under the columns, I can't help but wonder about their resemblance to the ancient Greek foundation I explored earlier. For the last four years prior to the World's Columbian Exposition, G. Brown Goode has been promoting[28] a new kind of fair design. In his lecture "The Museum of the Future" delivered before the Brooklyn Institute, he employs an architectural script with ancient Greece as the prototype.[29] Specifically, he advocates erecting local fairgrounds on a model of civic exchange, in effect arguing rhetoric as a context for his architectural model. With this model he claims that local fairs would be transformed from small community events into great expositions of museum-like quality. The museums of the future will offer the "most powerful . . . systems of teaching by means of object lessons."[30] His vision would mean amalgamating the particular or the local under a single roof, and under this roof is the house of rhetoric because the lessons are at some level about civic engagement through discourse.

Many object lessons came out of the Chicago fair—such as how to pronounce words and how to act in the food court.[31] They are not my focus today. I want to explore the architectural script imposed on the fair as a rhetorical experience with attention to the lesson on authority that the house imposes on all who enter it. So I pass under the columns—the peristyle—and enter the house of rhetoric by way of its columns that frame the entrance to its first plane. In their Greek prototype, these columns function architecturally as an "escape" from the wild, bestial, and other irrational forces. So as I pass through them, I also move across the palindrome of the <CIVIC>.

I escape—if you will—into the World's Columbian Exposition, what Daniel H. Burnham (the fair's consulting architect) predicted "would be the third greatest event in American history, following the Declaration of Independence and the Civil War."[32] Standing on the ground and from the perspective of the harbor, I see the U.S. Government building to the north. It is a small structure. From my guidebook, *The Time-Saver*,[33] I know it contains exhibits on George Washington, carrier pigeons, international currency, and the like. Beyond the Government Building, my map shows more buildings such as the Fisheries Building and the Palace of Fine Arts. To the south, the buildings include the Electricity Building, Machinery Hall, and the Railroad Terminal. The Railroad Terminal is a second main gate for arriving at the fair. Whether by steamship or by train, after passing through one of the main gates, I eventually pass the Administration Building. Now I am right smack in the middle of the Court of Honor.

The Court of Honor consisted of five neoclassical massive buildings, "with cornices a uniform height, painted a dazzling white, and supremely ornamented,"[34] and because of the dazzling white paint, the court area was called the "White City." As for the massive size of the buildings, Machinery Hall stands out: it was "six times the size of the Roman Coliseum."[35] Also in the Court of Honor stood the Manufacturers and Liberal Arts Building, which was the largest building in the world. It could hold one hundred thousand people and contained forty-four acres of exhibit pavilions from many nations. When William Dean Howells (as "Traveler") saw the Manufacturers and Liberal Arts Building, he was reminded again of "our national capitol" because the Manufacturers and Liberal Arts Building—like the Capitol—"shows its mighty mass" above the thicket around it and thus is the "light" on the "night of our Evolution."[36] Above all, Howells called the "White City" the first and full embodiment of "a real civic life."[37] The space—the Court of Honor—had become the "the glory that was Greece."[38]

To start with the first image, the ostensible reason why the "White City" would be extolled as the U.S. Capitol (and analogically the house of rhetoric) was its architecture. Meant to evoke core values, beliefs, and ideologies, the neoclassical building stylized a show of unity with "many opportunities" for a "diversity" of displays and exhibits. The consulting architects for the World's Columbian Exposition were Daniel H. Burnham and John W. Root. They hand-selected several other architects, including the firm McKim, Mead, and White, who leaned toward the classical. Their "influence is evident in scores of libraries, stations, educational institutions, and private houses scattered over the country."[39] When all the architects met to discuss the building for the fair, the firm made a strong case for the classical style. Charles McKim argued successfully that all the buildings be done in white, and the committee adopted the idea.[40] Absent from the initial meeting, however, was John Root, who was ill and died unexpectedly three days later. Root, it is fair to say, would have voiced a strong opposition to the firm's plan. Root wanted the fair to be an "expression of the heartland." He envisioned the buildings painted in a variety of colors. But under the sway of the classical style, other styles were dismissed. Thus, Montana's plan to build a pavilion in the shape of a mountain was rejected. The firm said it would be "an exceedingly ugly thing."[41] It also rejected South Dakota's plan to erect a pavilion in the form of a Sioux tepee. This, said the chief architect, would present "a rather startling effect from an artistic and architectural standpoint."[42] In the end, Montana, South Dakota, and other states were advised to make their designs coincide with the fair's overarching themes and evoke its meaning of civic unity.

Remarking afterward on the process of designing and building the World's Columbian Exposition, Daniel Burnham said that the buildings were what the Greeks and Romans would have wished "to create in permanent form."[43] When Henry Adams visited the "White City," he said he thought he had "leaped directly from Corinth and Syracuse" to Chicago.[44] The classical style had been imposed on all it contained, becoming the "first expression of American thought as a unity," observed Adams.[45] As a side note, he predicted that one day America would want to forget about politicians and remember these architects for their influence in shaping thought.[46]

And so, as I pass through the columns to enter the "White City," I also enter, by extension, the house of rhetoric. Architecturally, the columns signify the "escape" and thus the foundation rhetoric possesses about its context and itself. The Court of Honor symbolizes the ancient bēma–the place where the warrior-citizen stepped onto the platform and entered public life. It stands as the boundary separating the rational style of deliberation from what Isocrates and Cicero called the uncivil life of the beast, something akin to wild emotional discourse.

Figure 4.1. The Women's Building, World's Columbian Exposition. Courtesy the Field Museum, Chicago.

Finally, the Court of Honor stands as the boundary of the *ekklēsia*, the public assembly and attendant condition of authority.

But in all of this, there is no sight of the Woman's Building, and so I leave the court proper. From there I walk past several buildings, the Mines and Mining structure, and the Transportation Building. I walk sixteen acres past the Wooded Island. It is only then I saw the Woman's Building (figure 4.1). I laugh when I read in the *Illinois Quarterly* that the Woman's Building was "out of the way."[47]

It was more than three times larger than the Women's Pavilion in Philadelphia. Architecturally speaking, the Woman's Building was a masterpiece of the classical style. The consulting architect, Daniel Burnham, had reviewed Sophia Hayden's plans and deemed the building "in compliance."[48] Her design, which was chosen by a board of male architects, was described as "especially suited for the purposes for which it is to be used—it is chaste and timid."[49] Though impressive, the Woman's Building was chaste and timid because it was unequal in size to its classically styled counterparts in the Court of Honor. The 80,000-square-foot

Woman's Building was, in fact, the smallest building at the fair. It measured 200 feet by 400 feet. The total sum appropriated for it was less than $200,000, as compared to the appropriations in the millions for the other buildings.

Although the building was in the same style as its male counterparts, its white color left the impression that although the building was far from the main area, it remained entrusted to the model of women acting in the public sphere in a pure and good way. Its diminutive size in the architectural model of civic exchange communicated the message that women's work—no matter how accomplished it was—still held a subordinate status. Its location—about twenty acres from its massive male counterparts—reminded me of having to go down the stairs to the basement to see the Portrait Monument. The manner in which the building includes women in a system of exchange—for example, same architectural style but in a diminutive form—is pulled off tropologically by hypallage. I continue to decipher its capacity to make a hierarchical configuration while masking it in a strategy of diversity and democratization.

It is the second day at the fair. There is a third entrance to the fair, the gate to the Midway Plaisance or "Joy Zone." The Midway is spectacular, too. It doesn't have columns, but it does have visibility with George Ferris's wheel. Revolving almost 280 feet above the ground, it was the exposition's Eiffel Tower.[50] The Midway was not exactly a Coney Island, but then again, neither was its fun time entirely separate from the other exhibitions. The Midway strove to "bridge the gap between entertainment and education."[51] Somewhere between an amusement park and a serious and educational strip, all of the exhibits fell under the purview of the architectural model of civic exchange and everything in it was integrated with the teaching focus of the main fair.[52] This Midway, then, emphasized the "cultural aspects of people" in order "to encourage the study of ethnology."[53] All the exhibits were not built in a neoclassical style and thus could allow, say, a tepee where the exhibition area would not permit this of South Dakota. However, the exhibits in the Midway or Joy Zone were arranged in a style in keeping with the vision of the fair's architecture. The order of the exhibits would perform the unity of design. It would render a unified sociopolitical composition while keeping a diversity of displays and exhibits.

The entertainment venues in the Midway were exhibits of native villages. I picked up a pamphlet with pictures of many people, including a Samoan Warrior. I soon discovered these villages were arranged in an ascending order with the "lowest specimens" of humanity at the bottom and the "higher forms" at the top.[54] "Step this way," I hear a man at the midway gate say. I will not step further into their darkness, but I can't stop seeing, hearing, and smelling. Herein was my education, later to be interpreted by my guide Denton Snider. Presumably, the midway offered an opportunity to see people "of every hue, clad in outlandish garb, living in curious habitations, and plying their unfamiliar trades and arts with incomprehensible dexterity," as well as the opportunity "to listen to their barbaric music and witness their heathenish dances."[55] The people of the Da-homey village, for example, were described to the fairgoers as "pets of the public" and as "ancestors of voracious cannibals."[56] For the fairgoers' edification, Chief Rain-in-the-Face was dressed in the "aboriginal and wild west" costume of Indi-ans.[57] There were Amazons, the Wild West shows, and other curiosities.[58] By the time I reached "a large mechanical Uncle Sam" that delivered "40,000 speeches" during the course of the fair,[59] I had walked a strip of land a mile long.[60]

It was then I saw the Woman's Building, standing at the end of the Midway. In her novel *Sweet Clover: A Romance of the White City*, Clara Burnham takes this as-cending approach to the building: "You come out o' that mile-long babel . . . you pass under a bridge—and all of a sudden you are in a great beautiful silence. The angels on the Woman's Building smile down and bless you, and you know that in what seemed like one step you've passed out o' darkness and into the light."[61] Taking this approach as a mode of climbing up the stairs, the Woman's Build-ing was not the building beyond the pale of the Court of Honor. It was the exit out of that "mile-long babel," thus rendering it the rise to the top. According to the literary critic Denton J. Snider, one could "march forward" from the Mid-way, "starting with the lowest specimens of humanity," and then reach continu-ally "upward to the highest stage"[62] to arrive at the Court of Honor. According to Snider, the Court of Honor stood for the top of the stairs. So the Woman's Building headed the top of the Joy Zone. This is the perspective of Burnham, who ascends out of darkness. I had walked to the building the day before. If it stood at the top, it also stood near the bottom—signified by its size and magni-tude with respect to the exhibition proper. The Woman's Building was not ac-tually at the top of the stairs; rather, women separated the order from chaos.

Hypallage grounds the entrances to the Woman's Building in a way that de-fines women's evolving relationship in the house of rhetoric—one that gives them access but denies their authority. From one way, the building stands as site of women's inclusion in the exhibition proper but not the Court of Honor. Women are *in* but they stand in a place *below* the court and in this way their authority is denied. Their denial, however, is not flagrant like an epithet but is exchanged for their being at the top of the Midway. This rotates the up and down in a fash-ion that appears to be equal. They don't have authority in the World's Colum-bian Exposition, but their building and its location display their authority as a kind of lording over—albeit in a chaste and timid form—all that is part of the wild and bestial for which the columns at the main gate denote an escape from.

So this building renders women sort of a halfway house—halfway between the barbarians and the (male) humans.

The museum of the future that Goode saw in local fairs and imagined as an architectural script of civic exchange would impose its ideas "on all who entered it."[63] One of its strictest ideas of order and arrangement can be viewed as the warrior-citizen speaking in the middle.[64] The Midway and its ascending mile of exhibits reproduce the loot that the would-be fairgoer would take to the middle and exchange with others. This is the pattern that yielded to a system of deliberation with a prerequisite of authority to enter the *bēma*, the podium, or the moment of decision making. Before I locate the podium in the context of the fair, it is worth mentioning that several people in the Midway felt like loot. The people of the Dahomey village put up a sign requesting that visitors not ask them "annoying questions about cannibalism."[65] Henry Pratt, founder and builder of the Carlisle Indian School in Carlisle, Pennsylvania, predicted the exhibits would convince the whites of their superiority over Indians. Pratt urged the Bureau of Indian Affairs to avoid showing Indians in "aboriginal and wild west" costume because, he argued, the dress was designed to demonstrate to the whites that nonwhites were not civilized and thus lacked authority to participate as citizens.[66] African Americans organized and responded formally to their treatment within the fair as well. The most sustained response to problems of exhibition confronting a group was by the authors (including Ida B. Wells) of *The Reason Why the Colored American Is Not in the World's Columbian Exposition.*[67] Women lack the capacity to meet the requirement of deliberation and enter the sociopolitical realm with full status as decision makers. As a palindrome, the exhibits not only projected various people's future political status but also demonstrated that the people on display had no authority to deliberate, much less make decisions about their own image in the public sphere.[68]

The system of taking loot has two middle points at the fair. One of them is outside, appearing in the order and arrangement especially in the five white buildings as they make up the center of deliberative activity. Here many speeches are delivered, including Fredrick Jackson Turner's "The Significance of the American Frontier in American History." The other middle as it aims for the possibility of the inclusion of women is precisely at the juncture of the fair and the amusement park. The deliberative activity is not only from without but also from within.

To expose the inner activity of the building as it bears on the pattern of deliberation in which only the warrior-citizen has access to authority, I go back and take a look at how the debate between the Isabellas and the Auxiliary created an internal hierarchy that shows the two kinds of movements: one of the active inclusion of women in the building and one that separated women from it on the basis of authority. During the debate, both sides tried to influence the National Commission, which was given the power to appoint the Board of Lady Managers.

Trying to satisfy the two factions of women, the commission appointed two women from each state and territory, as well as the District of Columbia, eight members at-large, and nine additional delegates from Chicago, eight from the Auxiliary and one Isabella. All told, the committee was composed of 117 middle- and upper-class women, with an equal number of alternates, and "not a single colored woman on the Board proper."[69] Black women were upset because they had no representation on the board and because the board would not take up the question of their inclusion. Hallie Q. Brown sent a letter to each member of the Board of Lady Managers asking "the personal consideration of her plan of appointing some colored person." She said, "It seems to be a settled conviction among the colored people that no adequate opportunity is to be offered them for proper representation in the World's Fair. . . . Permit me to emphasize this fact, that this matter is in earnest discussion, among the representatives of the eight millions of the population of the United States."[70] The response was always the same: hands were tied. But as the protestors pointed out, "when it was ascertained that the seals and glaciers of Alaska had been overlooked" in some exhibit, it was easy for the president or a board proper to rectify those matters.[71]

In the end, one change was made. Imogene Howard, a black woman from New York, was appointed to the state board of management. There were a number of complaints about the makeup of the committee and the delegation of authority. Charlotte Smith of the National Industrial League complained that there were no factory workers on the board.[72] Ultimately blacks and working-class women played the same role as did the Woman's Building in the fair proper: they were in but their authority was diminished.

The World's Columbian Commission gave the Board of Lady Managers plenary power as "the channel of communication through which all women or organizations of women may be brought into relation with the Exposition, and through which all applications for space for the use of women or their exhibits in the building shall be made."[73] This channel of communication reveals the deliberative pattern on which the house of rhetoric is built.

I follow this internal channel as a splinter of the architectural model of civic exchange. I diagram the channel of communication with the three key roles of women at the fair scripted by the décor of the Woman's Building.

Outside the building is statuary. Above the outside door is the statue *Women's Virtue*. This is one that Clara Burnham saw first after she made her way out of the Midway. She described *Women's Virtue* as angels that "smile down and bless you."[74] This central statue was meant to depict the theme of good quality, good worth, and high merit. This image not only opens up a space for women within the newly constituted civic order that the exposition proclaimed but also presents women in public in a positive way. In this vein, the Board of Lady Managers became concerned about how to control the actions of working-class women coming to the fair. The Woman's Building, cast in the mode of women's virtue, provides an opportunity for "young ladies" to take over the drive "for equal rights."[75] In this way, the statue guides lower-class women to trade their identities from workers for (private) wages to workers for (public) causes. Toward this end, Bertha Palmer called a meeting in the spring of 1892 to see what could be done for the breadwinning, wage-earning, industrial women who might want to visit the fair. Since working-class women would not be able to afford room and board in Chicago and thus would be open to undue influences, a Woman's Dormitory Association was formed. In the end, the dormitory attracted various self-supporting women such as teachers and nurses; breadwinning or industrial women did come but they were in the minority. During the exposition, the dormitory provided room and board for 12,210 women and supervised their interaction at the fair. In exchange for room and board, the working-class women were given information and shared stories with other (mostly upper-class white) women about women's rights.

It was not who came to the dormitory but rather how unmarried, white, industrial women were viewed that ultimately separated them from the main building. The Board of Lady Managers used their authority to build a dormitory. They wanted to provide "for the great army of women that would visit Chicago." And so, they would need "a good clean safe home at reasonable prices . . . supervised by a refined, motherly woman who will have a watchful eye over unprotected girls."[76] Eventually, the board put Sada Hardington in charge of "this place of quiet," along with a staff of twenty-seven women, including one who acted as a security guard. Every hour wagonettes would take the women from the dormitory in Hyde Park to the entrance of the fair. Upon return to the dormitory, women could gather in one of "eight good-sized sitting rooms" for the exchange of ideas on the "progress of her sex."[77] The idea of *Women's Virtue*—that statue over the building—invokes a hierarchy among women and at the same time means to transform inequalities in matters of culture into equalities of woman's rights interpreted along merits of class and race. Like the exposition, the Woman's Building shaped the civic realm and enforced and supervised its social arrangements.

This is substantiated by the president's report on the fair. His remarks revealed that women earned the highest form of praise—not through their accomplishments but by overseeing the virtue of women. The idea of protecting women, the president observed, "evolved from the brains of women who labored without fee or reward in order that those of slender means might have the advantage of seeing the Exposition at a very small outlay."[78] Women acting ostensibly on behalf of single, white, working-class girls conceived "the largest building ever erected for women, by women, and entirely managed by them."[79] In effect, the Board of Lady Managers demonstrated by their decision to build and operate a dormitory that they could enact moral choice comparable to that of men. Embodying spaces of deliberation or rooms of discussion while being cut off from the world of politics, the women's dormitory and its organization prompted and enforced the idea of woman's virtue in a manner of the citizen-warrior.[80]

A second performance of women is reflected in the World's Congress Auxiliary. The stated purpose of the Congress of Representative Women was to show the progress of women since 1492. The Congress of Representative Women was part of the World's Congress Auxiliary, which served as the authorized adjunct of the World's Columbian Exposition. Its goal was to supplement the buildings and grounds with a comprehensive program of congresses with a wide range of topics "from medicine and surgery to Africa." All in all, the congress featured 1,283 sessions and 5,978 speeches by 3,817 speakers.

The first of the congresses was the World's Congress of Representative Women. Women gave speeches on a site called the "Art Palace." Between May 15 and May 21, there were 330 scheduled speakers and almost as many unscheduled ones. Although Susan B. Anthony, Lucy Stone, and a few other suffragists attended the congress, the focus of the speeches was not on suffrage. The subject that received the most publicity was dress reform.[81] Professor Ellen Hayes of Wellesley College delivered a talk on women's dress in terms of power and independence. There were talks on the "gymnastic costume" at Mount Holyoke. Lucy Stone spoke on the bloomer.[82] As for other speeches, events, and exhibits at the fair sponsored by women, the Illinois newspapers gave little room to them. Tired of the silence, Susan B. Anthony proposed forming a newspaper and staffing it with women. The newspaper was never formed. So these speeches bypassed political action and focused on the more male-accepted issues of dress and decorum—the "proper way" to disguise the female body.

The Board of Lady Managers had been given plenary power as "the channel of communication through which all women or organizations of women" had to go through in order to, according to Bertha Palmer, "be brought into relation with the Exposition."[83] As things and ideas and speeches passed through this channel, the Board of Lady Managers based their decisions on what fit into the theme of "Progress." In this vein, women from other parts of the world—Poland, Greece, Spain, and Brazil, to name a few—could speak critically on women's rights. Their criticism of women's progress was included while American speeches that were critical of progress were not included. This decision to include only critical comments of foreign women was meant to show off the progress of American women to the world. American women had no call to be critical, for they were the most advanced of all women in the world, so the thinking went. The speech of Callirrhoë Parren of Athens was typical. She spoke out against the exclusion of women from public office and industrial employment in Greece, only to proclaim American women as the most progressive women in the world.[84] In effect, the theme of women's place in history with its placement of American women at the highest level and foreign women at the lowest resembled the Midway's organization of cultures and offers a glimpse of the staircase running through the fair.

In broad terms, the World's Congress of Representative Women was meant to publicize the achievements of women, staging American women as leaders in science, education, and the arts. In their own words, "The special object" was "to show the capabilities of women for more varied employments, greater usefulness and higher happiness than she has hitherto enjoyed."[85] The congress organized the achievements of women but also transformed the achievements in a collection—a civic unity—that was primarily understood as a record of progress.

The statuary *Woman's Place in History* is the second of the three and was used to feature industrial, working-class women. Equality in employment and recognition of women's authority in the workplace were offered up as the building process for these women. As women were going to work, what would be their place? In his speech "The Industrial Emancipation of Women," the Honorable Carroll D. Wright, U.S. Commissioner of Labor, said, "Industrial emancipation, using the term broadly, means the highest type of woman. . . . Each step in industrial progress has raised her in the scale of civilization rather than degraded her."[86] So there was a sense within industrialization that working-class women were marching forward, but as the Woman's Building was poised atop the Joy Zone and at the bottom of the fair proper, so too this order of women existed with the working-class women. They were squeezed in between the upper-middle-class educated white women and black women and women from foreign countries.

The third and final role for women was to own the Woman's Building and all the exhibits that related to women, especially working-class women. Here the statue *Women as the Genius of Civilization* stood above the Woman's Building. It was meant to use art as a way to proclaim the role women play in generating a civic atmosphere. For example, the Woman's Building housed a bust of Harriet Beecher Stowe along with a cabinet containing forty-two translations of *Uncle Tom's Cabin*. On display were Adelaide Johnson's busts of Lucretia Mott, Elizabeth Cady Stanton, and Susan B. Anthony. At both ends of the Rotunda of the Woman's Building were murals filling the arch of the roof from east to west. One was Mary Cassatt's *Modern Woman*. The other was Mary Fairchild MacMonnies' *Primitive Woman*. The murals depicted the choices and the presence of what women ought to bring to mind in the public domain. In effect, the viewer of the murals in the Rotunda was given a script that drew upon society's most revered values and beliefs. Insofar as the viewers enacted the script within the architectural structure of the exposition, they followed a line of thinking that would return women's authority to their place, something akin to the private realm.

The central group in MacMonnies' mural was five women carrying antique water jars from a spring on their heads and hips, accompanied by small children. Agriculture was represented on the right side by a woman sowing seeds; a bearded patriarch was depicted on the left handing over the fruit of his hunt to women.[87] This mural contrasted with Cassatt's depiction of women clothed in contemporary dress. The central group featured women gathering fruit and represented, according to Cassatt, "young women plucking the fruits of Knowledge and Science."[88] According to Cassatt, the mural was meant to appear feminine and feminist. It accepted notions of femininity and rejected them by "subverting the traditional images of Woman, Madonna, Venus, Vanity, and Eve, in accordance with the aspirations of the movement of women to be '*someone* and not *something*.'"[89]

It appears that the majority of viewers preferred "Primitive Women." The MacMonnies' mural was considered "far more decorative."[90] It was valued for its symmetry, its inclusion of men and women, and its strength of composition held together by distant wooded hills. It was women pictured in a form of art not unlike the classical designed building in which the mural was hung. Cassatt's painting was considered "garish" and not held together by "a reasonable theory."[91] Frances Willard, who had been a professor of rhetoric at Northwestern University, did not like Cassatt's portrayal of women. She complained to Susan B. Anthony that "there were no men in the mural."[92] Writing on the art in the Women's Section in Chicago in 1893, Florence Fenwick Miller regretted the accordion skirts and the barely clothed women that Cassatt depicted, for it was too much like the oriental dancers in the Midway. The Woman's Building was meant to be an escape from the Midway and, with classic architecture, was certainly seen as above it and as part of the fair proper. MacMonnies, therefore, presented the most ordered and idealized version of both art and women. At her closing remarks at the fair, Bertha Palmer put the choice in perspective: "When America chooses a leader . . . she is not only a queen but queenly."[93]

The epithets (Jezebel, female monster, and so forth) by which public women were first seen in the house of rhetoric heightened attention and ultimately called for a decent way of talking about women in public. In the exchange of expressions, there was another exchange that went something like this. Women would be recognized publicly and at the same time the recognition would be translated as their proper place, thus limiting the condition of authority in terms viewed as appropriate to women's role. In the end, the reevaluation of public women prompted by hypallage adheres to the argumentative values of authority that deny it to women while increasing the impression that women are included but only in their proper place.

POSTSCRIPT

As we continue to consider how to build a house of rhetoric, it is crucial to realize that the tropes—antonomasia (chapter 3), hypallage (chapter 4), and paronomasia (chapter 5)—are used to describe how the house is set up to grant access and deny authority *later*. While the steps may not take place in an orderly fashion, the classification system stands as an indicator of the development of the denial of women's authority once women are included in the house of rhetoric. With this in mind, I leave Chicago and fast forward seventy-two years to the World's Fair in New York in 1965. While I never attended the fair, my husband did. As I was telling him about this chapter while walking on the Rail Trail on a fall day in 2006, we had the following conversation.

"I was at a World's Fair."

"Where?"

"New York in 1965. I think I still have the guidebook."

"Really?"

"Yeah."

"Where is it?"

"I think it's up in the attic. I am sure I can find it."

"I'll look when we get back home."

Fifty minutes later.

"I can't believe you still have your guidebook *New York World's Fair!*" I almost shout. For once I am glad for his "trash." "Who did you go with?"

"My dad, mom, and sister."

"Which sister?"

"Barbara."

"How did you get there?"

"Subway. It went right to the gate on the Shea Stadium side. My dad and I went to a baseball game. New York Mets and Pittsburgh."

"What about your mom and sister?"

"They had tea or something."

"Tea?"

"Yeah, there was some building for women."[94]

I look at the guidebook. I turn to the index and look up "women," which tells me to see the Better Living Center. Eventually, I learned that the Woman's Building in New York was called the Better Living Center. I later learned that the Better Living Center was "inspired by earlier fairs," especially the 1893 World's Fair in Chicago. I glance at the map in the guidebook and read the description of the Better Living Center: "Five fashion shows held every day."[95] I continue looking at the map and see a building called the Clairol Building.

"Do you remember the Clairol Building?"

"No. (Long pause.) I do remember that Mom and Barbara went somewhere to see what they would look like with red hair."

"Maybe they went to the Clairol Building. It's very close to the Better Living Center."

"Umm, I can't say."

I continue to read the guidebook.

"You went by subway to the fair in '65, right?"

"Yeah."

"Could you get there by water, like by boat?"

"Yeah, there were these hydrofoils that ran to the World's Fair Marina from Manhattan."

"Why didn't you take one?"

"Too expensive. For a round trip, the boat was about six bucks and the subway was about fifteen cents each way. My parents didn't have a lot of money."

"What would your entry into the fair have been like if you had gone by boat?" I asked.

"I don't know."

I look it up on the map and say to Jerry, "Well, it looks like you would have gone right into the Transportation Area. Did you go there?"

"Yeah, I guess."

"What did you see?"

"I don't know; I was about thirteen for God's sake."

I look up the Transportation Area. I read aloud: "'In between the marine entrance and the subway entrance was the Court of the President of the United States.' (Long pause.) Wow, this area reminds me of the Court of Honor," I mumble.

I study the map in the book. I see that the Better Living Center—the women's building—is far—very far—from the Court of the President.

"Little wonder women are so far from the presidency," I think.

5

Speakers As We Might Be—Now

[T]here is . . . one technique which they [women] may have invented—that
of plaiting and weaving. If that is so, we should be tempted to guess the unconscious motive for the achievement. Nature herself would seem to have the
model which this achievement imitates by causing the growth at maturity of
the pubic hair that conceals the genitals. The step that remained to be taken
lay in making the threads adhere to one another, while on the body they stick
into the skin and are only matted together.

—Sigmund Freud, "Femininity"

The question of souls is old—we demand our bodies, now.

—Voltairine de Cleyre, "Sex Slavery"

From the World's Columbian Exposition, I venture down the hall of the house.
My research quest takes me from the Woman's Dormitory to New York where
many of the working-class women, for whom the dormitory had been built, had
originated from. As I go, I see ahead a colossal mural hanging on the wall.

A hugely popular photograph of a mural—something akin to a sound bite—is
Edmunds E. Bond's "Weavers of Speech," c. 1915 (figure 5.1).

The black-and-white photograph was popularized in *An Ideal Occupation for
Women*, a pamphlet that the New York telephone company circulated in the first
decade of the 1900s.[1] This pamphlet was part of a media campaign[2] that included
the publication of stories (written by men) about being a Telephone Girl.[3]

The drawing depicts a woman of heroic proportions sitting next to a vertical, upright structure set up to hang telephone wires. Holding these wires like
thread, "Weavers of Speech" is the Telephone Woman. I use the character Telephone Woman to refer to young, white, single, working-class women. Normally,
a weaver's work does not entail speaking in public. However, this personification of a female worker appears as a weaver at a gigantic loom, the numerous
wires "crossing and recrossing as if in the execution of some wondrous fabric . . .
a wondrous fabric of speech . . . woven into the record of each day."[4] Weaving

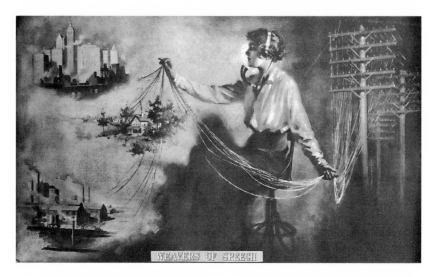

Figure 5.1. Edmunds E. Bond, "Weavers of Speech," 1915. Reprinted courtesy of the Boston Public Library, Print Department.

city, factory, farm and farm, factory, city in a fabric of speech day and night and night and day, Telephone Woman produces the rhetorical space of and for the public. Ironically, although they could not vote in the 1900 presidential election, telephone operators provided election services for men,[5] a degree of service that seemingly let working-class women edge closer to if not meet rhetoric's conditions of authority. Telephone Woman speaks, as it were, in public—a decisive turn for women in the house of rhetoric.

I stop at the mural where I find a group of working-class women in New York.

In the city, women were an important part of the marketing strategy of the Bell Telephone Company (AT&T) from the 1890s until the later part of the twentieth century. Early on, the company realized that single, white, working-class females between the ages of seventeen and twenty-four could help market the new technology and help spread its growth.[6] By December 31, 1895, the Bell Telephone Company had 14,699 employees, and virtually all the operators were women.[7] According to the census records, by 1910 there were approximately 52,000 single female operators in the United States.[8] How the telephone company realized that females were better than male operators and why they retained female operators as a labor force when automatic switching systems became available are some of the major critical questions that have been explored by a number of people working in history, labor studies, and business.[9] Little attention, if any, has been given to how these women affect and simultaneously are affected by rhetoric, namely, how the house produces the sign of a woman in it.

In this sojourn, I focus on how the jobs enabled the masses of women to move up the stairs, even obtaining access to rooms above the ground floor of rhetoric, giving them an opportunity to speak in public never before thought possible and what it meant for their authority.

I sit among a group of female telephone operators who had gone to Chicago and are returning home and going to work. I meet Amelia Schauer. Amelia tells me about her arrest. As she tells her story, Amelia leads the way, not by narrative line but across the mural hanging on the wall of the house now morphing into a sociopolitical sphere of city and street. Amelia's story, like Bond's photograph of a mural, displays the rise of working-class women and their newfound inclusion in the house. But when I ask the question what time o' night is it? another story of an arrest emerges, specifically how the house produces a genre-like figure "Telephone Woman," a creation who arrests women's authority.

In December 1895, Amelia ("Lizzie") Schauer, a blue-eyed, comely, working-class "girl" of seventeen, stepped out of her aunt's house at 432 Eighteenth Street and began walking to Mrs. Dittmyer's house at 16 First Street in New York; however, there was a question about the street number. Moments earlier, over a small supper, Maggie Osterburg told her niece that she was too poor to keep Amelia any longer but another aunt, Mrs. Dittmyer, had some money and was willing to pay for her housekeeping services. So off into the night Amelia went. According to the affidavit, Amelia stopped at a third aunt's house, Mrs. Raff at 620 Fifth Avenue, and borrowed ten cents for the bridge. Evidently a family friend, George H. Mackall, who had known Amelia's grandparents in Germany and who was known in the family as "Douglass," had agreed to meet Amelia at the bridge and escort her through the city to the Dittmyer residence. Although both Amelia and Douglass arrived at the bridge, their paths, for whatever reason, never crossed.

About 10:45 that evening Policeman Oppenheimer saw Amelia walking up First Street. Either Mrs. Dittmyer had moved or Amelia had the wrong address. Either way, she was lost. At 11:30 P.M. Policeman Reagan saw her talking to two men. Amelia, according to her own account, was looking for the house of her aunt and, not seeing the police officer, had stopped to ask directions of a man.

In the courthouse Policeman Reagan said he saw Amelia talking to "two Italians" in front of a "saloon." He arrested her, Reagan claimed, because "she seemed to be acting improperly," although in cross-examination, Reagan would admit he did not hear "what she asked the men." At any rate, this behavior of a woman, as well as the fact that an unaccompanied woman was out at night, was, in the mind of Reagan, presumptive evidence that Amelia was soliciting prostitution.

Reagan was not alone in his thinking. In the eyes of the law, Amelia was a "public woman," and Magistrate John O. Mott sentenced her to the workhouse on the charge of "disorderly conduct."

Fortunately, her three aunts employed a lawyer to get Mott to reopen the case. Mott agreed, but only after Douglass produced a certificate of examination from Dr. J. T. Deyo of 364 Ninth Street that showed Amelia to be a "strictly good girl," medically speaking. The doctor's examination impressed Mott, but it failed to change his judgment of the case.[10] Some newspapers, such as the *New York World*, made a fuss over Amelia and praised her as a "good girl."[11] Eventually, Assistant District Attorney Hennessy claimed the "girl's" only appeal was to the Court of General Session. In the end Justice Andrews, who presided over the Court of General Session said: "There is no evidence she is a girl of bad character."[12] And he added: "There is nothing for the Court to do but to discharge the prisoner from custody forthwith." When Peter Conlin, the chief of police, read the decision of Justice Andrews, the paper reported Conlin to say, "It always seemed clear to me that the police have no right to arrest women in the street on the bare suspicion . . . that the women are disorderly."[13]

If Peter Conlin's reply was intended to soothe, it also revealed an anxiety and perhaps even an anger about women's public activity and the continual rise of it. What is most surprising in the chief of police's statement, therefore, is not the mere possibility of a woman being seen in the city circa 1900 as a prostitute but something else: Conlin's statement creates the impression that, for many, it was quite normal to see a public woman as a "public woman." The Amelia Schauer case indicates a mind-set in the sociopolitical realm. The police, the aunts, the doctor, the lawyer, the court system, the oppressed, and oppressor all are caught up in the "circulation" of two phrases (public woman and "public woman") whose meanings are close but not identical. Within the sociopolitical realm and understanding where the rise of rhetorical woman lies there is enough leeway to confuse the imaginary "Amelia," the public woman who has a job as telephone operator and, for whatever reason, is out on the streets—working the night shift or going to a relative's home—with Amelia Schauer, "the public woman" who is out on the streets at night accused of soliciting sex.

At this point, I should mention that mostly white, middle-class, unmarried women who worked and spoke up (in settlement houses, as charity workers) outside the home (in public space)—such as Jane Addams, Florence Kelley, and Julia Lathrop (appointed first head of the federal government's Children's Bureau in 1912)—would define the public woman doing good works and speaking (up) well. However, a telephone woman was considered either lower or working class and, therefore, more easily confused with the political category of a "public woman" (read: prostitute)[14] than any of the women just mentioned. Remember that just a little more than two years before at the World's Columbian Exposition in Chicago, the working-class women were kept in dormitories so as to monitor their whereabouts. The image of a "public woman," therefore, implicates class in the movement of women gaining admittance in the house of rhetoric.

As telephone operators, women like Amelia were everywhere. First, they were in its main rooms—even those reserved for authority. By virtue of the telephone, a female operator could be (kind of) with men in their meetings. Invisible and speaking only a few words, her speaking, as an operator, enabled the process of decision making between men regarding public matters. Second, women were in the halls, even during the night. As more and more women entered the workforce as operators, male operators moved into higher positions in the Bell organization. What is crucial about this change is that by the late 1890s women were given the opportunity to work the night shift.[15] This newfound access to what men were saying—especially during the night—was also feared for the power it gave women. Telephone Woman could turn against the men she overheard. That a woman like Amelia could be (kind of) present with men in their offices and speaking between them prompted a vision of her telephone talk as a silent form of speech envisaged as a weaver. As such, her work, requiring her to speak, was cast as a form of subordination, either working a shift like a good wife or working a shift at night with a bridled tongue. As "speakers," these women gained entrée into the house of rhetoric and, at the same time, their authority was suspect.

With Amelia, I follow a turn marked by the intersection where she becomes a trope. On the stairs in the house, this trope displays a body of a woman where the active movement of inclusion runs back into—palindromically speaking— the opposite kind of movement that denies her authority. Specifically, the trope paronomasia isolates the conditions that the house of rhetoric grants for women's agency and authority. It intensifies the isolation through the repetition and replication of a public woman/"public woman" and identifies the use of paronomasia as its own conditions, setting up on the streets of New York the possibility and impossibility of women's authority. To illustrate these conditions in the house of rhetoric, I go, therefore, into its attic to take a look at stored images and how they, when invoked visually, can set up, through repetition, a paronomastic use of public woman/"public woman" in the sociopolitical world.

One of the oldest insights into the domain of rhetoric has it that the rhetorical activity peculiar to women is not speech. Greek women do not speak; they weave.[16] In this house are two prominent weavers: Penelope and Philomela. Each one uses deception. Penelope deceives through subordination while Philomela deceives through indirect power. As they portray these styles of deception in their work—or their weaving—they animate the linguistic structure of the trope paronomasia. I use their myths to actualize the two kinds of movements of women in the house of rhetoric.

Penelope is the good woman speaking well, but her speaking is in a form of silence that includes her in the house but separates her from authority in another room. When she spoke (up) to the bard and asked that he change his speech to the suitors, her son Telemachus ordered his mother, Penelope, to go to her room "and look to your own province, distaff and loom; . . . public speech shall be men's concern."[17] It is the man or son who commands authority.

The other woman who weaves is Philomela. She, too, is silent because her tongue was cut out by her sister's husband, Tereus, after he raped and brutalized Philomela. According to Apollodorus, Philomela wove pictures of the rape and sent them to her sister Procne.[18] In this way, Philomela's silence enacts a power equal to that of the man who raped her.

The major difference between them is that Penelope tricks the suitors, while Philomela tricks the head of household. One preserves male authority in the house while the other challenges it. Either way, weaving performs a trick of speech. Is the weaver of speech a public woman who preserves male authority or is she a "public woman" who can challenge it? This is the question over the use of space in the house of rhetoric that the trope structures and actualizes as it plaits women's status as speakers in the house.

The loom in the house of rhetoric is a telephone pole. "Weavers of Speech" (figure 5.1) places a figure, a goddess or heroine, next to a telephone pole as if the pole were a woman's loom and the telephone lines were her yarn. Given the opening epigraph from Freud, the telephone pole might be only about sex, but it is also about weaving. In this case the loom is set upright. Set upright (histos), the telephone pole is a loom whose beams in ancient Greece stood upright, instead of lying horizontal as in current-day looms.[19] The telephone pole and the loom represent yet another variation of a steep vertical climb—like a staircase. The weaver in the photograph may appear to be a public woman on the rise. This is evinced by the action of weaving. The warp and woof threads reveal at once not only an enthymematic structure (with the warp being the major premise and woof the minor premise), thus giving women a rational edge toward authority, but also a movement that may be cast as going up and going down. What is crucial to note at this point is how the move from a telephone pole to a loom (histon) continues the metonymical movement of adding women to the ancient house of rhetoric. The techne of rhetoric and the technology of speaking (on the telephone) are placed side by side. This action redistributes the technology of the United States with the art (techne) of rhetoric in ancient Greece.[20] So integrated, the generic representation of the two kinds of women includes not only items associated with weaving but also what their weaving has been associated with.

On the top of the beams—loom and telephone—hang the woof threads of Philomela. The woof threads are fragments of working women positioned in space as "public women" or prostitutes who pose a threat. With the loom set up in the house of rhetoric, I pick up the threads and follow the contour of how the sociopolitical realm pictured women appearing in it. At the beginning of the women's movement, popular theology represented women speaking in public in terms of social "pollution."[21] And finally, to be a woman and speak publicly was to be labeled a whore by the press; women who came to hear women were also called "whores and harlots."[22] Then it seemed impossible to escape the figure of Jezebel and the question of moral speech as she shadowed the body of a woman speaking in public.

But seeing Telephone Woman or Amelia as "public woman" was not like it was seventy-five years before. Now there is a general confusion between the terms public woman and "public woman" and a shadow of impropriety looming over the activity of women in public. Using the Amelia Schauer case as a point of reference of "public woman's" impropriety, I find other woof threads that reveal how a public woman is turning into a "public woman." Senator J. M. Sanford, speaking before the California State Senate around 1911, describes what happens to any woman who enters the public sphere. They "lose the esteem" and "respect of men."[23] Sir Almroth Wright's *The Unexpurgated Case against Woman Suffrage* (1913) presents another woof thread that structures women's activity under the name of a "public woman." Wright claims that a woman who enters public space has violated a rule of "nature." Violations of nature's rules incur a sanction that acts as proof that such a rule exists. When women defy the natural rule of law, they are penalized with the stigma of prostitution. Nature being what it is punishes women who break the law. Men are justified to speak of public women as "offensive and evil."[24]

From arguments against inserting the word *sex* in the Fifteenth Amendment fall additional woof threads. A good example is John F. Crosby's essay, which was awarded the Mallory Medal in 1910. Crosby argues that the two hundred thousand prostitutes in New York City could be "easily induced to vote, and that they would become a very powerful and pliant force" of political rings.[25] Just as "public" women "sell their own souls" so they would "readily sell their votes."[26] Echoing Crosby's line of reasoning is Mrs. Andrew A. George's statement before the Committee on Woman Suffrage in the U.S. Senate on April 19, 1913. Public women constitute a real danger to the polity. As Mrs. George puts it, reading from page 84 of Dr. Helen L. Sumner's book *Equal Suffrage—The Results of an In-*

vestigation in Colorado Made for the Collegiate Equal Suffrage League, New York State, "Prostitutes generally vote, and their vote is cast solidly for the party in control." And then Mrs. George turns to page 93 and says, "this trained investigator reports: 'The red-light district is freely used by the party in power, and its women [would be] compelled . . . to vote.'"[27]

This report as well as the award-winning constitutional essay, Senator Sanford's speech before the California Senate, and so on show the worry within the sociopolitical realm about women appearing in public as speakers. Its concern is revealed in the use of the word *trick*. As Sylvester Baxter notes, "trick" refers to "working time."[28] Using the technical term in telephony, telephone operators are classified as "a trick," "b trick," "c trick," and "d trick" according to whether their service is "for morning-afternoon, afternoon-evening, morning-evening, or all night."[29] The "trickiness" of Telephone Woman in the house of rhetoric means that she speaks and thus makes connections and disconnections, plugs and unplugs, wires and unwires, weaves and unweaves during the day and night.

Structured within paronomasia, female telephone operators are hired through references. The clergy is the preferred form of recommendation. Telephone women who were hired to speak in public are inspected and guaranteed as good: "Companies regularly send 'medical matrons' to visit applicants to determine that the home surroundings [are] healthful and proper."[30] This company practice goes along with the idea in the house of rhetoric that women's hearts lack the practical wisdom necessary to act deliberatively in the sociopolitical realm. If a woman is good, so to speak, then she is able to speak in public, like a telephone operator.

Now at the loom sits Telephone Woman. She is set up to enter in the public realm, characterized by the icons of industry, agriculture, and city. If she is a sexually ambiguous woman bound by Philomela's woof, she is also a virginal daughter loyal and obedient to her father, the New York Telephone Company. The loom consists of warp threads—those of Penelope.

The woof extending vertically in one direction is bound together by warp threads traveling orthogonally. The warp threads are used to make distinctions between public women and "public women." One key warp thread is the line of women going to work because they had to. No one denies that under certain circumstances—the death of a husband—a woman has to perform, has to enter, has to work in public space. In "The Diary of a Telephone Girl: The Work of a Human Spider in a Web of Talking Wires" (1907), the unknown author (probably the telephone company) suggests that women ought to be judged by their background, namely, who their mother and father were, and not by their clothing. In this manner, there is the issue of education. The longstanding rules of propriety make it unthinkable for women to be educated (like their male counterparts), but yet an education is a kind of guarantee that women who enter the sociopolitical realm as a public (telephone) speaker are subordinate. As Fairfax Harrison, president of the Southern Railroad Company, told his audience before the Alabama Girls' Technical Institute in 1914, "we must recognize the *necessity* for the industrial education of women . . . and acquire this viewpoint."[31] By spinning the yarn of "necessity," women speaking and acting in public are cast as "devoted servants of male overseers."[32] For their devotion, they deserve protection. Like Penelope, a public woman works quietly and faithfully. Writing against woman's right to vote, Almroth Wright summons the spirit of Pericles to protect the telephone women who were working and speaking in public. Quoting Pericles, he proclaims that no evil can be said "of woman in public so long as she confines herself to the domestic sphere."[33] That Telephone Woman works in a private space is evident by her Periclean trappings: loom and hearth. Because loom and hearth comprise a formal whole, a unified dominant image, Telephone Woman's work is cast as a public speaker in a realm associated with the private. She is in fact in her room. Telephone Woman is a helpmate to the public but has "no personal contact with the public." She is, therefore, respected and "held in the highest esteem of the land."[34]

In the logic of domesticity, the public woman/"public woman" becomes woven together where she inhabits public space privately and thus has no real contact with public deliberations. In teaching, for example, we encounter a parallel situation in which public women were fulfilled and influenced by the space of the hearth. Although women were speaking in public as teachers, which had been controversial in light of Paul's dictum in 1 Timothy 2:11–12 that a woman was neither to teach nor to usurp authority over a man, female teachers were regarded as public women working in a private space.[35] Minnie Bronson's analysis of teachers' salaries in 1910 depicts public-speaking women as at home with the children, if you will, and subordinate to public-speaking men: "The majority of male teachers are principals, supervisors, superintendents and college presidents or college professors, while the country school teachers, the kindergartners and under teachers are women."[36] Telephone operators are like teachers in that both professions are seen as fulfillments of woman's role as wife or mother.

Another thread forms public woman with respect to servitude and support associated with the image of the wife and mother. In his remarks "Should Women Vote?" Joseph Gilpin Pyle observes that servitude is the "law" of a good woman. Presumably, a "woman" who does not perform that role is sanctioned as "bad." Samuel Gilmore Anderson's sermon *Women's Sphere and Influence* describes the good woman as "a woman just out of sight over the hill who cheers the man."[37] In effect, Telephone Woman completes man's well-being. She is his conduit, his conductor, his cable, his flow area through which public speech passes. During the 1900 presidential election, telephone women working for the New York Telephone Company read bulletins, handled inquiries, and provided election services to "thirty-two Manhattan clubs and hotels and thirty-five country clubs, hotels, and associations in Westchester County."[38] Although public women were speaking in public, they were, in effect, out of sight. They were enabling the vote—the speech—of men, but they were not voters, decision makers.

On the eve of women's suffrage, just a year shy of the celebration of the Portrait Monument of Lucretia Mott, Elizabeth Cady Stanton, and Susan B. Anthony in the Capitol Rotunda, the image of public woman is becoming dominated by a view that separates her from and resists the image of a prostitute while distinguishing her public speaking as private, providing support for or facilitating life in the public sphere. A telephone woman stands outside industry, factory, and agriculture. Out of sight of the public realm, her loom and hearth were again engendering the very space that women had dared to leave.

In the structure of the trope where behavior is actualized in the palindrome of the <CIVIC>, the trick is turned back on "public woman," who is figured as a public woman who can enter the realm of men and make the inaudible audible. The trick, then, in rhetoric involves translating Philomela's night hours to Penelope's time of silence. This translation renders any trick—a, b, or c—as a faithful and loyal act of silence. It is this encoding of *trickiness in silence* that will enable the male speakers to become audible across industry, agriculture, and the city, while public women stay in their rooms, as it were.

POSTSCRIPT

The overturning of women's authority has not diminished as much as we might like to think. Here is an account of late twentieth-century women employees of a large corporation being shuttled from workplace to home by predominantly male taxi drivers, with women and drivers alike under strict orders by their respective supervisors about how to navigate the public. Here is Michael Huspeck's personal account.

> I was reminded of my three-year stint as a cab driver in St. Paul, Minneapolis, and then later Chicago. In St. Paul, "Radio Cab Co." had a contract with the Bell Company whereby every evening beginning at 10 P.M. and every half hour thereafter a lineup of cabs would be ordered to pick up Bell employees, all of whom were women. So at ten o'clock the call would be for the first 8 cabs in line to proceed to the Bell Company; at

10:30 the call might be for 6 cabs, at eleven o'clock for fourteen, etc. The employees had strict orders prohibiting them from initiating conversation of any sort with the driver. Similarly, all drivers were under strict instructions to refrain from any and all conversation with the Bell employees. Well, cab drivers can tend to be a chatty bunch, and on a hot and humid 4th of July eve, I "forgot myself" and asked one of the employees to roll up her window. "Why?" she asked. "Because," I sez, "kids have been throwing fireworks at passing cabs all evening, and I don't want one coming through the window." She audibly shuddered at my response. The next day I received a letter of reprimand from my superiors and was ordered off the Bell Co. lines for a month. No conversation permitted whatsoever! This was back in the early '70s.[39]

Huspek's account, at the very least, illustrates that as women rise in the house of rhetoric as "public speakers" (weavers of speech) they are also excluded from speaking. In the first part of the twentieth century, women were permitted into the workforce. This is equivalent to going up the stairs. But in the case of telephone women they had to comport themselves as public speakers but without authority, as suggested by the contradiction within the labor term "tricks." The trick of her speaking labor is equivalent to going down the stairs. At the same time, this vision of her in the public workplace is played out in the sociopolitical realm as she traverses its streets on the way to and from the workplace, which required that women endure the scrutinizing gaze and interrogations of patrol officers. To fast-forward to the later part of the twentieth century, the contradiction is obvious enough: there is a house of rhetoric that proclaims recognition of women's right to access public domains, and a house of assumptions and practices geared toward keeping women muted when in public domains and invisible when traveling public thoroughfares in order to reach such domains.

Surely there are other contingencies—for example, issues of class evoking the feeling that cab drivers are lowlifes—that shade and bear upon how women are seen in public in the 1970s. But the encounter between a cab driver and a Bell employee reveals how the house of rhetoric influences the tropical representation of women, and this shapes not only her body but the embodied practices in which she finds herself speaking. Although women are in public space, the public space itself has not changed its tropical structure of how women's access and yet their loss of authority can shade, overlap, and bear upon the other in a manner that renders them public women/"public women" (in sotto voce). As soon as speaking women enter the house, the perception of public woman/"public woman" (in sotto voce) kicks in, microphysically speaking, and they (and others such as cab drivers) become defined by it, the transmitters of it, and subject to its power. Put another way, the trope called paronomasia—embodied as public woman—is still with us, and it is actualizing behavioral attitudes from within its enactive microphysics of power. Now that we know there is an opening in oppositional discourse, we must attend to it. While it may be possible to find or invent a new trope from within the tropical array of the opening and then draw that trope through the warp that I have been opening up throughout this book, my hunch is that a trope is not enough and that we have to make a new house. It is my hope that we can find a blueprint from which to work. Only in a new space will public woman get her body back and with that body emerge as a leader, decision maker, person-in-charge, deliberator—a woman in public, in other words.

6

Walking the Milky Way

Easy to go there, but hard to come back; and then you must write it all down on a stone. Finally, if you are lucky enough and if the right reader comes along, the stone will speak.

—Margaret Atwood

The top picture on p. 124 (figure 6.1) is the Portrait Monument as it stands in the Capitol Rotunda. The picture below it (figure 6.2) shows the back of the monument, its rough stone. What the pictures do not show is a group of high school students. They are standing in the front of the monument but their backs are to it because their attention is focused on the teacher standing in front of them. Instinctively, I decide to join the high school students. Along the wall behind them is a bench. I sit down and listen. As the teacher talks, she motions up and as she does, she says to her students, "Look at the ceiling. The painting you see is Constantino Brumidi's *The Apotheosis of George Washington*."

She tells us that the painting is an eye.

A student in the back of the group starts joking around with his friends about the painting seeing things.

The teacher easily hears what he says to his friends but she doesn't miss a beat. She tells us that Daniel is on to something. She says, "*The Apotheosis of George Washington* has a nickname. It's called 'the eye of the Rotunda.'"

We hear about how the eye sees and oversees the past, present, and future through themes selected by a joint committee of the House of Representatives and the Senate.[1] The list (I learn eventually) included "the discovery of America; the settlement of the United States; the history of the Revolution; or the adoption of the Constitution . . . the subjects to be left to the choice of the artists under control of the committee."[2]

As the teacher talks, I begin thinking more about the Rotunda having an eye that could encapsulate all in its gaze, and about how the eye could see into the past to anticipate something in the future.[3] I am not thinking in a science fiction way but in a rhetorical way. The eye of the Rotunda manifests scene paint-

Figure 6.1. A. Johnson's Portrait Monument to Lucretia Mott, Elizabeth Cady Stanton, and Susan B. Anthony, Washington, D.C. Photograph courtesy Dave Swanson.

Figure 6.2. Behind the Portrait Monument. Photograph courtesy Dave Swanson.

Figure 6.3. Lucretia's eyes. Photograph courtesy Dave Swanson.

ings and reflects the future as it comes out of the past so that the scene paintings acquire a deliberative capacity. I now remember Aristotle, who says in his
Rhetoric, "Now the style of public-speaking [political deliberation] is exactly like
scene-painting."[4] It is no stretch of the imagination, therefore, for me to fix my
eyes on the stone eye sockets of the Portrait Monument and wonder what the
scene painting in front of them might tell about the future of women's status in
(the house of) rhetoric. If I could just see what the stone eyes see, I might, so my
rhetorical reasoning goes, be in a position to pursue the question, whither rhetorical women? I have to put my eyes physically in the back of the stone heads.
By inserting my eyes in the stone sockets, the statue is able to look at the future
in front of them, while I, being the eyes in the backs of their heads, obtain a future perspective on the past.

I get up from the bench and use the two rectangular stone base slabs to climb
up on the back of the fourteen-thousand-pound sculpture (figure 6.2). I step up
on the black Belgian marble base and then to the white Carrara marble base.
Given my height, I can just put my eyes in the stone eye sockets of Lucretia Mott
(figure 6.3). What I see "with Lucretia's eyes" is John Gadsby Chapman's *The
Baptism of Pocahontas* (1840).[5]

The teacher gathers her students around this painting. With their backs to me, I consider myself fortunate since I can hang about the statue (without being seen) and reflect on Chapman's painting—the deliberations it holds. The students are shuffling and moving about, and so at first I can't see a lot of the painting. The teacher acquaints them with the artist, telling them that Chapman was one of four artists chosen by the Rotunda Commission (joint committee of the House of Representatives and Senate). Then she tells them about the project. Chapman's "assignment," she says, was to select one of the themes (she told us about earlier) and visually tell the story of America. Her voice drones on.

The Baptism of Pocahontas is a screen for Virginia, distinguishing it as a space of power. Actually, in Chapman's description of his work, the screen is depicted as a house where all the colonists gather. One by one, the settlers left their "houses"— "the sick and hurt excepted"—and repaired to one location. Using the metaphor of pine columns to depict the house, the location is set in the woods of Virginia.[6] Cast in the context of a baptism, the figure of Pocahontas is, therefore, "inseparably interwoven" with the "very existence" of the "great Confederation."[7] The painting mingles "religious" with "patriotic sympathies."[8] While Chapman's painting contextualizes the conception of America in Virginia, it recognizes Pocahontas's "life and actions"—her rescue of Captain John Smith from death—as an historical event of undue influence, thus rendering her a leader. In the words of Chapman, Pocahontas "has descended to posterity as the great benefactress, the tutelary genius of the first successful Colony planted within the limits of the United States" and thus "deemed a fit subject of a National Picture, painted by order of Congress."[9] While not stated explicitly in his government pamphlet, Chapman leads the reader to assess his grand theme on the grounds that it "pays tribute to the contributions made by both Native Americans and women to the history of this country."[10] According to the Office of the Curator, U.S. Capitol Complex, the painting signifies women's inclusion within the walls of the house.[11]

As the teacher describes Pocahontas's inclusion, I remember what she told her students earlier about the women in Constantino Brumidi's *Apotheosis of George Washington*—that "eye of the Rotunda" that beholds them.[12] Pointing her finger toward the ceiling, she said, "See the woman holding the transatlantic cable? That's Venus." Evidently, the cable was being laid at the time Brumidi painted his fresco. "There are others [women]. Class, see! There is Minerva and Liberty."[13]

As I stare back from the future, I notice something. Venus holding the transatlantic cable reminds me of the mural "Weavers of Speech" with the figure of heroic proportions holding the telephone wires to connect industry, farm, and city. Propositionally speaking, does the eye of the Rotunda foresee the claims that will be made about telephone women like Amelia? So my thoughts go with the clouds and the floating figure of George Washington.

It is the sound of laughter that brings my thoughts back to the present moment. Eventually, I have an unobstructed view of the Pocahontas painting. I settle in, leaning my weight against the stone, and begin to reflect on what is in front of my/Lucretia's eyes: the future of women in rhetoric. Given her power of life and death, a power not uncommon to some Native American women,[14] Pocahontas seemingly possesses the authority to lead the "political destiny of the United States."[15] Her power is also evinced by the posture of several white men— such as the minister and her husband-to-be—surrounding her. Cast to pay homage to Pocahontas, their bodies dignify her act of saving a life and thus her capacity for decision making. Insofar as she has power (over life and death), what will become of her authority once inside the <CIVIC>, I wonder?

I hear the teacher talking about how the painting includes Native Americans, and I tune back in.

"There is 'Nantequaus.' He is Pocahontas's favorite brother."[16]

But Nantequaus is positioned very differently. Unlike his white counterparts who gaze upon the kneeling Pocahontas, Nantequaus's head turns away as Alexander Whiteaker, the Anglican minister in Jamestown, renames her "Rebecca," declaring that she "openly renounced her 'Countrey Idolatry.'"[17] The teacher points out Pocahontas's oldest sister. With her down-turned mouth, she appears anxious. There is also her uncle, Opechankanough.[18] His head is turned down. Opechankanough appears sullen, his whole body poised in agony at the moment Pocahontas becomes Rebecca. Perhaps his gesture foreshadows the massacre he will execute later. The teacher moves away from the painting, leading her students to Statuary Hall.

I am alone now (except for the guard who is herding stray students). As my eyes adjust to seeing both ways—behind me and in front of me—I become aware of Sojourner Truth arising out of the present circumstances. In the mode of the teacher, Truth speaks. That is, the name swapping and the embodied actions of Pocahontas's family—her brother, sister, and uncle—are Truth's envoys.[19] The down-turned corners of her sister's mouth, the turning away of her brother's head, and her uncle's down-turned head and body provoke Truth's *performance*— her promise to come out to tell what time o' night it is. All told, the embodied actions of the sister, brother, and uncle are tropes. Collectively, they expose a separate but interrelated movement happening within the (pine) columns of the house (in the painting). While Pocahontas is included (in the scene and in the Rotunda), her authority is usurped. And so even though I/Lucretia stand face-to-face with a painting that ostensibly declares the historical role of women, the

Portrait Monument's authority in the Rotunda is just not palpable. By extension, the same goes for women in rhetoric.

Now what? Where do I go?

As a start, I decide to take seriously Aristotle's notion that scene painting is a metaphor—a style really—for deliberative rhetoric. In this manner, I use Chapman's painting as a point of entry where I might step forward. How do I enter a painting? Supposing I do "get in," how would I go and where? Eventually, I will tell you about the road ahead, how it crosses in the fashion of chiasmus between two groups of women, broadly identified as Cherokee and American. But that would be to get ahead of myself. For now, I pause here and reflect on the painting of Pocahontas to find a way to pass through (the house of) Virginia and to that world (of which Chapman's government pamphlet writes) where Native Americans and women made contributions to the history of the United States. Through metaphorical leaps, I go from Pocahontas in the painting to someone the whites called the "Pocahontas of the West." This is Nanye'hi, one of several Cherokee chiefs. Being aware of the rhetorical use of epithets in the house to swap women's authority for something else, I steer clear of that trap and instead follow this woman Cherokee chief in Tennessee. Through associative links I discover the authority Nanye'hi possessed was the kind unimaginable among the whites. As coincidence would have it, I also find Frances Wright. Wright may have bumped into Nanye'hi on a road in Tennessee. As I imagine them meeting, the encounter may have emboldened Wright to speak publicly and dare to ask, "Does speech have a sex?"

So my journey now comes full circle, but I have not returned to the same place from which I set off. Although I am still *actually* in the Rotunda after traveling through a painting, I do not see the same old Rotunda I stood in at the outset of my quest. I'll go so far as to say that the Rotunda is imprinting a house of rhetoric—becoming.

This chapter ventures a fresh start, and it also concludes my journey. *The House of My Sojourn* charts where I have been and what I have experienced concerning women's place in the house of rhetoric. The old house, it seems, can only turn down women's authority any time they make additional headway. It does so by rotating women's speaking (uttered for the purpose of adding, including, and inserting themselves) into its own house version of metonymy (undergirded by the palindrome), and this version has sufficient variations (antonomasia and epithet, hypallage, and paronomasia) to swap women's authority for a subordinate form of it, thus denying them equal inclusion. So in the end, this is why I think we should abandon the seventy-year-old project of finding and recuperating rhetorical women for future prosperity. Rather, we need to figure out a way to recuperate women's rhetorical excellences while simultaneously altering the conditions that make her exclusion happen again and again. And that means that I have yet to consider how another house might point toward another beginning of rhetoric, a structure allowing the full inclusion of women. From here on, I sketch out the possibility of doing just that. After setting up an imaginary meeting between two women, I turn to its hypothetical results. I use them to set up a different blueprint, an alternative method to do rhetorical historiography while at the same time point toward modeling a new house of rhetoric.

Now I enter Chapman's painting. I leap from Pocahontas to the "Pocahontas of the West," and as I do Nanye'hi becomes the subject. As she becomes the subject, the scene shifts from Virginia to Tennessee. Then Virginia's principal players—the minister, Nantequaus, Opechankanough, and so on—fade away, and as they fade out, other figures come to the fore. They are Frances Wright, Andrew Jackson, and Thomas Jefferson, to name a few. The painting's theme shifts from a woman (Pocahontas) being changed (via baptism) to women (Nanye'hi and Wright) acting as change agents. Besides the transformations of actor, scene, and theme, there is the transfiguration of houses and the plot within. Instead of a house set amid pine columns reminiscent of a house and a baptism, there is a road and a semblance of a meeting between two interlocutors—Nanye'hi and Frances Wright. The road is like a house. Being an icon for a "public square (the agora),"[20] the road sets the stage for an imaginary meeting fashioned in the mode of deliberation. Being imaginary, I structure the meeting tropically as chiasmus—literally a crossing. The letter "X" concretizes a public space on the road and the event. I begin by introducing the two women.

Nanye'hi (Anglicized as Nancy) is one of the most famous Cherokee leaders and chiefs. She is better known by her married name, Ward, or Nancy Ward (c. 1738-1824).[21] As we already know, Frances Wright (1792-1852) was one of the most famous pioneer orators of her time.[22] While Wright has been reclaimed to rhetorical studies, Nanye'hi has not. In an effort to motivate the action, I provide information about Nanye'hi and her rhetorical activities. Again, my purpose in recovering information about Nanye'hi is not to argue for the inclusion of a Cherokee orator within the Indo-European tradition of rhetoric but rather to fuse the different trajectories of Nanye'hi's and Wright's speaking "careers." Then based on that fusion, I describe the variables I believe are capable of altering the house and offer a vision of it that is compelling enough to see people—men and women—participating in it.

Set on the road, Nanye'hi and Wright were linked by one close historical circumstance: they were two "first" women of historical note to speak publicly on political causes and assert women's right to speak before the women's movement was truly under way in the United States. Being first constitutes the trajectory on which each traveled the road during the course of her "career." In 1818, Nanye'hi was an old woman nearing the end of a very distinguished appointment to the office of Ghighua, the head War Woman, or "Most Honored Woman" or "Beloved Woman" of her tribe, while the young twenty-something Wright had not yet begun her public-speaking career for which she would be recognized years later as a "Great Champion" of women's rights on the dedication page of *History of Woman Suffrage*.[23] But this detail of 1818 is less about age and youth than it is about what distinguishes these women with respect to oratory: Nanye'hi stands at the end of a long line of Cherokee women who spoke publicly as leaders;[24] Wright stands at the beginning of a long line of American women who would come to speak in public on women's right to speak or act as a leader.[25]

Their "firstness" is the initial event or road condition in which the trajectory of their "careers" cross and in which I imagine them making contact. This is where the trope of chiasmus comes in. I imagine one line of the chiasmus "X" as Nanye'hi's trajectory and the other line as Wright's. Each line consists of the two women's many similarities and differences—for example, being first and last. Working in simultaneity, they set up the opportune moment for Nanye'hi and Wright to meet, hypothetically speaking.

As for their resemblances, both were out of step with their times, so to speak. Nanye'hi was unusual because she was behind her time. The Cherokee expected women to speak at treaty meetings and to participate in public deliberations. The whites found her odd and wrote in their journals about her speaking.[26] Wright was unusual because she was ahead of her time. When Wright stepped on the platform in the New Harmony Hall on July 4, 1828, to address the small utopian community in Indiana, she created a new beginning for women and public speaking in the United States.[27] At that time, it was outrageous for a woman to speak, and, as such, her speaking led to this question circulating in the press at the time: "Is it proper for a woman to address a public assembly?"[28]

Nanye'hi played a prominent role in war and civil councils. She exercised considerable rhetorical skill in negotiating with men on land transactions and speaking at treaty conferences. Her rhetorical power emanated from her bravery in battle *and* her childbearing body. These dual capacities signified her ability to command because any right to public office was traced by the Cherokee directly to the labors of a woman. It is she who both gives life in birth and takes it in battle.[29] Epitaphs used in conjunction with Nanye'hi's name implicated her political status. "One Who Goes About" (from Nunne-hi, the legendary name of the Spirit People of Cherokee mythology) is the "tribal myth-name for 'spirit people.'"[30] Her name meant that her voice was imbued with authority. As John P.

Brown explains, "The head of the Women's Council was the Beloved Woman of the tribe, whose voice was considered that of the Great Spirit, speaking through her."[31] Her epithet "Beloved Woman" was a title of authority.

Wright, on the other hand, was not expected to speak in public. When she did speak, she was not honored but called epithets, names meant to discount her authority. Wright's name was swapped frequently for "Aspasia" (a name swapped for the sign of the prostitute), "bitch," and "female monster."[32] Wright's power was linked to monstrous sexuality, which was captured in her epithet "Aspasia," who is traditionally cast as the mistress of Pericles of ancient Athens.[33] It was not uncommon for women speaking in public to be called "Aspasia" as an indirect form of condemnation.[34] Aspasia also meant *hetairos*, a "courtesan," as opposed to a "common prostitute." Calling Wright the "New Aspasia" linked her rhetorical force to the traditional (and often feared) power of female sexuality.[35] Following the "New Aspasia," the press labeled women who spoke in public as "whores and harlots,"[36] as they did women who went to hear women speak in public.[37] Seen as having no legitimate authority, women who spoke in public were also called bitches.

Not only did Nanye'hi and Wright differ in the respect attributed to them by their audiences, but they differed politically as well. Whereas Nanye'hi was not opposed to slavery and in fact was the first slave owner among the Cherokee of Tennessee,[38] Wright opposed slavery. Wright used a good portion of her inheritance to establish a settlement on the Wolf (aboriginal name Margot) River in Tennessee called Nashoba (from the Chickasaw word *wolf*).[39] Nashoba was an experimental community meant to reform the South's "peculiar institution"[40] out of existence. Wright was intent on ending slavery.

The two women also differed on racial issues. Nanye'hi spoke well toward whites. She said, "The white men are our brothers. The *same house shelters* us, and the same sky covers us all."[41] The Cherokee allegory of a house made of sky—concretely a seven-sided structure modeled after the Pleiades—stood for cosmic space, a model of the universe.[42] Her constant cry for peace stemmed not only from a vision of Cherokees and whites living harmoniously under the same roof and walking the White Path (Milky Way) but also through the central image of house, which put rhetorical deliberations among all into practice. Her metaphor of "house" ties back to the original metaphor for this book—that rhetoric is a house that covers us all and envisions humans solving differences with words, not violence. But as we now know, the original house of rhetoric let women in while it denied their authority to influence public action.

In contrast to Nanye'hi, Wright expressed a racist fear of American Indians. She thought they were "dangerous and inferior," saying, "The savage with all his virtues is still savage."[43] For Wright, peace did not mean negotiation or reconciliation with "Indians" but their removal. As she put it, "The increase and spread of the white population at the expense of the red is, as it were, the triumph of peace over violence."[44] Their marked disparity of political beliefs exemplifies the diversity of backgrounds among women who advocated women's involvement in political deliberations.[45] It also signals the difficulties ahead when imagining a new house of rhetoric built from these disparities.

Let me now bring these two women together and see what we might learn from their hypothetical meeting. Actually their paths may have crossed briefly in Tennessee, but nothing pinpoints the exact time and place of their possible encounter. The meeting is not an actual one; rather, I use history to set up an imaginary one. Somewhat ironically, I think the meeting might have been facilitated by two very famous men who knew both women—namely, Andrew Jackson and Thomas Jefferson. Whether they met, literally or not, their paths crossed symbolically through the Jackson and/or Jefferson link. Using what Jackson and Jefferson said about these two women, I bring the two women together on the road.[46]

I pick up their roads in Tennessee. On one side of the chiastic road stand Nanye'hi and the speeches she gave in various towns in Tennessee before and leading up to the land cessions in 1817-19. On the other side is Wright, who will not give any speeches for several more years. I depict Wright on horseback riding to Nashville with George Flower, a friend of Lafayette, to get together with General Jackson.[47] The purpose of Wright and Jackson's meeting was to discuss the location of an experimental community. Around 1825, about a year after Nanye'hi died, Wright was in search of land to establish an experimental colony; she had written a letter to Jefferson and asked him to endorse her project to establish a colony in Tennessee. He wrote back from Monticello on August 7, 1825: "To Miss Fanny Wright, every plan should be adopted, every experiment tried, which may do something toward the ultimate object."[48] Jackson suggested land along the Wolf River around Memphis. One semblance of a road to Memphis was the Cherokee trace. Wright "rode miles on horseback" through Tennessee and "occasionally slept in the forest at night."[49] About that ride, the *New York Times* reported: "there were undoubtedly Indians."[50] At any rate, these roads were sites of exchange, particularly business transactions, between the settlers and Cherokee, especially after 1804. Theda Perdue describes how the Cherokee National Council granted to white settlers five-year leases for "houses of entertainment" along the Cumberland Road as well as issued permits to various skilled workers such as blacksmiths and millers for business establishments.[51] Back on the other side of the road in the southern part of Tennessee near the Occoee (aboriginal name *ócoee*) River was the Inn at Womankiller Ford. It was operated by Nanye'hi in her later years. Even if Wright never visited the Inn at Womankiller Ford, she doubtless would have heard of it as it was one of the most popular inns for travelers, partially because of Nanye'hi, who was dubbed among the whites the "Pocahontas of the West."

In a chiastic manner, Nanye'hi is, therefore, moving both near and far from Wright relationally, and vice versa. Clearly, Nanye'hi is far from Wright and Wright is far from Nanye'hi in all kinds of relational ways—culture, religion, race, politics, age, and so forth. But at the same time they are far, they are also *exactly as near as they can be*. This is where one line crosses over the other one. So chiasmus is not *just* a representation of diagonal markings; rather it shapes or forms something and that something can become real. Therefore, to push the circumstances of chiasmus even more, could the young Wright have met the old Nanye'hi on the road?

Although there is no evidence, the circumstances of chiasmus make the encounter plausible. In particular, there is material relevant to each woman in the documents of Thomas Jefferson and Andrew Jackson. Jefferson mentions Nanye'hi in his letter to Colonel Campbell from Richmond on February 17, 1781. He writes that he is "much pleased at the happy issue of the expedition against the Cherokees. I wish it to be used for the purpose of bring[ing] about peace." After addressing the question of boundaries, he advises Campbell that "[t]he prisoners you have taken had better be kept for the purpose of exchanging for any of ours taken by them. Nancy Ward [Nanye'hi] seems rather to have taken refuge with you. In this case, her inclination ought to be followed as to what is done with her."[52] Jefferson not only singled out Nanye'hi from other Cherokee prisoners (men, women, and children) but also let her decide her fate. Jefferson obviously knew of Nanye'hi and apparently respected and admired her enough to use her authority to decide what should be done with the captives. Nanye'hi's authority is credited among the whites for having saved the life of a white settler (Mrs. Bean). For this act, Nanye'hi earned the title "Pocahontas of Tennessee" among the whites.[53] There is a fictionalized account that popularized Nanye'hi as Pocahontas, and this is the associative link (I mentioned earlier) as I made my way through a painting hanging on the wall in the Rotunda.[54] At any rate, it was not unusual for a government official to focus on Cherokee who were cooperative with the whites. Saving the white settler appeared to the whites as an act of cooperation.[55] Why Nanye'hi used her highest authority to save a life is not mentioned among the Cherokee. What is significant to the Cherokee is that Nanye'hi is a chief. They say she possesses the power to decide matters of life and death. This is the highest form of female leadership.[56]

Jackson also knew both women. Within Jackson's letters is (the only) copy of Nanye'hi's speech of May 2, 1817. The speech is part of the land cessions of 1817-19.[57] On that day, Nanye'hi addressed a large audience concerning land cessions, the speech that General Jackson carried with him. In the speech she urges the chiefs to keep away from "paper talks" or treaty negotiations with the whites. Without talks it would be impossible, she says, "to remove us all."[58] Because Jackson carried Nanye'hi's speech with him, it is reasonable to suppose he showed a copy of the speech to Wright.

For whom was that speech intended? History does not tell. He may have carried Nanye'hi's speech for a government official to prove that this female leader was no longer a model of cooperation and, therefore, could not be trusted by the whites, as Jefferson once had. Would Jackson, knowing of Wright's intellectual sympathy for a policy of Indian removal, tell Wright what Nanye'hi said? At the very least, Jackson may have wanted Wright to know the speech's contents, especially given Wright's desire to buy land. After all, Nanye'hi was a Cherokee arguing against selling any more land. She and other Cherokee women planned to resist the 1817 cessions.[59] Could it be that Jackson showed Wright the speech because in so many ways he could see that the young Wright was very much like the old Nanye'hi?

At any rate, Nanye'hi made an impression on Jackson, who kept her speech among his possessions. In addition, she made an impression on Jefferson as well, who did not keep her as a prisoner. Also Jackson and Jefferson personally interacted with Frances Wright on political matters and did not obstruct her plans. In this way, both men set up the conditions for contact between the women. The speech that Jackson carried with him may be proof that Wright had a prototype of a woman speaking in public on political matters. As Jackson and Wright rode their horses across Tennessee, I see him telling her about a female Cherokee chief named Nanye'hi who spoke at treaty meetings. Perhaps Wright responded that she had heard of such a woman through Jefferson. I visualize Jackson telling Wright what Nanye'hi said about white women's authority and how it is denied by men. The outspokenness of both women—for example, Nanye'hi on the political status of women among whites and Wright on the political status of blacks—puts their similarities and differences into play as chiasmus.

Nanye'hi and Wright make contact at the point where they dare to rebuke white male audiences regarding women's political status in deciding affairs of state. In this manner, I picture Wright hearing Nanye'hi say, "I know that you [white women] are always looked upon as nothing."

This statement represents the imaginary meeting. It represents point B where each line of the "X" crosses over the other. Point B or the middle enables Wright to see from point A or her line (of speaking) to point C or Nanye'hi's line (of thinking).[60] In chiastic fashion, Wright sees in Nanye'hi the possibility of women speaking in public. After leaving Tennessee, and eventually going on to Indiana, Cincinnati, and New York, I envision Wright entering the house (of rhetoric), marching down the hall, and saying, "I shall venture to ask, whether [speech] has any sex: and I shall venture to ask, whether they count for nothing, for something, or for everything, the influence of women in the deliberations and business of public life."[61]

With this scenario, it is possible to surmise that Wright came to public speaking through Nanye'hi's influence. At the very least, there seems to be Native American influence on the feminist's movement.[62] I would argue that the hypothetical meeting produced a vision of a house of rhetoric in which women speak in public and thus are included. As I look back and retrace the steps Wright took, I now catch a glimpse of her regenerative vision of a house of rhetoric, one equal for all. When public spaces, such as in New York, closed their doors to her, refusing to let her enter and speak,[63] she used her personal wealth to buy a church, reforming it as a meeting house where women and men were not only given the opportunity to speak on political matters but also were offered lessons in how to debate.[64] Wright's speaking activities bring before my eyes a remodeled house of rhetoric. I also see through eyes facing the future in the deliberative mode that the house is one where women have access but not authority. The painting of Pocahontas signifies this effect of the imaginary meeting.

The house that Wright saw did not feature the variable of authority alongside inclusion. Without both variables coupled equally, the house of rhetoric reverts to its palindromic ways. Nowhere is this reversion more vivid than in the case of Cherokee women. They, like Pocahontas, lost their authority to lead and act as decision makers after they were included within the nascent civic realm and its pine-columned and, metaphorically, Athenian-modeled house of rhetoric. In fact, leaders like Nanye'hi were troped or rotated by the troops. The figure of Aspasia was given to the Cherokee women in exchange for their rhetorical authority. The tropical exchange—hypallage, to be exact—of Nanye'hi for Aspasia is evinced in essays. Here is a portion of one essay written by a Cherokee woman: "How often we have heard it reiterated that the destiny of the world depends on women—that woman is the appointed agent of morality—the inspirer of those feelings and dispositions which form the moral nature of man. . . . Many are the instances recorded in history, which may be mentioned in proof of this. I will speak of some of the most notable ones. First, of Aspasia of Athens . . . in eloquence she far surpassed all of her contemporaries."[65] In the house of rhetoric, a Cherokee woman learns to eulogize an ancient Greek woman, not a female chief. As the Cherokee woman was writing her essay, praising Aspasia of Miletus and holding her up as a newfound heroine, the press and editorials were representing (troping) Wright as "Aspasia-like." Aspasia-like women were viewed negatively, cast by the media as prostitutes leaning on would-be leaders and exercising undue influence by "sitting in the laps of the highest and lowest" of men.[66] This role model strips the Cherokee women of their own role model (via the action of antonomasia) and replaces it with a Greek one. This is not much of a lesson.

With "Lucretia's eyes," I now see that Wright's vision (or its appropriations) is partially regenerative. Launched by Wright's question "Does [speech] have a sex?" the vision foresees of a house of rhetoric of full equality. For almost two centuries, the house that Wright saw has offered women reliable and continual entrée. It is no exaggeration to say that as women moved from the back porch through the rear door in 1828 into the house, the changes to the house were dramatic during the years that followed. Women were in rhetoric, crowding around the edges of its rooms, advancing: they were speaking in public, they were using the rhetorical process to gain political stature, and they were rising with public authority as decision makers, leaders, and persons-in-charge. The house is filling; however, it is not yet a house where *any woman* can be elected president of the United States.[67] The house of rhetoric is not compelling when it comes to women/minorities and their truth of authority.

What if I were to return to the imaginary meeting with a wish? I wish to make contact with Nanye'hi so I can deliberate an alternative house in which women possess authority and function as leaders and decision makers within it. I now remember Chaim Perelman and Lucie Olbrechts-Tyteca, who claim in their *New Rhetoric* that deliberating and *wishing* are conjoined. Comparing a wish to Alice's desire to make contact with a caterpillar in *Alice in Wonderland*, Perelman and Olbrechts-Tyteca write that a *"wish"* sets up a possibility for entering into deliberation.[68] Now I make contact with the Cherokee for the sake of deliberation. I also wish to hear through their speeches how the variable of authority functions.

Since Nanye'hi and the speeches that are connected with her are unfamiliar to most in rhetorical studies, I begin with a brief introduction of her life. With this background, I contextualize her voice in the Cherokee house as well as introduce the speakers I encounter. Nanye'hi was born in 1738 at Chota where her mother, Tame Doe, was a member of the Wolf Clan of the Cherokee Nation. Nanye'hi was the grand-niece of Old Hop, a leading chief of the Cherokee Nation, and a niece of Chief Attacullaculla, a skillful leader and known to the whites as "Little Carpenter" primarily for his rhetorical ability to construct "win-win" agreements.

In 1755, Nanye'hi went to the Taliwa battlefield in Georgia with her husband, Kingfisher, and a war party of five hundred to fight against the Creek. During the battle, she lay beside her warrior husband, chewed bullets, and passed them on to him.[69] When Kingfisher was killed, Nanye'hi took his rifle and fought in his place alongside the warriors who eventually defeated the Creek. When the battle was over and the spoils of war were divided among the Cherokee, Nanye'hi was given one of the black slaves who had fought alongside the Creek. This gift to her invokes images of the "booty" being divided up among winning Greek warriors, except a woman is included in the project. The gift also "made her the first Cherokee owner of a black slave and she was responsible for introducing her people to [the institutional system of] slavery as it was used in the south."[70]

By her personal lineage and display of courage, Nanye'hi was destined for leadership. Shortly after the Battle of Taliwa, she was elected to the office of Ghighua (pronounced Agi-ga-u-e), which is translated as "Very Much Beloved Woman" or "War Woman" and sometimes "Pretty Woman." With this title she served as the leader of Chota, which was signified by the color "white" and designated as a "peace" town and a "mother" town, "a designation of the oldest Cherokee town."[71] Given her political status as Ghighua in Chota, her voice/speeches were mixed, therefore. Situated in the "white peace" of Chota, her voice in the town was to advocate peace. However, the Ghighua played a key role in war. One of her duties was to prepare the "Black Drink" (made from the leaves, tops, and shoots of winterberry) for the ceremony preceding war.[72] Thus, her knowledge of purification put her at the center of the preparations for war. In this way, the Ghighua's voice was also that of "War Woman."

Nanye'hi was also head of the Women's Council, a senate-like body in the Cherokee Nation that was asked to choose war or peace over the vote of the Cherokee Council of Chiefs. The Ghighua was distinguished from the rest of the women who comprised the council. Although a place was reserved for women in the council house and although women could express their views (a practice the whites referred to as "petticoat government"), only the Ghighua could vote or take part in the deliberations of the chiefs. Distinctively, Nanye'hi sat with the Peace Chief and the War Chief in the "holy area" near the ceremonial fire.[73] In some ways, the holy area invokes the central hearth around which the ancient Greeks gathered to make decisions. Like the Peace and War Chiefs, the Ghighua could oppose decisions made by the headmen or chiefs who made up the National Council. In the event that she believed a chief's actions to be unworthy, she had the power to institute proceedings to remove the chief. In some cases, her speech was more powerful than that of the head chief's speech, for it was believed that the voice of the Great Spirit spoke through her.[74] In terms of power and authority, Nanye'hi was able to grant clemency to prisoners (such as Mrs. Bean), sparing them from death even as the preparations for their execution were under way.[75] She could negotiate treaties with enemies and establish coalitions with friends. Thomas Nuttall, a botanist who lived among the Cherokee in Arkansas in 1819, was told by Nanye'hi's people that "her advice and counsel bordered on the supreme and that her interference was allowed often to be decisive even in affairs of life and death."[76] In short, Nanye'hi had authority that was "well established by years of precedent, and was unquestioned by the warriors, head men, and chiefs, as well as the ordinary citizens of the tribes."[77]

When Nanye'hi spoke at various treaty meetings, her authority was not recognized among the whites. After Americans established settlements like Nashville—an affront to the Transylvania Treaty of 1775, which was "not to allow any [white] person to settle below a place called the narrows,"[78]—some of the Cherokee, egged on by British agents, argued for raiding the settlements. In this debate, Nanye'hi argued against war. As their debate raged on, Thomas Jefferson in June 1780 ordered Colonel William Campbell to punish the Chickamaugas—a Cherokee group who wanted to go to war. Dismayed by the taking of Chota, Dragging Canoe, the principal voice of war among the Chickamaugas, urged his militant band to attack the weaker but expanding white settlements in the Cumberland basin before they had time to grow strong. They did, and their attacks on the settlements led Colonel Campbell to issue an ultimatum to all the Cherokee chiefs: within two moons, six of their chiefs were to report to Joseph Martin, Indian agent for Virginia and North Carolina, at Long Island on the Holston, to arrange for a treaty. The chiefs were upset, to say the least.[79]

The Long Island Treaty meeting began July 26, 1781. The commissioners started the talks by (again) telling the chiefs that the British could no longer furnish them aid and had been defeated. As such, the Cherokee had no choice but to turn to the Americans for help. Corn Tassel, opened the talks for the Cherokee, blaming their militancy on several whites as well as on one of their own leaders, Dragging Canoe. John Sevier then replied that he did not hate the Cherokee but fought them to protect his own people. At this point, Nanye'hi approached the treaty commissioners and spoke. Her speech (which is less than fifty English words) is one of the earliest instances of a woman speaking in public in the United States. In light of her opening words, she knew (I will say more about this later) that among the whites, women had no power to deliberate and thus no authority to speak in public. She began, therefore, "You know that women are always looked upon as nothing."[80]

Then she made a brief statement for peace and closed her speech with a plea to let white women, too, hear the words, the argument for peace. Colonel William

Christian responded by saying he was "surprise[d]" how "soft & tender" the words are coming from a "woman" and especially an "unlearned" one. "No man can hear it [her speech] without being affected by it." But after this opening bit of praise, he simply told her to be "still and quiet at home."[81]

While a few claimed that Nanye'hi's speech made an impression on the commissioners,[82] most did not.[83] Among those who sided with the historical view that claimed she failed to impress was Theodore Roosevelt, who noted that "Nancy Ward" brought "overtures of peace," but the commissioners "would not listen" to her because she was a woman.[84] When Theodore Roosevelt suggested that Nanye'hi was not heard because of her sex, he also made it clear that the refusal to listen to Nanye'hi was not because of race.[85] It was because she was a woman. This refusal to listen to a woman is further corroborated when, in a later speech, Nanye'hi opened her address to her male audience saying, "tho I am a woman giving you this Talk, I am in hope that you and all the men in Congress will pay particular Attention to it."[86]

That the whites refused the authority of Nanye'hi as well as Cherokee women created a crisis in the Cherokee system of rhetorical deliberation. I follow these reverberations, cast by Cherokee speeches/voices regarding the denial of women's authority, by first setting up the question and then the problem of judgment that the denial entails. I begin with Attacullaculla's question, one he asked a governor and other officials at a council meeting. This situation—of question and response—contains first impressions as to what female authority means in the context of deliberation.

Chief Attacullaculla (Nanye'hi's uncle) asked the whites something like this: Aren't women present when white men deliberate matters of public policy? After telling the governor "that I and all the warriors with me are resolved to go to war [Revolutionary War]," Chief Attacullaculla told the governor that "some of the women" desired to speak with him. Apparently, Attacullaculla then startled the Carolinians by asking why all the speakers sitting at the council table were male. According to the minutes of the meeting, "The Little Carpenter [the name the whites gave to Attacullaculla] observed to his Excellency [Governor Lyttleton] that the White Men as well as the Red were born of Women and that it was customary for them [the Cherokee people] to admit Women into their Councils and desired to know if that was not the custom of the White People also."[87] There was no response, except to say, I'll get back to you on that. Actually, it took several days for Lyttleton to "get back to" Attacullaculla on that. Attacullaculla waited and waited. Having other things to do, he grew tired of waiting for the governor's response and sent Chief Woolenawa to sit and wait for the answer. Eventually, the answer came. Lyttleton said: Men would "share their council with them [women]" but not now. Women would speak "when they [White Men] know their [women's] Hearts to be good."[88] That the Cherokee waited until they knew exactly what it meant that women were absent from the table indicates the Cherokee sensed something. The governor's rhetorical deliberations did not share the same structure of decision making as did their house. The Cherokee house appears to operate with both men's and women's authority. How does women's authority function? What role do women's performances play in making judgments? To answer this question, I again follow the Cherokee responses.

The scene now is Colonel Martin's house and the talk involves another matter and another set of negotiators. The actors are Colonel Martin (plus some of his commissioners) and Chief Corn Tassel (and other male chiefs). It is worth noting that white men freely admit Native American men to their private domicile—standing metaphorically as a house of rhetoric—but they do not admit Chief Nanye'hi. It is not her exclusion per se but what her exclusion means that reveals how the variable of authority functions. Nanye'hi's exclusion from the house of rhetoric is so problematical for Corn Tassel that he fears that the talks stand in grave danger of losing their power to bind people together through words. As Attacullaculla's question reveals, there is no house of rhetoric without women's authority being present. The system of deliberation fails, leaving the trace of its failure in empty "paper talk." What happens next is telling as Corn Tassel seeks to keep the house of rhetoric stable and upright despite the absence of women. Corn Tassel does everything he can to conjure the presence of the absent and excluded Nanye'hi, thus attempting to preserve the sanctity of gathering as a realm of decision making.

On Friday, July 31, 1781, the chiefs assemble at Colonel Martin's house for the treaty. Corn Tassel opens the talks. Corn Tassel insists that since he opened the talks, it is only right for him to close them, thus hoping to give them organic unity by restoring some sense of women's authority to them. He closes them, saying, "Before I leave my elder Brothers I want to give out my Talk. Brothers when I first come the paths were [very?] bad but now I make them straight & clear. The path was spoiled by both sides before but now is made clear. We been four days since we began to clear. We all met with good Talk in our mouths and we will part in same way."[89] As he closes the talks, he makes it very clear that Nanye'hi should have opened the talks. This is because her authority is attached to life and death, thereby giving *meaning* to the deliberation, and because her political status is inextricably bound to the Spirit World, where truth and honor reside. Since the system of rhetorical deliberation has been violated, Corn Tassel makes an attempt to repair the damage to the great house made of sky ("that shelters us all") in which everyone speaks and dwells. In this way, the judgment—the end of deliberation—is not completely reduced.

To discern how Corn Tassel's closing words attempt to embody Nanye'hi, it is first necessary to go back to the opening of the deliberations. He opens with, "I belong to Telliko [a region of Tennessee spelled today Tellico; its aboriginal name is Ptsaliko or Saliko] and am the first man who took pity of our Women & Children and took hold of them while [Beloved] came in to open the way."[90] He goes on to say, however, that the commissioners were not willing to let a woman open the negotiations; they would only speak with men. Corn Tassel attempts to preserve the dignity of their house made of sky and the speaking practices it upholds by saying, "While [Beloved Woman Nanye'hi] came in to open the way. . . . [It was only] All the Head Men [who] have talked throughout the Treaty with you. And [so] as the first man to begin the good Talks, I am now going to finish them."[91] The Cherokee way, Corn Tassel reminded the commissioners, which envisioned a house in which all adults could speak, had not collapsed completely, as he invoked the principles of the body of speech—the head and feet, introduction and conclusion. By invoking these principles, Corn Tassel is concerned with the parts of speakers, not the parts of a speech. Speakers embody the sanctity of rhetorical deliberation.

For comparative purposes, I go to the Greek house, specifically its edifice metaphor.[92] Within this context, the substance that rhetoric possesses about itself is highly integrated in terms of the body. But the body in this palindromic space refers not to anyone but to speech composition. The goal is to make a beautiful speech out of body parts such as the introduction and conclusion. If words are put together well, they will make a beautiful speech just as stones laid down well will make a beautiful house. Based on manifest relations, an architectural structure equals the delivering of rhetoric. Architecturally speaking, the speech that integrates its (body) parts serves as the source of inspiration. So the edifice metaphor deals with exterior connections between words and images. Based on manifest relations between speech and body, the house of rhetoric in the Greek style is highly compressed and contracted around particular types/voices deemed to have authority to speak and to inspire. Eventually, the particular types (of voices) have no real physical presence. In effect, there is no warrior-citizen. His bones are concepts. Especially in the hands of Aristotle, the bones comprise rhetoric as civic discourse but there is no body, not even any speeches, within his *Rhetoric*.

The Cherokee house is a context of embodied speaking, and this activity entails the conditions of rhetoric's existence. What emerges poignantly from these scenes—the council meeting and the treaty meeting in Colonel Christian's home—is the variable of authority and how it performs rhetorically. Within the context of the Cherokee house, authority functions to integrate the entire presence of chiefs/bodies with the context and substance of rhetoric. That this is so is evinced by the chiefs' invoking what the whites denied: the authority of Nanye'hi. Within the Cherokee house, the integration of many chiefs and the attendant values (of peace, war, and so forth) they reflect during the deliberative process comprises the foundation of inspiration for determining a course of action. This foundation coordinates the variables of inclusion and authority, and they, in turn, set up the parameters of a new house of rhetoric. At the very least, this Cherokee design offers to rhetoric the spaciousness that it deserves during deliberations.

I climb down the Portrait Monument. As I set one foot on the base, I see a security guard. His presence prompts my memory of the beginning of my journey. I pause and reflect on where I have been and what I have seen. I have a tropical method for deciphering the question of authority as more and more women gain access to the house. I used this method extensively over the course of my sojourning. It also enabled me to venture in the deliberative mode through a painting. Now as I return to the Rotunda, I carry two decisive variables—inclusion and authority—that are connected.

As I put one foot (quietly) on the floor, I wonder if these variables of inclusion and authority are fluctuating in our contemporary world. Do they ever converge, even fleetingly but long enough to materialize an image—an image of a house in the building process?

As the guard turns his head and looks my way, I freeze in time like all the statues around me. Then something—it's the movement of people—catches me unawares. As I stand alongside the Portrait Monument, I am in the Rotunda, but I am not in the same place I was when I began my climb on the statue.

In the middle of the Rotunda is Rosa Parks. As the people move around her body, I catch a glimpse of a house.

After Rosa Parks's death, the House of Representatives approved a resolution on October 28, 2005, to allow her body to lie in honor in the Capitol Rotunda.[93] As it stood, the Capitol Rotunda could not accommodate her body because there are laws that pertain to Rotunda space. In fact, to insert her body required a formal decision-making process—Senate Concurring Resolution 61—as well as a new design by the Capitol architect.[94] Appointed by the president, the Capitol architect took the necessary steps to carry out the design of public space for the viewing of the first American who had not been a military figure or government official[95] and the first woman[96] to receive this honor.

As Parks's body lay in state in the Capitol Rotunda thousands of people stood patiently in long lines that wound for blocks around the Capitol complex and public leaders of all stripes observed her passing. Three ex-presidents attended her memorial event; the current president attended; long lines of mourners filed past her coffin over a period of three days; and television viewers across the country followed the coverage of these events.

The talk was surprisingly about the future. How is it that a figure from the past did not engender a reflective mood but rather conversation that pointed to the future? How is it that a memorial service, an event that is intrinsically retrospective, turned predictive, forward looking? More specifically, how could a corpse, the remains of a person no longer there, an object of the past, be so much about the future of rhetoric?

In much the same way that people spoke of how Parks and the movement she had been instrumental in was an indicator of a better future, so it is possible to see the activity her corpse embodies as creating a new house. How does her body—a woman and a minority—engender a house without a staircase capable of overturning women's authority? In the same way that Corn Tassel evoked the absent Nanye'hi to establish the Cherokee pattern of deliberation, so the people coming to view and pay their respects evoke the presence of a woman in the Rotunda. They evoke her presence by what they do; they perform a circular pattern as they move around Parks. But their movement is not limited to the citizen-warrior who moves in boustrophedon fashion—that plowing action that creates a palindrome. The movement to and around Parks involves everyone without distinction. Through their contact, bodies *interact*, which traces out a form. This form constitutes space.[97] Embodied activity "builds up the objective world."[98] Embodied activity engenders a house—the house of rhetoric. Rhetorically speaking, humans are "forming animals."[99]

As the people stream in the Rotunda and move around the body, they plow the Milky Way, metaphorically speaking, and craft a house made of sky.[100] The people per*form* Parks's inclusion and her authority, something a palindromic realm derails them from doing. If the palindrome of the <CIVIC> were to permit the authority of a woman, it would require, you see, a rhetorical architect—something akin to a Capitol architect. A rhetorical architect would take the theoretical steps necessary to carry out the design of public space regenerated as a realm of the <CIVIC> without a boundary of authority.

The inclusion of Rosa Parks in the Rotunda in conjunction with the embodied activity—that array of movement composed of U.S. presidents and ordinary citizens around the middle—bears witness to her authority to act as a leader. The variables, although in fluctuation, have generated a house. After the body is removed and the people disperse, they leave behind them a Rotunda—concrete and unaltered. So a statue of Rosa Parks does not a new house of rhetoric make. Is it any wonder that Michelle Obama would dress like Sojourner Truth for the dedication of the Rosa Parks statue? In effect, Truth is coming out to tell us that it is still night. But to the extent that the people left behind their footprints—a measure of movement unwavering in its pattern that connects a woman's body with authority—the house of rhetoric is in the building process—approaching the dawn. In this manner, the footprints represent a new house. If the feet of the people go back and forth as they did using the boustrophedon effect, they build a house. But if the movement goes in a new manner, a manner of movement that features a willingness to participate with the other as did Rosa Parks one day on the bus, then we could use our bodies to architect a new space. So rather than feet as a standard of measurement, we can use our feet to create a house, one that can be just as solid, canonical, and binding if human civic discourse were designed to include women as persons with authority.

Now I head north after leaving the capital. I am on the roadway, what Ovid calls the Milky Way.[101] I have no house, only a way to transfigure one. What makes the house of rhetoric morph is a new standard of construction that measures space not in feet, so to speak, but by feet moving. In the house made of the Milky Way, movement means women and men are participating equally with authority.

What Gaston Bachelard says about space could just as easily be said about the spatial qualities of the house of rhetoric: "Space calls for action, and before action, the imagination is at work."[102] I wish: That a people should work rhetoric more than any other people and more than at any other thing.

Notes

INTRODUCTION

See Stone, "The Condition of Women." The speech continues, "They pelted her with ink stones; they jeered at her as she went in the street; they threw bad eggs at her as she stood on the platform; some of the women for whose sake she endured all this were ready to drive her from the field." See also "Insult to Woman."

1. "President Obama Speaks at Signing of Executive Order Creating White House Council on Women and Girls."

2. See Hawhee, *Bodily Arts.*

3. I am aware of the term *archi-techne* from Irigaray, *The Forgetting of Air in Martin Heidegger.* However, my use of archi-techne is more in line with M. M. Bakhtin's thinking than with Irigaray's. This gets confusing because Bakhtin uses the term *architectonics,* but he does not mean anything like McKeon's sense of the term. McKeon, "Introduction." For Bakhtin, architectonics "is first and foremost a style of seeing the world, and only after that—a style of working the material." Bakhtin, *Art and Answerability,* 202. As a brief aside, an architectonic à la McKeon means that all the parts of rhetoric create a system. The primary reason for thinking of rhetoric along an architectonic line of thought is for elevating the status of rhetoric. As championed by McKeon, architectonic refers to all the parts in Aristotle's conceptualization of rhetoric—from parts of other treatises (such as the *Politics* and *Ethics*) to parts of rhetoric (such as the three "proofs": logos, pathos, and ethos). Collectively, they feature how the parts coalesce to effect the systematization of rhetoric as well as raise rhetoric to the status of an art. A model based in an architectonics, therefore, "always already" puts women at risk because it steers an investigation toward the *necessity*—perhaps the tragedy—of hierarchy that holds the parts together. Accordingly, an architectonic approach forgets the lived experiences of women

as it attends to how the parts complete or actualize rhetoric as a way to make claims on the world and other participants in it. In this way, an architectonic—in the interest of unifying the parts under, say, the *pistis* or "proof" of ethos (character)—makes its claims on the ends of rhetoric, and those marked as female or "woman" are reduced or subordinated to the whole. An architectonic approach takes little notice of the claims made about women's authority.

4. Anaximenes, *Rhetorica Ad Alexandrum*, 1420.26–21a.2.

5. Griffin, "The Edifice Metaphor in Rhetorical Theory," has traced this history from the ancient Greeks to the modern period.

6. However, concealed in the temporal aspect of techne is a sense of space and building: "the word *technē* belongs to the verb's root *tec*," writes Heidegger in "Building Dwelling Thinking," 337. With respect to rhetoric as space, see Sutton, "On the Structure of Rhetoric in Aristotle"; and Mifsud, Sutton, and Fox, "Configurations." Most scholars in rhetorical studies today approach space as rhetorical and thus stop short of envisaging rhetoric qua rhetoric as space. On place-making as rhetorical, see, for example, Code, *Rhetorical Spaces*; N. Johnson, *Gender and Rhetorical Space in American Life*; N. Johnson, "Reigning in the Court of Silence"; Marback, "The Rhetorical Space of Robben Island"; Mountford, "On Gender and Rhetorical Space"; and Mountford, *The Gendered Pulpit*.

7. Sloane, preface, xi.

8. See, for example, Vitanza, *Negation, Subjectivity, and the History of Rhetoric*.

9. As Nietzsche tells it in his "History of Greek Eloquence (1872–1873)," it is only with the political form of democracy that rhetoric begins. Rhetoric "has become the greatest instrument of power *inter pares* [among equals]." *Friedrich Nietzsche on Rhetoric and Language*, Gilman, Blair, and Parent, 214.

10. See, for example, Farrell, *Norms of a Rhetorical Culture*; Foss and Foss, *Inviting Transformation*; Hauser and Grim, *Rhetorical Democracy*; and Ivie, "Rhetorical Deliberation and Democratic Politics in the Here and Now."

11. James, *The Question of Our Speech*, 10.

12. Of all the arts rhetoric alone "controls 'opinions about things' and *hence the effect of things upon men*." Nietzsche, "History of Greek Eloquence (1872–1873)," in *Friedrich Nietzsche on Rhetoric and Language*, ed. Gilman, Blair, and Parent, 213.

13. Gilman, Blair, and Parent, *Friedrich Nietzsche on Rhetoric and Language*, 214.

14. Considering the art (techne) rhetoric as an old *technology* that was once new, it also preserves its newness—the context in which deliberation is defined—while being old. For a similar kind of argument about new media, see Gitelman, *Always Already New*.

15. See, for example, Isocrates, "Panegyricus."

16. Gilman, Blair, and Parent, *Friedrich Nietzsche on Rhetoric and Language*, 211.

17. Atwill and Lauer, *Perspectives on Rhetorical Invention*, xx.

18. In 1983, the name of the association was Speech Communication Association.

19. Office of the Curator, "Architectural Features and Historic Spaces," the Architect of the Capitol, Capitol Complex, February 2001, http://www.aoc.gov/cc/architecture/index.cfm.

20. Brandell, "Out of the Broom Closet and into the Rotunda."

21. We had read, for example, K. Campbell, "The Rhetoric of Women's Liberation"; Hillbruner, "Frances Wright"; and Kendall and Fisher, "Frances Wright on Women's Rights."

22. See, for example, Allen, *The Concept of Woman*; Deslauriers, "Sex and Essence in Aristotle's *Metaphysics* and Biology"; Horowitz, "Aristotle and Woman"; Irigaray, "Place, Interval"; and Sparshott, "Aristotle on Women."

23. Oliver, *The History of Public Speaking*, 449. However, the chapter "The Great Debates That Shaped Our Nation" does not mention any women.

24. I shouldn't have been too surprised given my familiarity with a number of key historical studies such as de Beauvoir, *The Second Sex*; Berg, *The Remembered Gate*; Lerner, *The Woman in American History*; and Noble, *A World Without Women*.

25. In many ways, Ferraro echoes my point in her interview on the *Today Show*. See "Twenty-Year Anniversary of Geraldine Ferraro Being Selected as the First Female to Run for Vice President," *Today Show* (National Broadcasting Company, 2004).

26. Kenneth Cmiel makes a similar point: "Residues of ancient taboos persist [in the twenty-first century] far beyond any 'official' end to barriers [in the nineteenth century] against women speaking in public" (*Democratic Eloquence*, 71).

27. See also Brownmiller, *Femininity*; Jamieson, *Eloquence in an Electronic Age*; and van Zoonen, "The Personal, the Political, and the Popular." The Web sites Emily's List and Women's Media Center posted examples of sexism.

28. See http://www.figarospeech.com/it-figures/2005/8/1/if-bill-had-great-interns-then-hillary.html.

29. Adams, "Not in Kansas."

30. Peyser, "Ok, I Give Up—She Just Won't Die."

31. See, for example, "911 Tapes Released; Stocks Surge; Donda West Autopsy; Ghost Flights; Minding Your Business" (Cable News Network, 2007); "The 'B' Word: Tough Question," *World News with Charles Gibson* (American Broadcasting Companies, 2007); "Bomb Parts on Board? 50,000 Volts of Electricity; Tagging Taggers; Shifting Gears?; Scouring the Web; Gerri's Top Tips," in *CNN Newsroom* (Cable News Source, 2007); "For November 14, 2007," *Hardball* (Voxant, Inc., 2007); "For November 15, 2007," *Countdown* (Voxant, Inc., 2007); "Latest Polls Show Shake-Ups in '08 Race; Democrats Playing Politics with Iraq?" *Hannity & Colmes* (Fox, 2007); "McCain Answered Woman Who Rapped Clinton," *Nightline* (American Broadcasting Companies, 2007); "Mud Slinging Erupts in U.S. Presidential Campaign," *Show* (Australian Broadcasting Corporation, 2007), "O. J. Simpson to Face Trial; Interview with Colorado Congressman Tom Tancredo; John McCain and the B-Word," *Out in the Open* (Cable News Network, 2007); Keith Olbermann, *Countdown* (2007); "Unscripted Moments on the Campaign Trail," *The Bryant Park Project* (National Public Radio).

32. After Anne Hutchinson spoke up, John Winthrop referred to her speaking as "a-whoring from God." Crawford, *Four Women in a Violent Time*. When Hutchinson was killed in an Indian massacre, the Puritan leaders expressed pleasure in what they claimed

was God's exposure of the Jezebel. Winthrop reveled, "God's hand is apparently seen herein, to pick out this woful [sic] woman, to make her . . . an unheard-of heavy example" (108). She "has been cast down" due to her "speaking out like a Jezebel" (137). Jezebel, a character from the Old Testament (1 Kings 18:4, 1 Kings 16:32–33, 2 Kings 9:30–37), was eaten by dogs after being put to death for her wickedness.

33. Gage, *Woman, Church and State*, 262.

34. "McCain Answers 'How Do We Beat the Bitch,'" http://www.youtube.com/watch?v=fnvPpSta7WQ. The question was put to John McCain by a female constituent in November 2007. He laughed, as did seemingly everyone else at the (de facto) town hall meeting in Hilton Head, South Carolina, before calling it an excellent question.

35. Templin, "Hillary Clinton as a Threat to Gender Norms," 32. The fantasy is not limited to Clinton. Consider the witch and teeth imagery of "Chainsaw Drew," the epithet used to rename Drew Gilpin Faust, the first female president of Harvard University. See Heinrichs, *Figures of Speech Served Fresh*.

36. Jamieson, *Eloquence in an Electronic Age*, 67. In colonial America, the scold or the "unquiet woman" was submerged in water "where she could choose between silence and drowning. When the stool was raised, the drenched, breathless woman was offered the chance to renounce her verbal past. . . . Her submergence and submission invited silence from women who might otherwise be disposed to disrupt the social order with speech." See also Brownmiller, *Femininity*, 112.

37. While the images may illuminate Clinton's potential, they also intend to fix our attention on "everywoman" who would dare follow her footsteps. The witch, the bitch, and the teeth of the zipper on a gagged mouth engender a discursive "thing" to invite silence from any woman who would dare speak as Clinton speaks—with authority.

38. *Bill Moyers Journal* (PBS, 2007).

39. Ibid.

40. Jamieson, *Beyond the Double Bind*, 16. See also Mandziuk, "Dressing Down Hillary."

41. On the recurrent irony of the public and private transformation of "woman," see Hahn and Borisoff, "How Do We Keep Women in their Place if Woman Is Place?"

42. *Video: Maddow, Ferraro on Gender Factor* (MSNBC, 2008), http://www.msnbc.msn.com/id/21134540/vp/24722757#24722757 (accessed May 20, 2008).

43. Goldenberg, *Madam President*, 31.

44. Ibid., 32–33.

45. Steinem, "What Women Need to Rise."

46. Clark, "Rhetoric, Social Construction, and Gender"; N. Miller, "Rereading as a Woman."

47. On the urgency of linking theory and history to feminism, see Scott, *Gender and the Politics of History*.

48. I mean something other than Aristotelian rhetorical theory and its receptions, especially as they lean toward man as a disciplinary figure and a tradition of great men who canonize theory as civic discourse. This Aristotelian theory—as a result of its vocabulary, categories, and terminology—disposes a cultural order in the house of rhetoric. However,

this cultural order creates a problem of equality in democracy due to the relation it sustains between rhetoric and women. I argue that we need to leave behind this order. On the problems of articulating rhetoric and feminism, see Poster, "(Re)Positioning Pedagogy." So why not just begin anew and leave Aristotle behind? Here's why: Aristotle's text comprises the field of principles that form a house of rhetoric. It is odd to posit a text as the house of my sojourn. But no other comparable situation exists in any other discipline. Gross and Walzer write, "Because Aristotle situates his reflection in opposition to Platonic and Sophistic versions of rhetoric, even those who might have preferred a different starting point have tended to frame their views with reference to his position." *Rereading Aristotle's Rhetoric*, x. The upshot of Aristotle's opening remarks on rhetoric was to render his work not only the core of civic discourse but also the middle of a disciplinary practice. They go on to write, "No other discipline would claim that a single text so usefully informs current deliberations on practice and theory." See also Gross, "Renewing Aristotelian Theory." Having said that a single text informs the disciplinary practice, I do not mean to suggest that a single text represents the house of rhetoric but gives to the house its definition or shape through a "near total domination" of Aristotle's *Rhetoric*. See Wardy, "Mighty Is the Truth and It Shall Prevail?" 56. There are, of course, other rhetoricians and other texts on rhetoric. See, for example, Walker, "Before the Beginnings of 'Poetry' and 'Rhetoric'"; and Wardy, *The Birth of Rhetoric*. Moreover, someone may ask, what about Cicero? The history of rhetoric, viewed at large, presents Cicero quantitatively more often than Aristotle. However, as Wardy, *The Birth of Rhetoric*, 108, writes, *Rhetoric* "achieved a position in the regiment of canonical handbooks equaling Cicero's in influence." I would add that the concept of rhetoric is shaped by Aristotle, for rhetoric is defined by Aristotelian vocabulary, categories, and definitions. Cicero, therefore, is conceptually bound to Aristotle. Roland Barthes in the chapter "L'Ancienne Rhétoriques, Aides-Memoire" illustrates the point nicely when he asks rhetorically, "Isn't all rhetoric (if we except Plato) Aristotelian?" He explains, "All the didactic elements which feed the classical manuals come from Aristotle." Even Cicero comes from Aristotle. "Cicero is . . . a certain pragmatization of Aristotelian theory and therefore [says] nothing really new in relation to this theory." By "nothing really new," Barthes suggests that Ciceronian rhetoric "owes everything to Aristotle [e.g., topics], including the de-intellectualization of Aristotle, which is a fear of system." Barthes, *The Semiotic Challenge*, 220. Barthes's reading is not totally fair, as Liu, "Disciplinary Politics and the Institutionalization of the Generic Triad in Classical Rhetoric," makes clear. It does, I believe, make sense to connect rhetoric as a conceptual site of civic discourse to the house that Aristotle built. How would one recognize rhetoric as the house that Aristotle built rather than, say, Isocrates? One way would be to count the number of copies of Aristotle's *Rhetoric* that have been printed and sold. The copies could be put side by side and presumably would make a space comparable to or larger than any other set of relevant texts, such as texts on rhetoric by Isocrates or Cicero or Kenneth Burke. We could also consider other ways to measure the house of rhetoric by a text. To that expansive space of *Rhetoric* created out of sold and printed copies we might add to it numbers, namely numbers of translations or the number of times the text was used as required reading in the classroom or the number of times the book was checked out of the library. I might follow the same procedure with other rhetorical treatises such as those by Cicero or Kenneth Burke. Afterward, I could compare the size of each. The results may or may not warrant my claim that Aristotle dominates the imagination of rhetoric. Paradoxically, it really does not matter if *Rhetoric* constitutes the largest or smallest textual space in history. Size does not make the house. The significance of Aristotle and his text to a contemporary world is measured by its "overweening influence," according to Gaonkar, "Contingency and Probability," 160. The *Rhetoric* is influential and dominates the space of speech because it supplies the principles—the language, the grammar, the categories, and the vocabulary—from which we mold and tender our conceptual understanding of speech as civic discourse and our speaking practices. For example, most of the terminology, vocabulary, definitions, and categories central to the idea of speech are derived from Aristotle. As Jacob Klein has observed, "It is perhaps no exaggeration to state that something like three-quarters of all existing scientific and philosophic terminology is either determined by Aristotle's . . . vocabulary or can be traced back to it" (*Lectures and Essays*, 179). Structurally, *Rhetoric* gives the field the language with which to understand the art and the formal tools with which to apply the art to lived experience. Interaction is imagined, talked about, rationalized, and idealized in the construct of a text. A house that is built and always already in the building process—supplied by Aristotle's language, vocabulary, and terminology—comprises everything from our judgments of women as civic orators to our rules for deliberating national issues such as war and peace. T. Morris, *If Aristotle Ran General Motors*, is but one recent example of how Aristotle's vocabulary, language, and categories continue to frame our thinking about decision making. By adopting the text's precepts and by using and incorporating its procedures and methods, we constitute and are constituted by this language, vocabulary, and terminology to the extent that each time we reclaim something of *Rhetoric*, whether it is the word *rhetoric* itself or rhetorical ideas found in business, we make and are made by the textualization of speech.

49. Pirsig, *Zen and the Art of Motorcycle Maintenance*, 102.

50. "And if some say that women have no soul, they speak a truth they are unaware of, because—except for the *neutre*, also a benefit of our time—women do not actually have rhetoric; rather they are always the same demand for a 'man'; and in this they are betrayed . . . even before being born." Michelstaedter, *Persuasion and Rhetoric*, 76.

51. Goldenberg, *Madam President*, 32. See also Eicher-Catt and Sutton, "A Communicology of the Oval Office as Figural Rhetoric"; and Gutgold, *Paving the Way for Madam President*.

52. Jamieson, *Beyond the Double Bind*; Jamieson, *Eloquence in an Electronic Age*, 67–89.

53. Van Zoonen, "The Personal, the Political, and the Popular," 292–93.

54. Goldenberg, *Madam President*, 89–162.

55. Tuchman, Daniels, and Benét, *Hearth and Home*; Woodall and Fridkin, "Shaping Women's Chances."

56. Victoria Farrar-Myers, "Money and the Art and Science of Candidate Visibility,"

in *Rethinking Madam President: Are We Ready for a Woman in the White House?*, ed. Lori Cox Han and Caroline Heldman (Boulder, CO: Lynne Rienner, 2007).

57. Woodall and Fridkin, "Shaping Women's Chances," 83.

58. See B. Anderson, *Joyous Greetings*; Crawford, *Four Women in a Violent Time*; Cutter, *Unruly Tongue*; Jamieson, *Beyond the Double Bind*; Kamensky, *Governing the Tongue*; Kleinberg, *Women in the United States*; Levander, *Voices of the Nation*; Matthews, *The Rise of Public Woman*; and Rupp and Taylor, *Survival in the Doldrums*.

59. See, for example, K. Campbell, *Man Cannot Speak for Her*; K. Campbell, "Style and Content in the Rhetoric of Early African-American Feminists"; Glenn, *Rhetoric Retold*; Hillbruner, "Frances Wright"; Jarratt, "Sappho's Memory"; Kendall and Fisher, "Frances Wright on Women's Rights"; O'Conner, *Pioneer Women Orators*; Logan, *"We Are Coming"*; Logan, *With Pen and Voice*; Portnoy, *Their Right to Speak*; Ratcliffe, *Anglo-American Feminist Challenges to the Rhetorical Tradition*; Sutherland and Sutcliffe, *The Changing Tradition*; Wertheimer, *Listening to Their Voices*; Yoakam, "An Historical Survey of the Public Speaking Activities of American Women"; Yoakam, "Pioneer Women Orators of America"; and Yoakam, "Women's Introduction to the American Platform."

60. See, for example, Brake and Neuleib, "Famous Women Orators"; Brake, "Women Orators"; C. Brown, *Dynamic Communication Skills for Women*; Butler, *Time to Speak Up*; Garland, *Public Speaking for Women*; Richardson, *The Woman Speaker*; and Stone and Bachner, *Speaking Up*.

61. As for similar kinds of publications, see Egermeier, *Girls' Stories of Great Women*; Mosley, *The Suffragists in Literature for Youth*; and Vrato and Clinton, *The Counselors*. I want to stress that the problem of exclusion is not confined to an academic discipline. It is a problem within the sociopolitical realm. In a recent issue of *Glamour*, a popular women's magazine, Representative Beatrice Lanzi (D-RI) told her readers that the face of the politician in the United States has not been and still is not the face of a young woman. Elected to public office at age twenty-five, Lanzi related—in an interview titled "Uncle Sam Needs You"—several mistaken-identity gaffes, including being mistaken for the house page and being stopped by the door attendants at the Rhode Island legislature because they did not believe that she was really a representative. When she is out in public with her husband, he is thought to be the representative. In the year 2000, women held 65 of the 535 seats in the U.S. Congress (12 percent). Of those women five were under forty years of age. (See B. Anderson, *Joyous Greetings*.) Lanzi notes a decrease of young women in politics by comparing and contrasting the number of seats held by men and women under the age of forty in the U.S. Congress and in her home state: "Of the 37 women in the Rhode Island legislature, two are under 40. By contrast, of the 111 men in the legislature, 34 are under 40. This means that while young women [under 40] make up 1.4 percent of the Rhode Island legislature, young men [under 40] make up 23 percent." Although the percentage of seats that women held in 2000 represents an increase of women, especially compared to the 1980s, the Congressional Research Service pointed out that at the current rate of growth, it would take 432 years before women would have a majority in the House. See Scull, "Women Members of Congress." Writing

at the end of the twentieth century, some contend that because the number of women entering college and studying in typically "male" fields such as business are increasing so rapidly, women will achieve parity by 2010. See Ehrenreich and Tiger, "Who Needs Men?" Finally, in 1997 Secretary of State Madeleine Albright hosted a party of women from all over the world to draw attention to the "political progress of women." World-wide there are ten UN ambassadors and seventeen speakers of parliament. According to "Women Leaders Decreasing Worldwide," the number of women in parliament "has declined from 15% in 1988 to less than 12% today." According to the same article, this recent decline is a "result" of more countries turning toward "democracy." Citing the *Los Angeles Times* (September 9, 1997), the article says that when countries turn toward democracy patriarchal systems resurface.

62. See Biesecker, "Coming to Terms with Recent Attempts to Write Women into the History of Rhetoric"; Biesecker, "Negotiating with Our Tradition"; and K. Campbell, "Biesecker Cannot Speak for Her Either."

63. As interest in adding women to the pages of texts and in putting them in positions of leadership, power, and authority continues to grow, arguments concerning the methods of achieving the goals of inclusion have begun to unfold. What are the forces of exclusion? How might rhetorical women be inserted into the institutions associated with public speaking? Since the early 1990s, a few, very important controversies have arisen and now press the attention of many feminists. In rhetorical studies, the controversy arises on the various ideological and political questions relevant to the task of putting or inserting women into the public sphere. Because a number of special issues of journals over the past decade of the twentieth century, namely *Rhetorica, Rhetoric Society Quarterly, College English, Philosophy and Rhetoric,* and *Southern Communication Journal,* have already provided opportunities for feminists to explore the implications of these questions in essays, discussions, and comments, I will not try to give an account of the various positions held. For a brief and excellent summary, see Ballif and Morgan, introduction, 2. See also K. Campbell, "Feminist Rhetoric." For a selection of research, see, for example, Ede, Glenn, and Lunsford, "Border Crossings"; Bizzell, "Feminist Methods of Research in the History of Rhetoric"; Wu, "Historical Studies of Women Here and There"; Biesecker, "Coming to Terms with Recent Attempts to Write Women into the History of Rhetoric"; Conners, "The Exclusion of Women from Classical Rhetoric"; Gale, "Historical Studies and Postmodernism"; Gearhart, "The Womanization of Rhetoric"; Glenn, "Comment: Truth, Lies, and Method"; Jarratt, "Comment: Rhetoric and Feminism"; N. Johnson, "Reigning in the Court of Silence"; Liu, "Disciplinary Politics and the Institutionaliza-tion of the Generic Triad in Classical Rhetoric"; Norton, "Rhetorical Criticism as Ethical Action"; Nuyen, "The Rhetoric of Feminist Writings"; Rushing, "Introduction to Femi-nist Criticism"; and Sutton, "The Taming of the *Polos/Polis.*" For book-length projects, see, for example, Atwill, *Rhetoric Reclaimed;* Enoch, *Refiguring Rhetorical Education;* Bal-lif, *Seduction, Sophistry, and the Woman with the Rhetorical Figure;* Glenn, *Rhetoric Retold;* Hawhee, *Bodily Arts;* Portnoy, *Their Right to Speak;* Ratcliffe, *Anglo-American Feminist Chal-lenges to the Rhetorical Tradition;* and Sutherland and Sutcliffe, *The Changing Tradition.* Suf-

fice it to say that *The House of My Sojourn* centers attention on a common insight that has begun to emerge from among the conversations—books, journal articles, convention papers, review essays—to which various communities in rhetorical studies have been engaged. The emergence of this insight is especially timely for it gives shape and direction to spelling out with some specificity the problem as I see it. In spite of radical differences among these feminists as to methodological procedures for altering the current situation of rhetorical women, all of them to some degree point to the foundation (ground) as impeding the development of rhetorical women. It is to a problematical ground, replete with its categories and definitions, that Karlyn Kohrs Campbell gestures when she urges feminists in rhetoric to do "battle" with the "ideological criteria" of rhetoric and "rethink its fundamental assumptions" ("The Sound of Women's Voices," 212, 214). It is that foundation that Barbara Biesecker looks to when she insists that feminists must first challenge the criteria to which "any particular discourse is assessed" ("Coming to Terms with Recent Attempts to Write Women into the History of Rhetoric," 23). In this vein, Diane Helene Miller cautions feminists about evaluating rhetorical women through categories provided by the foundation, for these categories have already been used to exclude women from rhetoric ("The Future of Feminist Rhetorical Criticism," 375). For a recent summary of the debate among feminists over methods of inclusion, see Meyer, "Women Speak(ing)." To write from a feminist perspective does not mean that I assume automatically the grounds of rhetoric to be sexist. It may very well be, as Celeste Condit has indicated, that fault lines do not simply follow a patriarchal influence ("Opposites in an Oppositional Practice," 223). In this manner, I join current discussions of the problem of including women in rhetorical histories, theories, and practices by approaching public speaking in and through several critical observances of women as public speakers drawn from a variety of verbal and visual forms. In this vein, see, for example, N. Johnson, *Gender and Rhetorical Space in American Life*; and Jorgensen-Earp, "The Lady, the Whore, and the Spinster." I, however, differ from such cases in that I seek a theoretical intervention by delineating the main ways women's inclusion poses a serious challenge to the future of women *in* rhetoric.

64. Portnoy, *Their Right to Speak*.

65. Enoch, *Refiguring Rhetorical Education*.

66. This line of reasoning follows from a number of thinkers such as Foucault, "Of Other Spaces." See Biesecker, "Michel Foucault and the Question of Rhetoric"; the notion of the chronotope in Bakhtin, *The Dialogic Imagination*; Bialostosky, "Architectonics, Rhetoric, and Poetics in the Bakhtin School's Early Phenomenological and Sociological Texts"; Bialostosky, "Aristotle's *Rhetoric* and Bakhtin's Discourse Theory"; and Peeren, *Intersubjectivities and Popular Culture*.

67. Eakins, "The Evolution of Rhetoric," 195, 197.

68. Clinton, H., "Hillary's Remarks in Washington, DC, June 7, 2008."

69. "My exclusion in rhetoric is changed by knowing that women participated in rhetoric." This is adapted from Scott, *Gender and the Politics of History*, 31.

70. These perspectives include post-structuralism, psychoanalysis—particularly Lacanian—

and myth and communicology. Except for the mythical and communicological, many of these are summarized in note 63. For the mythical, the most notable examples can be found in the scholarship of Janice Hocker Rushing. See, for example, three of her essays: "Evolution of 'The New Frontier' in *Alien* and *Aliens*"; "Power, Other, and Spirit in Cultural Texts"; and "Putting Away Childish Things." As for communicology, especially as it relates to agency, see, for example, Eicher-Catt, "A Communicology of Female/Feminine Embodiment"; and Eicher-Catt, "Non-Custodial Mothering."

71. See, for example, Ede, Glenn, and Lunsford, "Border Crossings"; Foss and Foss, *Inviting Transformation*; and Foss and Griffin, "A Feminist Perspective on Rhetorical Theory."

72. Wertheimer, *Listening to Their Voices*, 13n4, sums up the score of the debate: "Barbara Biesecker launched a fairly strident attack against Karlyn Kohrs Campbell's 'women's history approach' in her essay 'Coming to Terms with Recent Attempts to Write Women into the History of Rhetoric' (1992). I have read Biesecker's essay several times and believe that she did use Campbell's work rhetorically—as a foil against which to develop her own views; she could have written her essay without the polemical confrontation, but the clash gave the piece a kind of gusty energy. Unfortunately, what may have been originally a capitulation to 'scholastic' form became transformed into genuine conflict—somewhat personal in nature—by the journalistic practice of allowing an author who was attacked the opportunity to defend herself in print."

73. See, for example, Blair, Brown, and Baxter, "Disciplining the Feminine"; Dow, "Feminism, Cultural Studies, and Rhetorical Studies"; Foss and Griffin, "A Feminist Perspective on Rhetorical Theory"; Norton, "Rhetorical Criticism as Ethical Action"; and Shugart, "Counterhegemonic Acts."

74. See, for example, Meyer, "Women Speak(ing)."

75. Clinton, "Hillary's Remarks in Washington, DC, June 7, 2008."

76. Cox, "Memory, Critical Theory, and the Argument from History"; Hennessey, "A Theory of Memory as Applied to Speech"; Hoogestraat, "Memory: The Lost Canon?"; C. Irwin, "Rhetoric Remembers"; Jarratt, "Sappho's Memory"; Lentz, "From Recitation to Memory"; Struever, "Rhetoric: Time, Memory, Memoir"; Sutton, "Hippias of Elis."

77. Clinton, "Hillary's Remarks in Washington, DC, June 7, 2008."

78. Jamieson, *Beyond the Double Bind*, 20.

79. Clinton, "Hillary's Remarks in Washington, DC, June 7, 2008," emphasis added.

80. C. Irwin, "Rhetoric Remembers"; Weaver, *Visions of Order*, 42-43.

81. Weaver, *Visions of Order*, 5-6.

82. As Hillary Clinton said, "[t]hink of the suffragists who gathered at Seneca Falls in 1848 and those who kept fighting until women could cast their votes."

83. Atwill and Lauer, *Perspectives on Rhetorical Invention*, xx.

84. See also Shenandoah and George, *Skywoman*.

85. The angle brackets signify <CIVIC> as an ideograph. An ideograph, according to Michael McGee, "is a figure" or trope, but the brackets indicate a code or body of regulations. The code is observed by fixed and dominating customs or habits as in rule of the road. McGee, "Ideograph," 378.

86. My view of the body is quite different from that of the body in Hawhee, *Bodily Arts*. She links the verbal art of speaking with the athletic contests of the gymnasium on the basis of "rhythm, repetition, and response" that effectively realizes the concept of rhetoric. The body has the capacity to generate a concept of rhetoric after recognition. The movement I focus on is not that realized in the gymnasium and used to conceptualize rhetoric; rather, I focus on how the body moves, whose body can move, in what direction the body can move, and so on. This movement shapes rhetoric. I have discussed this movement in terms of dance and partnering in Sutton and Mpofu, "Figuring Reconciliation."

87. Aristotle, *Metaphysics*, 1.998a.20–29.

88. Woolf, "Shakespeare's Sister," 16. In my mind, Woolf exemplifies the differences between Shakespeare and Shakespeare's sister in two ways: through the body and through space. While opportunity is more often than not linked to time (*kairos*, opportunity or right time) among rhetoricians, I think Woolf envisions opportunity as space, particularly the possibility of women embodying space wherein they can create ideas. Following this line of thought, I have not a room in mind but a house. To work like Virginia Woolf does for Shakespeare's sister and extend it to rhetoric, it would be fair to say that work entails creating an opportunity for her to rise up in the flesh and speak as a leader in a house of rhetoric. Toward that end, she will need a space, and the space must be not only of her own but also of a house of rhetoric that heretofore does not exist.

89. Qtd. in Levander, *Voices of the Nation*, 17.

90. See also V. Turner, *Blazing the Trail*.

91. F. Wright, *Course of Popular Lectures*, 32.

92. Truth, *The Women Want Their Rights!*

93. "Michelle Obama Honors Sojourner Truth, Wears Striped Skirt."

CHAPTER 1

Nietzsche, *The Twilight of the Idols*, sec. 11.

1. Yoakam, "An Historical Survey of the Public Speaking Activities of American Women." See also Yoakam, "Pioneer Women Orators of America"; and Yoakam, "Women's Introduction to the American Platform." Compare Platz, *The History of Public Speaking*. Platz notes the modern status of oratory, particularly its relation to the public forum and the school curriculum in the wake of World War I (283). The discussion of women amounts to one sentence on Susan B. Anthony (251). To put this one sentence in perspective, neither the chapter "The American Period," which includes an antislavery section, nor the chapter "The World War Period" includes women orators.

2. Yoakam, "An Historical Survey of the Public Speaking Activities of American Women," 519.

3. Garland, *Public Speaking for Women*; Richardson, *The Woman Speaker*.

4. Cf. *Liberator*, October 1, 1852.

5. Richardson, *The Woman Speaker*, 16-17.

6. Ibid., 17.

7. Ibid. Less than one-fifth of respondents to a 1936 Gallup Poll approved of married women working. For discussion, see Kleinberg, *Women in the United States*, 219.

8. Garland, *Public Speaking for Women*, 152-53.

9. Butler, *Time to Speak Up*, 115.

10. Ibid., 117.

11. Ibid., 119.

12. O'Conner, *Pioneer Women Orators*.

13. Ibid., 98-99. O'Conner is following Lester Thonssen and A. Craig Baird. She quotes them, writing, "The *Rhetoric* [of Aristotle] is the most literate and forthright analysis of the art of speaking in print."

14. See J. Q. Adams, *Lectures on Rhetoric and Oratory (1810)*.

15. Egermeier, *Girls' Stories of Great Women*.

16. Ibid., v.

17. Vrato and B. Clinton, *The Counselors*.

18. Brake, "Women Orators." Brake reports that A. Craig Baird's *American Public Addresses, 1740-1952* contains no speech text from a woman orator, even though Baird claims to present a "cross-section of the leading figures and their productions" (21). See also Brake and Neuleib, "Famous Women Orators."

19. Oliver, *The History of Public Speaking*; F. Wright, "Address, Delivered in the New-Harmony Hall"; *New Harmony Gazette*, July 9, 1828.

20. Oliver, *The History of Public Speaking*, 447.

21. C. Brown, *Dynamic Communication Skills for Women*.

22. The result of Campbell's analysis was presented as a lecture at Tulane University, New Orleans, and is discussed in Spitzack and Carter, "Women in Communication Studies," 419-20n5. See also K. Campbell, "The Communication Classroom."

23. K. Campbell, *Man Cannot Speak for Her*.

24. Stone and Bachner, *Speaking Up*, 5.

25. Mueller, "Aphasia," 211.

26. Vonnegut, "Listening for Women's Voices." See also K. Campbell, "Hearing Women's Voices." Cf. Fallon, "Planning for the Year 2000."

27. Cf. Enos, "On the Trail of Ancient Rhetoric."

28. Bachelard, *The Poetics of Space*, 4.

29. Hyperides, "Funeral Speech," col. 3.

30. I would say the description is a definition. Anaximenes, *Rhetorica Ad Alexandrum*, 1420.26-21a.2. That there is no definition of rhetoric in *The Rhetoric to Alexander* is the view of O'Rourke, "Anaximenes, *Rhetorica Ad Alexandrum*." This house "definition" does not challenge the definition of rhetoric as the art of persuasion. It complements the ordinary view and centers more attention on the structure or space of rhetoric than on temporality. There is also the issue of authorship. While most believe that Aristotle is not the author of *The Rhetoric to Alexander*, Nietzsche says in his "Aristotle's Writings on Rhetoric," "The *rhētorikē pros Alexandron* is, with the exception of the first and last chap-

ter, ascribed to the rhetor Anaximenes Lampsakus (by Spengel)." Gilman, Blair, and Parent, *Friedrich Nietzsche on Rhetoric and Language,* 197, emphasis added.

31. Aristotle, *Metaphysics,* 1041b.5–10.

32. Bachelard, *The Poetics of Space,* 4.

33. Lévy-Bruhl, *How Natives Think,* 107–8; Cassirer, "Mythic, Aesthetic, and Theoretical Space," 14.

34. A boundary is a limit and definition of a thing. See Aristotle, *Metaphysics,* 1031a.1. So in this way, the glass ceiling forms a boundary claiming male authority for the house.

35. I am presenting rhetoric as a space. There is no concept of space in Aristotle. "Perhaps the most surprising thing about Aristotle's *Physics* to a present-day reader is the absence of the concept of space." Sachs, *Aristotle's Physics,* 105. I recognize there is some sense of space in the notion of an *aggeion.* It acts like a vessel and has the function of containing goods that are in motion and holding bodies in place vis-à-vis decision making. Aristotle, *Metaphysics,* 1043a.16–17. Aristotle characterizes an *aggeion* as a city that holds men and as a ship that holds sailors. Aristotle, *Metaphysics,* 1023a.16–17; Plato, *Theaetetus,* 7.197e. The U.S. Capitol, therefore, is like an *aggeion.* It is active, not empty, in configuring lived experiences. It contains or holds bodies in place and stabilizes (like pillars) their practices. What is common, then, to the inanimate and animate senses of an *aggeion* is that the contained—whether speech or men, respectively—is subject to limits, organization, and stability. Whenever an *aggeion* functions to hold, it acts as a motif of container or house and whenever it functions to manage impulsivity or appetite, it acts as a motif of constraint or domestication and thus is active and engaged in the dialectical tensions that shape it.

36. On rhetoric as a productive art and the implication of this, see Atwill, *Rhetoric Reclaimed.*

37. See, for example, Fortenbaugh, "Aristotle on Slaves and Women"; Sparshott, "Aristotle on Women"; and Horowitz, "Aristotle and Woman."

38. Aristotle, *Metaphysics,* 1022b.1.

39. At first glance it seems odd to return to myth, especially in the wake of poststructuralism's analysis of myth as a problematic form of concealment. Cassirer, "Mythic, Aesthetic, and Theoretical Space," 9, says myth in the twentieth century can be a technique manufactured by the political state according to the same methods "as machine guns or airplanes." For a full discussion of the limits and possibilities of myth, see Cassirer, *The Myth of the State,* 282. The myth I have in mind is animated within the "social imaginary," defined "as the ways people imagine their social existence, how they fit together with others, how things go on between them and their fellows, the expectations that are normally met, and the deeper normative notions and images that underlie these expectations." Taylor, *Modern Social Imaginaries,* 23.

40. Burke, *The Philosophy of Literary Form,* 20.

41. Qtd. in Rykwert, *The Dancing Column,* 122.

42. Of the many myths and origins of rhetoric, see Wilcox, "Corax and the Prolegomena."

43. Although Aristotle offers no full description of rhetoric's development and names

no founders, he does mention the art emerging out of the mythic topic of tyranny. See Aristotle, *Politics*, 1305a.1–5. On the myths of rhetoric, see, for example, Cicero, *De Inventione*, I.II.2; Isocrates, "Antidosis," 1.67; and Isocrates, "Nicocles or the Cyprians," 2.254–56.

44. See, for example, Farenga, "The Paradigmatic Tyrant"; and Farenga, "Periphrasis on the Origin of Rhetoric."

45. Qtd. in Sprague, *The Older Sophists*, 80C.1, emphasis added.

46. Qtd. in Farenga, "Periphrasis on the Origin of Rhetoric," 1035, emphasis added; Rabe, *Prolegomenon Sylloge*.

47. Croix, *The Class Struggle in the Ancient Greek World*, 11.

48. Emile Benveniste, *Indo-European Language and Society*, trans. Elizabeth Palmer (Coral Gables, FL: University of Miami Press, 1973), 371.

49. *Oxford English Dictionary Online* (Oxford University Press, 2003), http://oed.com/.

50. Cicero, *De Inventione*, I.II.2; Isocrates, "Antidosis," 254–56; Isocrates, "Nicocles or the Cyprians," 1.67; Plato, *Protagoras*, 322–23C.

51. Isocrates, "Antidosis," 253.

52. Euripides, *Euripides*, Vol. 3 201ff.

53. Several times Aristotle does use *anthropos*, the inclusive word for humans, instead of *aner*, man. However, he excludes women from the process of decision making and thus rhetoric and politics. See, for example, Fortenbaugh, *Aristotle on Emotion*. I would add that this organization is a solution to philosophical questions of the day, namely questions of virtue appropriate to the sexes and different kinds of people, such as slaves. The philosophical solution is to argue that women's capacity for virtue is very limited and in fact lacks the capacity for deliberation. While many argue that Aristotle is not sexist, his model of rhetoric is designed to exclude women. See Dobbs, "Family Matters"; Levy, "Does Aristotle Exclude Women from Politics?"; Swanson, *The Public and the Private in Aristotle's Political Philosophy*; Smith, "Plato and Aristotle on the Nature of Women"; and M. Katz, "Ideology and 'the Status of Women' in Ancient Greece." This model is a problem for us today because rhetoric acts as a means of deliberation that eventuates in judgment, and judgment is thought to reflect the views of all.

54. Fortenbaugh, "Aristotle on Slaves and Women," 137. Aristotle, *Politics*, 1377b.7–11, describes political authority as ruling over another man (of the same type) comparable to a citizen-warrior

55. Aristotle, *Rhetoric*, 1391b8–16. Cope, *The Rhetoric of Aristotle*, 2:176, elaborates this section: "But as a general rule it is only the person who decides the points in question in political (public . . .) contests that is absolutely (strictly and properly) to be called a judge [decision maker]."

56. Fortenbaugh, "Aristotle on Slaves and Women," 135.

57. See Sutton, "The Taming of the *Polos/Polis*."

58. Aristotle, *Politics*, 1277b.23.

59. For discussion of *idios*, see Poster, "Being and Becoming," 8; and Glenn, *Rhetoric Retold*, 1.

60. Sutton and Mifsud, "Figuring Rhetoric," 32. See also Booth, *The Rhetoric of Rhetoric.*

61. Yartz, "Aristotle on Monsters."

62. Grassi, *Rhetoric as Philosophy,* 22.

63. See also Sutton, "Rhetoric and the Peacock."

64. Aeschylus, *The Oresteia,* 33.

65. See Lawler, *The Dance of the Ancient Greek Theatre,* 46.

66. Euripides, *Euripides,* line 750.

67. See, for example, Allen, *The Concept of Woman.* It is worth mentioning that the sophist Prodicus develops a female personification of virtue and vice to talk about deliberation. Virtue stands for the life based on reasoned principles, while vice is linked to an undisciplined form of reasoning that resembles laziness. The point is: can a woman be virtuous? The question is not whether she is a good girl but rather this: can she render decisions based on a highly disciplined method of reasoning? See Allen's discussion of the sophists in *The Concept of Woman,* 38–46. See also Goffman, "The Arrangement between the Sexes."

68. Rykwert, *The Dancing Column,* 122.

69. Ibid.

70. See Sutton and Mpofu, "Figuring Reconciliation."

71. Rykwert, *The Dancing Column,* 64.

72. Aristotle, *Politics,* 1252b.15.

73. Detienne, *The Masters of Truth in Archaic Greece.*

74. Salkever, "Women, Soldiers, Citizens."

75. Except for the Amazons (if they ever existed), only men went to war. Sobol, *The Amazons of Greek Mythology.*

76. Demosthenes, "First Philippic," 1.4–1.5.

77. Homer, *Odyssey,* trans. A. T. Murphy, 2.37.

78. Detienne, *The Masters of Truth in Archaic Greece,* 102.

79. As I talk about the temporality of speaking in the middle, I am working from within physical space rather than metaphysical space conceived in terms of voice. For a recent discussion of metaphysical space, see Doxtader, "Characters in the Middle of Public Life." Specifically, the way I distinguish a physical approach from the metaphysical one is that a physical approach emphasizes the kinds of (temporal) movement that are possible in a spatial arrangement. For example, when Professor Kostas E. Beyes gave his multimedia presentation "The Trial of Socrates" at the Thirteenth International Conference on Greek Philosophy in Rhodes, Greece, on August 18–25, 2001, sponsored by the International Center for Greek Philosophy and Culture, Department of Philosophy, University of Athens, he noted the spatial arrangement of the courtroom: As each judge (for the trial of Socrates) was drawn, he would immediately enter the courtroom in a way that made it impossible for anyone from either side of the litigants to approach him and speak to him in private. In other words, it matters how people enter space and how entrances open and close off communicative interaction because this movement shapes the event.

80. Dupriez, A Dictionary of Literary Devices, A–Z, 82.

81. Pausanias, Description of Greece, 5.17.6.

82. Anaximenes, Rhetorica Ad Alexandrum, 1420b.26–1421a.2, emphasis added.

83. Aristotle, Eudemian Ethics, 1220a.37–20b.6.

84. Chamberlain, "From 'Haunts' to 'Character'," 97.

85. Aristotle, Eudemian Ethics, 1220b.10–11.

86. Aristotle, Rhetoric, 1408a.29–32.

87. Ibid., 1356b.35.

88. For a full treatment of the enthymeme in relation to character, see Sutton and Mifsud, "Figuring Rhetoric."

89. Aristotle, Rhetoric, 1372b.16–18.

90. Habits are like nature because the distance between the sign for habit—"often"—and the sign for nature—"always"—is not great. Aristotle, Rhetoric, 1370a.7–13.

91. Aristotle, Rhetoric, 2. See also Cope, The Rhetoric of Aristotle, 1:1; Grimaldi, Studies in the Philosophy of Aristotle's Rhetoric, 1–2; and On Rhetoric, 28–29.

92. Sutton and Mifsud, "Figuring Rhetoric," 32. For commentary, see Cope, The Rhetoric of Aristotle, 3:94–95; and On Rhetoric, 239–40.

93. Deslauriers, "Sex and Essence in Aristotle's Metaphysics and Biology"; Horowitz, "Aristotle and Woman"; Morsink, "Was Aristotle's Biology Sexist?" Saxonhouse, "Family, Polity, and Unity," 208, writes, "Whether this want of 'authority' in the women's deliberative capacity inheres in the soul itself or becomes manifest in groups of men who would scorn it coming from a woman is unclear in the text" of Aristotle, Politics, 1260a–60b.31, and Aristotle, Rhetoric, 1367b. According to Horowitz, "Aristotle and Woman," there is some evidence that Aristotle assumed her lack of authority on a biological basis since he theorized that a woman's womb lacked potency. Aristotle, Generation of Animals, 778a.1, 772b.27–33. Insofar as the Greek term akurios describes her womb, her political character, and her speech, her capacity to reason and deliberate is not sound and trustworthy. The word akurios condenses and legitimates, as Bourdieu, Masculine Domination, 23, explains the embodiment of domination: "a relationship of domination by embedding it in a biological nature that is itself a naturalized social construction." For discussion, see Sutton, "Intersections."

94. Aristotle, Historia Animalium, 608b.6–14. See also Aristotle, Rhetoric, 1368b.13, 1391a.25, 1396b, 1408b.5, which describe feminine speech in terms of excess, of reasoning loosely, and of lacking persuasiveness.

95. Fay, Eminent Rhetoric, 9.

96. Aristotle, Rhetoric, 1354b.7; Chantraine, Dictionnaire étymologique de la langue grecque, 2:601.

97. Cope, The Rhetoric of Aristotle, 1:53.

98. According to Peters, Greek Philosophical Terms, 96–97, "Aristotle (History of Animals 514a and Parts of Animals 656a) was not convinced by the evidence on the brain theory propounded by Socrates in Plato's Timaeus 44d. Despite the continuation of this debate in Cicero (Tusculanae Disputationes I.9.19), Aristotle's view is the one that prevailed."

99. Fortenbaugh, "Aristotle on Slaves and Women," 138.

100. Benveniste, *Indo-European Language and Society*, 411.

101. Aristotle, *Rhetoric*, 1367b.27. See also Anaximenes, *Rhetorica Ad Alexandrum*, 1443b.28.

102. Horowitz, "Aristotle and Woman." See also Allen, *The Concept of Woman*; and Sutton, "The Taming of the *Polos/Polis*."

103. Quintilian, *Institutio Oratoria*, 8.6.40–43.

104. See Sutton, "The Death of Rhetoric and Its Rebirth in Philosophy."

105. Unlike Thucydides' *History of the Peloponnesian War*, there are no speeches to speak of in Aristotle's *Rhetoric*.

106. Becker, "The Rhetoric of Architecture"; O'Connor, *The Athens of America*.

107. Whately, *Elements of Rhetoric*, 18–19.

108. Genung, *Handbook of Rhetorical Analysis*, 279.

109. Ibid., 285.

110. Heinrichs, "How Harvard Destroyed Rhetoric," 37.

111. "The Aristotelian Renaissance in Contemporary Rhetorical Theory."

112. Farrell, *Norms of a Rhetorical Culture*; Furley and Nehamas, *Aristotle's Rhetoric: Philosophical Essays*; Garver, *Aristotle's Rhetoric*; Gross, "Renewing Aristotelian Theory"; Gross and Walzer, *Rereading Aristotle's Rhetoric*; Hauser, "Aristotle on Epideictic"; Rorty, *Essays on Aristotle's Rhetoric*; Neel, *Aristotle's Voice*.

113. Hauser and Grim, *Rhetorical Democracy*; Hauser, "Aristotle on Epideictic"; Ivie, "Democratic Deliberation in a Rhetorical Republic"; Ivie, "Rhetorical Deliberation and Democratic Politics in the Here and Now"; Mouffe, *The Return of the Political*. See also D. Allen, *Talking to Strangers*.

114. See, for example, "Oration on Eloquence, Pronounced at Harvard University, on Commencement Day," in Bingham, *The Columbian Orator*, 32.

115. As Tom Frentz forever points out, of course, there's always Robert Pirsig's *Zen and the Art of Motorcycle Maintenance* as a stunning counterexample.

116. Qtd. in Levander, *Voices of the Nation*, 17.

CHAPTER 2

Qtd. in *On Rhetoric*, 243.

1. Although I spent several years on this project, it comes nowhere near the length of time it took to relocate the Portrait Monument in 1997. According to Michael Kilian, "Several legislative attempts were made to restore the statue to the Rotunda, but each was resisted fiercely by conservatives who considered it a rallying symbol for liberal women's rights activists." At the 1997 ceremony Rep. Carolyn Maloney (D-NY) noted the last move from the crypt/basement was the fourth attempt. The fourth one launched in 1992 by Woman Suffrage Statue Campaign co-chairs Karen Staser and Joan Meacham finally succeeded despite criticism that the sculpture was too heavy, the move up from

the basement too costly, and the work "too ugly." Kilian, "Out of Capitol Cellar." See also "Late Debut for Statue," *Pittsburgh Post-Gazette*, June 27, 1997.

2. The reinstallation of the Portrait Monument, which "originally had been planned for the 75th anniversary of women's suffrage, was delayed in part by demands from the National Political Congress of Black Women that the statue be remade to include a likeness of Sojourner Truth, a Civil War–era African-American woman abolitionist and feminist." Kilian, "Out of Capitol Cellar."

3. See Marlene Lang, "Rosa Parks Deserves Memorial, But Not on Portrait Monument," *Daily Southtown*, November 6, 2005.

4. Ibid.

5. "Why Whitewashed Inscription Was Turned to the Wall." See also A. Johnson, "Memories of a Pioneer Feminist."

6. The phrase "the woman movement" is nonstandard usage and there are several examples of it. The full inscription copied by curator Charles Fairman is published in "Why Whitewashed Inscription Was Turned to the Wall." Rep. Constance Morella of Maryland said the women's statue "symbolizes a fundamental and sacred part of American democracy," giving the right to vote to "52 percent of Americans." Kilian, "Out of Capitol Cellar."

7. Brandell, "Out of the Broom Closet and into the Rotunda"; Office of the Curator, "Relocation of Portrait Monument to Lucretia Mott, Elizabeth Cady Stanton, and Susan B. Anthony," Office of the Architect, Capitol Complex, April 2001, http://www .aoc.gov/cc/art/rotunda/suffrage_move.htm (accessed April 28, 2000).

8. Jones, "Suffrage Statue to Miss Ceremony."

9. "Why Whitewashed Inscription Was Turned to the Wall," 8.

10. Ibid.

11. Ibid.

12. Schiavone, "Even in Stone, Suffragettes Cause a Stir on Capitol Hill."

13. Kilian, "Out of Capitol Cellar." The article mentions that Abraham Lincoln is considered ugly, but no one uses the grounds of his ugliness to warrant the exclusion of his statue from the public sphere.

14. Kilian, "Out of Capitol Cellar."

15. "Someone get these bitches out of our faces, please." See Lang, "Rosa Parks Deserves Memorial, But Not on Portrait Monument." See also Jones, "Monument to Suffragists Stuck in Basement for Now."

16. Truth, *The Women Want Their Rights!*

17. Ibid.

18. Yoakam, "Pioneer Women Orators of America," 256.

19. O'Conner, *Pioneer Women Orators*, 42.

20. "Another Woman Orator."

21. See Willard and Livermore, *A Woman of the Century*; and Saxonhouse, "Family, Polity and Unity," 208.

22. The promise according to Burke is an "effect" of "admonition" or "instruction"

or "charting" of rhetoric capacity for persuasion. It is the function of political deliberation to have a "prophetic" character and in this way have a bearing on matters of welfare, hence of ethics and politics. See Burke, *The Philosophy of Literary Form*, 296. On the
prophetic character (*prophainesthai*) of rhetoric, see Grassi, *Rhetoric as Philosophy*, 20.

23. This is the quadripartite ratio as described by Quintilian, *Institutio Oratoria*, 1.5.38.
For discussion, see Sutton and Mifsud, "Figuring Rhetoric," 37.

24. Steven Mailloux, "Afterword: A Pretext for Rhetoric: Dancing 'Round the Revolution,'" in *Pre/Text: The First Decade*, ed. Victor J. Vitanza (Pittsburgh: University of Pittsburgh Press, 1993), 299. This expressive, enactive, and deliberative behavior that gives
tropes a kind of agency is an implication of Ballif and Morgan, introduction, 4.

25. See Spence, *Figuratively Speaking*, 9–17.

26. See Jakobson, "The Metaphoric and Metonymic Poles"; Lacan, "The Agency of
the Letter in the Unconscious or Reason since Freud," 156–60; and Krippendorff, *On
Communicating*.

27. George Lakoff and Mark Johnson, *Philosophy in the Flesh: The Embodied Mind and
Its Challenge to Western Thought* (New York: Basic Books, 1999), 37–38.

28. Cixous and Clément, *The Newly Born Woman*; Fernandez, *Persuasions and Performances*; White, *Figural Realism*; White, *Metahistory*. See also Kirby, *Indifferent Boundaries*;
and Spence, *Figuratively Speaking*.

29. Lacan, "The Agency of the Letter in the Unconscious or Reason since Freud," 160.

30. Fernandez, *Persuasions and Performances*, 46. When metonymy's certain power of
addition is not subsumed by metaphor, it offers a radical form of prefiguring any field,
making it open to a supplement, which is the implication of this book's coda. The supplement adds on but not in a manner that assimilates the other. Rather, the other enlarges
the field with its particular complexity. For discussion, see Jane Sutton and Mari Lee
Mifsud, "Alliostrophic Rhetoric," in *Advances in the History of Rhetoric*, forthcoming.

31. Spence, *Figuratively Speaking*, 19.

32. Hirschman, *The Rhetoric of Reaction*, 43–80.

33. Preminger, *Princeton Encyclopedia of Poetry and Poetics*, 499.

34. Heinrichs, *Figures of Speech Served Fresh*.

35. Mifsud, Sutton, and Fox, "Configurations."

36. Paul Ricoeur, *The Rule of Metaphor: Multidisciplinary Studies of the Creation of Meaning
in Language*, trans. Robert Czerny (Toronto: University of Toronto Press, 1977), 143.

37. Fay, *Eminent Rhetoric*, 4. A trope is a form of behavior that has been abstracted
from the body.

38. Compiled from R. Anderson, *Glossary of Greek Rhetorical Terms*, 23; Dupriez, *A
Dictionary of Literary Devices, A–Z*, 52; Gilman, Blair, and Parent, *Friedrich Nietzsche on
Rhetoric and Language*, 53, 59; Richard A. Lanham, *A Handlist of Rhetorical Terms*, 2nd ed.
(Berkeley: University of California Press, 1991), 17; Preminger, *Princeton Encyclopedia of
Poetry and Poetics*, 40; and Quintilian, *Institutio Oratoria*, 8.6.29.

39. J. Anderson, "Sexual Politics," 11. See also "Embattled," *New Yorker*, February 26,
1972, 26.

40. Stiller, *Commune on the Frontier*, 235.

41. "McCain Answers 'How Do We Beat the Bitch,'" http://www.youtube.com/watch?V=fnvPpStaTWQ.

42. "Simpson to Face Trial," 13. See also " Democrats Battle President Bush over War Funding; New York Governor Acknowledges Defeat over Driver's Licenses for Illegal Aliens; McCain-CNN Beef," *The Situation Room* (Cable News Network, 2007); "Hillary Hits Back," *CNN Reliable Sources* (Cable News Network, 2007).

43. Perelman and Olbrechts-Tyteca, *The New Rhetoric*, 172.

44. Ibid., 174.

45. "911 Tapes Released"; "The 'B' Word"; "Bomb Parts on Board?"; "For November 14, 2007"; "For November 15, 2007"; "Latest Polls Show Shake-Ups in '08 Race"; "McCain Answered Woman Who Rapped Clinton"; "Mud Slinging Erupts in U.S. Presidential Campaign"; "Simpson to Face Trial"; Olbermann, "Countdown"; "Unscripted Moments on the Campaign Trail."

46. R. Anderson, *Glossary of Greek Rhetorical Terms*, 121; Dupriez, *A Dictionary of Literary Devices, A–Z*, 213; Lanham, *A Handlist of Rhetorical Terms*, 86; Preminger, *Princeton Encyclopedia of Poetry and Poetics*, 358–59; Quintilian, *Institutio Oratoria*, 8.6.23; Thomas O. Sloane, ed., *Encyclopedia of Rhetoric*, 363.

47. Valian, *Why So Slow?*

48. Ibid., 125–28.

49. There is an example in Rushing, *Erotic Mentoring*, 146–48, in which a female college president has to sometimes give her ideas to men in her cabinet so that they can get "heard." This has several variations, such as having an idea "reduplicated" by a male colleague and then heard by the committee as though for the first time to "even not getting called on in [her] group—the presidents of the university system" (147). And "you have to be careful, said the 70-something-year-old president, because if you speak assertively, they will make that a weapon against you" (148).

50. "Who's Still Talking"; "Who's Talking Now."

51. "Who's Talking Now."

52. *Who's Talking? An Analysis of Sunday Morning Talk Shows*, 7, emphasis added.

53. Ibid.

54. "Who's Talking Now."

55. See the 2008 vice presidential debates at http://www.youtube.com/watch?v=89FbCPzAsRA.

56. Couric, "One-on-One with Sarah Palin."

57. Laura Bush told CNN's Zain Verjee on September 24, 2008, that Palin "does not have foreign policy experience" but downplayed it, saying Palin is a "quick study." See http://politicalticker.blogs.cnn.com/2008/09/24/laura-bush-says-palin-lacks-foreign-policy-experience/.

58. R. Anderson, *Glossary of Greek Rhetorical Terms*, 93; Dupriez, *A Dictionary of Literary Devices, A–Z*, 328–30; Gilman, Blair, and Parent, *Friedrich Nietzsche on Rhetoric and Language*, 79; Lanham, *A Handlist of Rhetorical Terms*, 110; Preminger, *Princeton Encyclopedia of Poetry and Poetics*, 602, 81–82; Quintilian, *Institutio Oratoria*, 9.3.66–67; Sloane, *Encyclopedia of Rhetoric*, 553–54.

59. "U.S. Military Women Cast Off Abayas."

60. The U.S. military reversed its policy three days after McSally told CBS News correspondent Lesley Stahl on 60 Minutes on January 20, 2002, that the policy flies in the face of the U.S. Constitution. Three days after 60 Minutes aired the show, Gen. Tommy Franks, head of the U.S. Central Command, sent an order via e-mail to commanders in the region that said wearing the abaya "is not mandatory but is strongly encouraged." CBS News (January 22, 2002) reported that according to Central Command spokesman Col. Rick Thomas, "McSally's lawsuit did not inspire the policy change." Colonel Thomas continued, "The policy was under review before the lawsuit was filed, so the change was not a direct result of that [lawsuit]." Moreover, "McSally's lawsuit, filed in federal court in Washington, also challenges policies requiring servicewomen to be accompanied by a man whenever they leave their base and to ride in the back seat of a car. Women are not allowed to drive in Saudi Arabia. Thomas said those policies remain in effect." See "U.S. Military Women Cast Off Abayas."

61. See Hariman, Popular Trials; and Mele, "Legal Subjects."

62. Hariman, Popular Trials, 20. See also Bender and Wellbery, The Ends of Rhetoric, 25–26.

63. The transcript is from CNN; the link is http://www.cnn.com/2007/POLITICS/07/23/debate.transcript/.

Chapter 3

Perkins and Wolfson, Frances Wright, Free Enquirer, 338.

1. Jones, "Monument to Suffragists Stuck in Basement for Now"; Kilian, "Out of Capitol Cellar."

2. Stanton, Anthony, and Gage, History of Woman Suffrage.

3. Long before Frances Wright, women—Margaret Brent of Maryland in 1647, Abigail Adams of Massachusetts in 1776—had spoken on women's rights. For a discussion of Frances Wright as the first woman to appear on the American platform, see Hillbruner, "Frances Wright," 19; Kendall and Fisher, "Frances Wright on Women's Rights," n. 1; C. Morris, Fanny Wright, 1; and Yoakam, "Women's Introduction to the American Platform," 157. Frances Wright was from Scotland and not American born. The first American-born public speaker was Marie W. Stewart, who lectured to a woman's club in Boston. See O'Conner, Pioneer Women Orators, 53–55.

4. Perkins and Wolfson, Frances Wright, Free Enquirer, 338.

5. See Heinrichs, Figures of Speech Served Fresh.

6. See figure 2.3.

7. Zaeske, "The 'Promiscuous Audience' Controversy and the Emergence of the Early Women's Rights Movement," 192–94. The description of the audiences as "promiscuous" has a varied "unsexed" history extending "at least as far back as Ben Johnson." By the 1820s, the notion of "promiscuous audience" was linked to the sexed body of "woman."

8. "Fanny Wright," Philadelphia Mirror, July 23, 1836.

9. Stiller, *Commune on the Frontier*, 169. Wright points out the prejudice against women speaking in public. See F. Wright, *Course of Popular Lectures*, 32.

10. Perkins and Wolfson, *Frances Wright, Free Enquirer*, 341–42.

11. "Mrs. Frances Wright Darusmont."

12. Ibid.

13. "Female Liberty of Speech."

14. O'Conner, *Pioneer Women Orators*, 185.

15. Winslow, *Woman as She Should Be*, 18.

16. Ibid., 19.

17. Gardner, *Woman Suffrage*, n.p.

18. Qtd. in Berg, *The Remembered Gate*, 72.

19. Waterman, *Frances Wright*, 169.

20. "Woman's Sphere."

21. O'Conner, *Pioneer Women Orators*, 40.

22. There were women's "colleges," such as the Young Ladies Academy of Philadelphia, which opened in 1787. Students learned French, music, and so forth. For discussion of women and education, see Noble, *A World Without Women*, 250–51.

23. Gilbert, *Memoir of Frances Wright*, 59.

24. Perkins and Wolfson, *Frances Wright, Free Enquirer*, 329. For the lectures and speeches, see F. Wright, *Course of Popular Lectures*.

25. In 1837, the General Association of the Congressional Ministers issued a "Pastoral Letter" to the churches under their care warning them against letting women speak in public. Cf. "Province of Woman"; L. Stone, "Workers for the Cause." The "Pastoral Letter" is included in Reid, *Three Centuries of American Rhetorical Discourse*, 315–23.

26. Gilbert, *Memoir of Frances Wright*, 32.

27. O'Conner, *Pioneer Women Orators*, 51.

28. Hays, *Lucy Stone*, 23; Kerr, *Lucy Stone Speaking Out for Equality*, 17–19.

29. Blackwell, *Lucy Stone*, 17.

30. The *Liberator* is one of the few newspapers in the United States that published the speeches of women. One of the earliest publications was in 1832. Maria W. Stewart, who is considered the first woman public speaker in the United States, gave a series of lectures that appeared in the newspaper from April 28, 1832, to May 7, 1832.

31. *Liberator*, January 7, 1832.

32. Blackwell, *Lucy Stone*, 16.

33. Hays, *Lucy Stone*, 47.

34. See, for example, L. Stone, "Letter to Hannah Stone."

35. Hays, *Lucy Stone*. Fairchild was not alone. The faculty and the male student body were opposed to the women's rights movement·

36. Ibid., 71.

37. Reid, *Three Centuries of American Rhetorical Discourse*, 316.

38. *Mrs. Willard Reviewed*; see also Hays, *Lucy Stone*, 38.

39. Gage, *Woman, Church and State*, 478–81.

40. L. Stone, "Letter to Francis and Hannah Stone" (1843); cf. Blackwell, *Lucy Stone*, 71; Kerr, *Lucy Stone Speaking Out for Equality*, 33–34; O'Conner, *Pioneer Women Orators*, 69n116.

41. Thome spoke of an inclusive rhetoric. See his "Address to the Females of Ohio," delivered at the Anti-slavery Anniversary, April 1836, Cincinnati, Ohio.

42. Hays, *Lucy Stone*, 65.

43. "Resolved: That Women Should Not Study Politics," Blackwell Family Collection, Library of Congress, Washington, DC.

44. O'Conner, *Pioneer Women Orators*, 69.

45. L. Stone, "Letter to Francis and Hannah Stone." Cf. Hays, *Lucy Stone*, 72.

46. F. Stone, "Letter to Lucy Stone."

47. Ibid.

48. L. Stone, "Letter to Hannah Stone."

49. See Hyman, "The Greek Slave by Hiram Powers."

50. Gibbs-Smith, *The Great Exhibition of 1851*, 129.

51. Genung, *Handbook of Rhetorical Analysis*, 285.

52. O'Connor, *The Athens of America*.

53. Ibid., 188.

54. Genung, *Handbook of Rhetorical Analysis*, 285.

55. Or "the woman with a rhetorical figure," as Michelle Ballif puts it in *Seduction, Sophistry, and the Woman with the Rhetorical Figure*.

56. "Greek Women"; Kasson, *Marble Queens and Captives*, 57.

57. *Liberator*, November 15, 1863.

58. O'Conner, *Pioneer Women Orators*, 31.

59. *Liberator*, July 9, 1952.

60. Hays, *Lucy Stone*, 91; Kerr, *Lucy Stone Speaking Out for Equality*, 51–52.

61. Blackwell, *Lucy Stone*, 89–90.

62. Berg, *The Remembered Gate*, 140.

63. *Beulah* was nearly a best-seller and won critical acclaim. See the introduction by Fox-Genovese, *Augusta Jane Evans: Beulah*.

64. "Woman on the Platform," *Liberator*, November 4, 1853. For a defense of the admission of women to the State University of Michigan, Ann Arbor, and for their admission to Cornell, see "Women in Cornell University," *Woman's Journal*, April 16, 1870.

65. *Woman's Journal*, January 29, 1870.

66. For example, see "Address of Frances E. Willard, president of the Woman's national council of the United States at its first triennial meeting, Albaugh's opera house," Washington, D.C., February 22–25, 1891.

67. Stevenson, "Miss Willard as University Woman & Educator."

68. By June 13, 1874, Willard resigned her office as dean as well as her professorship. Unstated issues with the all-male Board of Trustees and disagreements with the faculty were the reasons. Flexner and Fitzpatrick, *Century of Struggle*, 175.

69. Yoakam, "Pioneer Women Orators of America," 256.

70. L. Stone, "Workers for the Cause."

71. Stanton, Anthony, and Gage, *History of Woman Suffrage,* 1:53.

72. See *Liberator,* October 8, 1852; O'Conner, *Pioneer Women Orators,* 31.

73. *Liberator,* October 20, 1837.

74. The tropes are metaphor, metonymy, antonomasia, metalepsis, synecdoche, catachresis, and allegory. See Quintilian, *Institutio Oratoria,* v.3.9.1.5.

75. For a discussion of the accidental and how it is related to the feminine/female, see Yartz, "Aristotle on Monsters."

76. Stiller, *Commune on the Frontier.*

77. Perkins and Wolfson, *Frances Wright, Free Enquirer,* 334.

78. Stiller, *Commune on the Frontier,* 170.

79. Qtd. in ibid., 247.

80. Ibid., 7.

81. Quintilian, *Institutio Oratoria,* v.3.8.3.21.

82. Line of a poem (by William Cullen Bryant) chastising Frances Wright. Qtd. in Stiller, *Commune on the Frontier,* 175–76.

83. For further information and discussion on Aspasia with respect to speech and rhetoric, see Glenn, *Rhetoric Retold,* 36–44; Carlson, "Aspasia of Miletus."

84. A number of scholars have made this observation. See, for example, Glenn, *Rhetoric Retold,* 24–26.

85. "Female Depravity"; see also "Female Profanity."

86. "A Sermon of the Public Function of Woman by Theodore Parker."

87. Qtd. in Crawford, *Four Women in a Violent Time,* 108. Cf. Matthews, *The Rise of Public Woman,* 26–28.

88. "Female Depravity."

89. C. Morris, *Fanny Wright,* 293, 67. There may be more to this epithet than what I say here. As Rushing, *Erotic Mentoring,* explains, sacred prostitutes had extreme power over men insofar as their sexuality was the path to spiritual enlightenment. I wonder if this epithet might have implied women's power in its very naming—and that's why the fear is so intense. As Tom Frentz (personal e-mail, November 12, 2008) asks, "For if the female body (sex) is linked to the soul (spirit), then what, pray tell, can puny male reason have to do with real power?"

90. Stiller, *Commune on the Frontier,* 235.

91. See *Liberator,* October 24, 1835; "Society of Females."

92. See *Liberator,* October 24, 1835; "Society of Females." On the rape metaphor in the history of rhetoric, see Vitanza, *Negation, Subjectivity, and the History of Rhetoric.*

93. "Society of Females."

94. "Female Profanity."

95. Kennedy's translation does not elaborate on the view of women. Aristotle, *Politics,* 1269b.12–23; Aristotle, *Rhetoric,* 1361a.6–12; Cope, *The Rhetoric of Aristotle,* 79; Grimaldi, *Aristotle, Rhetoric I,* 1:110.

96. L. Stone, "The Condition of Women"; L. Stone, "Workers for the Cause."

97. Stiller, *Commune on the Frontier*, 170.

98. Qtd. in ibid., 165; Waterman, *Frances Wright*, 162; *New Harmony Gazette*, December 10, 1828.

99. Stiller, *Commune on the Frontier*, n.p.

100. Qtd. in Waterman, *Frances Wright*, 169. Cf. L. Stone, "Workers for the Cause."

101. Weimann, *The Fair Women*, 538.

102. "Women on the Grand Jury."

103. L. Stone, "Workers for the Cause."

104. Jamieson, *Beyond the Double Bind*, 16.

105. Qtd. in Jamieson, *Eloquence in an Electronic Age*, 69.

106. See, for example, Allen, *The Concept of Woman*; Deslauriers, "Sex and Essence in Aristotle's *Metaphysics* and Biology"; Horowitz, "Aristotle and Woman"; and Morsink, "Was Aristotle's Biology Sexist?"

107. *Bill Moyers Journal* (PBS, 2007).

108. That women, as Jamieson, *Eloquence in an Electronic Age*, 68–69, explains, are biologically unsuited for political activity is a residue of an Aristotelian view (Aristotle, *Politics*, 1335b).

109. See Crawford, *Four Women in a Violent Time*.

110. Boswell, *The Life of Samuel Johnson*, 280. In the 1920s, the Johnson cliché constituted a stock argument against women preaching. For discussion, see Inez Haynes Irwin, *Angels and Amazons* (Garden City, NY: Doubleday, 1933), 297–99.

111. Couric, "One-on-One with Sarah Palin"; Komblut, "So What Is Fair Game with Sarah Palin?"

112. "The Women Orators."

113. *Liberator*, January 28, 1853. See also "A Sermon of the Public Function of Woman by Theodore Parker"; and "Women Behind the Throne."

114. Kramer, "Liberty, Equality, Sorority."

115. Some of Erskine's fiction includes *The Private Life of Helen of Troy*, *Adam and Eve: Though He Knew Better*, and *Penelope's Man: The Homing Instinct*. *American Character and Other Essays* and the *Delight of Great Books* are two of his seven collections of essays. He also published *Collected Poems, 1907–1922*.

116. Erskine, *The Influence of Women and Its Cure*, 11.

117. Ibid., 125.

118. Ibid., 136–51.

119. For a wider historical perspective, see Ward, "Women and Latin Rhetoric."

Chapter 4

Qtd. in Stanton, Anthony, and Gage, *History of Woman Suffrage*, 4:213. Lucy Stone was very ill and died around the time of the fair on October 18, 1893.

Burnham, *Sweet Clover*, 24.

Qtd. in Stanton, Anthony, and Gage, *History of Woman Suffrage*, 4:213.

1. Howells, *Letters of an Altrurian Traveller*, 21.
2. Sullivan, *The Autobiography of an Idea*, 324.
3. The Field Museum Library in Chicago has three images of this building. Two refer to the building as the Woman's Building and one calls it the Women's Building. I use the term Woman's Building.
4. Snyder-Ott, "Woman's Place in the Home," 8.
5. See figure 2.4.
6. Hamilton, *The Time-Saver*. See also Burnham, *Sweet Clover*; and Holly, *Samantha at the World's Fair*.
7. Sullivan, *The Autobiography of an Idea*, 324.
8. Weimann, *The Fair Women*, 3.
9. Ibid.
10. Ibid.
11. Ibid., 2.
12. Benedict, *The Anthropology of World's Fairs*, 39–40.
13. See the comments of Mrs. Rachel Foster Avery (chairman of the Columbian Exposition Works, 1893) regarding Susan B. Anthony's work on the Columbian Exposition in Stanton, Anthony, and Gage, *History of Woman Suffrage*, 4:233.
14. Weimann, *The Fair Women*, 4.
15. Ibid.
16. Dorr, *Susan B. Anthony*, 304.
17. Rydell, *The Reason Why*, 67.
18. "Mrs. Palmer's Address," 42–43.
19. Ibid.
20. Eagle, *The Congress of Women Held in the Woman's Building*, 28.
21. R. Johnson, *A History of the World's Columbian Exposition*, 4:201.
22. Eagle, *The Congress of Women Held in the Woman's Building*, 28.
23. Ibid.
24. Ibid., 29.
25. Ibid., 27.
26. Ibid., 26.
27. Qtd. in Stanton, Anthony, and Gage, *History of Woman Suffrage*, 4:213.
28. Goode, *The Museums of the Future*.
29. Ibid.
30. Ibid.
31. See, for example, Holly, *Samantha at the World's Fair*.
32. Findling, *Chicago's Great World's Fairs*. The Congressional Committee report of May 20, 1892, announced that there would be "nothing like it in all of history." The exposition would "stand alone." See Burg, *Chicago's White City of 1893*, 75.
33. Hamilton, *The Time-Saver*.

34. Findling, *Chicago's Great World's Fairs*.

35. Ibid., 18.

36. Howells, *Letters of an Altrurian Traveller*, 22–23.

37. Ibid., 34.

38. Ibid., 28.

39. Morison and Commager, *The Growth of the American Republic*, 2:297.

40. Findling, *Chicago's Great World's Fairs*, 15.

41. Ibid., 19.

42. Ibid.

43. Qtd. in Morison and Commager, *The Growth of the American Republic*, 2:297.

44. H. Adams, *The Education of Henry Adams*, 285.

45. Ibid., 288.

46. Ibid., 286. I would add that maybe rhetoricians will one day want to forget the ancient Greek philosophers and remember the architects and designs of the buildings in ancient Athens. See Mifsud, Sutton, and Fox, "Configurations."

47. Janieson, "Women's Rights at the World's Fair, 1893," 7.

48. Weimann, *The Fair Women*, 174.

49. Janieson, "Women's Rights at the World's Fair, 1893," 7.

50. R. Johnson, *A History of the World's Columbian Exposition*, 4:77–80.

51. Findling, *Chicago's Great World's Fairs*, 16.

52. Benedict, *The Anthropology of World's Fairs*, 49.

53. Findling, *Chicago's Great World's Fairs*, 27.

54. See *Midway Types*, n.p.

55. R. Johnson, *History of the World's Columbian Exposition*, 4:433–34.

56. *Midway Types*, n.p.

57. Badger, *The Great American Fair*, 105. Henry Pratt objected to native dress because it kept a "valueless past" alive. His project involved converting the Indians to Christianity, a process that would make them suitable for citizenship.

58. See *Midway Types*, n.p.

59. Benedict, *The Anthropology of World's Fairs*. The picture of a mechanical Uncle Sam speaking is depicted on a souvenir trade card.

60. Badger, *The Great American Fair*, 107–9.

61. Burnham, *Sweet Clover*, 24.

62. Rydell, "All the World's a Fair," 122.

63. Goode, *The Museums of the Future*, 433.

64. See Bourdieu and Darbel, *L'amour de l'art*, 62. Cf. Duncan and Wallach, "The Universal Survey Museum," 457.

65. R. Johnson, *History of the World's Columbian Exposition*, 4:437.

66. Badger, *The Great American Fair*, 105.

67. Rydell, *The Reason Why*.

68. See Massa, "Black Women in the 'White City'"; Rudwick and Meier, "Black Man in the 'White City.'"

69. For a list of the appointments, see *Official Directory of the World's Columbian Exposition, May 1 to October 30, 1893*; and Rydell, *The Reason Why*, 70–75.

70. Rydell, *The Reason Why*, 71–72. At the time of the fair, blacks made up one-eighth of the entire population of the United States (74).

71. Ibid., 74.

72. Weimann, *The Fair Women*, 43.

73. *Report of Mrs. Potter Palmer* (Chicago, 1891), 7–8.

74. Burnham, *Sweet Clover*, 22.

75. *Chicago Tribune*, May 2, 1983.

76. Weimann, *The Fair Women*, 327.

77. Janieson, "Women's Rights at the World's Fair, 1893," 10; Weimann, *The Fair Women*, 327.

78. Weimann, *The Fair Women*, 331.

79. Ibid.

80. Blackwell, *Lucy Stone*, 282.

81. See, for example, *Chicago Tribune*, May 17, 1893.

82. Weimann, *The Fair Women*, 532–37.

83. *Report of Mrs. Potter Palmer*, 7–8.

84. Excerpts of speeches are included in Weimann, *The Fair Women*, 544.

85. Ibid., 530.

86. Stanton, Anthony, and Gage, *History of Woman Suffrage*, 4:214.

87. F. Miller, "Art in the Women's Section of the Chicago Exhibit," xiv.

88. Qtd. in Pohl, "Historical Reality or Utopian Ideal?" 303.

89. Ibid., 304; Andrew F. Wood, "Managing the Lady Managers: The Shaping of Heterotopian Spaces in the 1893 Chicago Exposition's Woman's Building," *Southern Speech Communication Journal* 69 (2004): 289–303.

90. F. Miller, "Art in the Women's Section of the Chicago Exhibit," xiv.

91. Weimann, *The Fair Women*, 317.

92. Ibid., 314.

93. Eagle, *The Congress of Women Held in the Woman's Building*, 817.

94. N. Wood, *Official Guide: New York World's Fair*; Weimann, *The Fair Women*, 598.

95. N. Wood, *Official Guide: New York World's Fair*, 68.

Chapter 5

Freud, "Femininity," 132.

Cleyre, "Sex Slavery," 350.

1. *An Ideal Occupation for Women.*
2. Danielian, *A.T.&T.*
3. Baxter, "The Telephone Girl"; "The Diary of a Telephone Girl."

4. Kern, *The Culture of Time and Space,* 69.

5. Marvin, *When Old Technologies Were New,* 219.

6. Green, "The Impact of Technology upon Women's Work in the Telephone Industry."

7. Danielian, *A.T.&T.*

8. Hill, "Women in Gainful Occupations, 1870 to 1920."

9. See Green, "The Impact of Technology upon Women's Work in the Telephone Industry"; Lipartito, "When Women Were Switches."

10. "Must Go to the Workhouse."

11. "The Night of Horror."

12. "Writ for Amelia Schauer."

13. "The Girl Schauer Is Set Free."

14. Marvin, *When Old Technologies Were New.*

15. Schmitt, "I Was Your 'Hello Girl.'"

16. "Dissoi Logoi," 50.

17. Homer, *The Odyssey,* trans. Walter Shewring, 9.

18. Apollodorus, *The Library,* 3.14.8.

19. McEwen, *Socrates' Ancestor.*

20. Barthes, *Mythologies;* Jakobson, "The Metaphoric and Metonymic Poles."

21. "A Sermon of the Public Function of Woman by Theodore Parker."

22. C. Morris, *Fanny Wright,* 63, 293.

23. Sanford, *Extracts from a Speech against Woman's Suffrage.*

24. A. Wright, *The Unexpurgated Case against Woman Suffrage,* 13.

25. Crosby, "The Advisability of Inserting the Word *Sex* before the Word *Race* in the Fifteenth Amendment to the Constitution of the United States," 13.

26. Ibid.

27. George, *Woman Suffrage,* n.p.

28. Baxter, "The Telephone Girl," 237.

29. Ibid.

30. Lipartito, "When Women Were Switches," 1089.

31. Harrison, "An Address before the Alabama Girls' Technical Institute," emphasis added.

32. Marvin, *When Old Technologies Were New,* 219; L. Stone, "The Condition of Women"; L. Stone, "Workers for the Cause."

33. A. Wright, *The Unexpurgated Case against Woman Suffrage,* 13.

34. *An Ideal Occupation for Women,* 9.

35. For discussion, see "The Doctrine of St. Paul Concerning Women"; "Paul Concerning Women"; and "St. Paul Once More."

36. Bronson, *The Wage-Earning Woman and the State,* n.p.

37. Pyle, *Should Women Vote?* n.p. *Woman's Sphere and Influence,* n.p.

38. Marvin, *When Old Technologies Were New,* 219.

39. Michael Huspack, e-mail message to author, February 3, 2005.

CHAPTER 6

Atwood, *Negotiating with the Dead*, 180.

1. Webster, "Writing History/Painting History," 36.
2. Ibid.
3. See Knox, *Backing into the Future*.
4. Aristotle, *Rhetoric*, 1414a.5. It is worth mentioning that by linking the deliberative genre to scene painting (a plastic art), Aristotle expands the genre to include not only time but also space.
5. John Gadsby Chapman's *Baptism of Pocahontas* can be seen at http://www.aoc.gov/cc/art/rotunda/baptism_pocahontas.htm (accessed November 19, 2000), the Web site of the Architect of the Capitol.
6. Chapman, *The Picture of the Baptism of Pocahontas*, 7.
7. Ibid., 4.
8. Ibid., 5.
9. Ibid., 3, 4.
10. Webster, "Writing History/Painting History," 38.
11. Office of the Curator, *Works of Art in the Capitol Complex*, Office of the Architect, Capitol Complex, February 2001, http://www.aoc.gov/cc/cc_art.htm (accessed March 16, 1999).
12. For a detailed description, go to http://www.aoc.gov/cc/art/rotunda/apotheosis/apotheosis/index.cfm (accessed July 2000), the Web site of the Architect of the Capitol.
13. The Capitol Historical Society uses the images of Venus, Minerva, and Liberty as proof that women are included in the history of the United States. See Scull, "Women, Art and the Capitol."
14. Foreman, *Indian Women Chiefs*.
15. Chapman, *The Picture of the Baptism of Pocahontas*, 5.
16. Ibid., 6, 9.
17. Ibid., epigraph.
18. Ibid., 9.
19. In his official description of the painting, Chapman recognized the injustices against the Native Americans. Perhaps Opechankanough tacitly embodies Chapman's view as Sojourner Truth. Ibid., 3. See also "The Cherokees."
20. Bakhtin, *The Dialogic Imagination*, 131. Earlier in the text, he says a "meeting" emphasizes "the public and the rhetorical side of the individual" (110).
21. As for full-length biographies, Pat Alderman has written a book on Nancy Ward within the context of Cherokee life, culture, and government, as well as a script for a documentary film prepared by East Tennessee State University Studios. In contrast, a romance, founded on and interwoven with history, is King, *The Wild Rose of Cherokee or Nancy Ward*. These sources include Burns, *Military and Genealogical Records of the Famous Indian Woman: Nancy Ward*; Kasee, "Ward, Nancy"; Lillard, "The Story of Nancy Ward";

and McClary, "Nancy Ward." Tucker, "Nancy Ward," places Ward's role in the Cherokee nation in cultural perspective. Here, the reader catches a glimpse of women's rights in a non-Indo-European culture as demonstrated by the role of "Beloved Woman" within the context of the Cherokee nation. Ward is seen as a respected chieftain and thus as their negotiator for Cherokee land with the encroaching American people. Shoemaker, *Negotiators of Change*, shows that Nancy Ward's influence spanned cultures, though she has been seemingly lost in the annals of history. It is no surprise that other Native American communities have struggled with women's roles, both within their own culture and as part of the male-dominated Western culture of American society. Devens, *Countering Colonization*, provides an historical accounting of the changing attitudes within the Native American community. Here it becomes evident that the imposition of the male-dominated Christian belief system had a profound impact on every American tribe that it touched. Kidwell, "Indian Women as Cultural Mediators," demonstrates how central Native American women have been in the struggle to maintain their own culture while becoming a part of the larger Western culture forced upon them. Women of other Native American peoples felt the effects of Nancy Ward's place of power in a male-dominated world. Farley, *Women of the Native Struggle*, and J. Katz, *I Am the Fire of the Time*, bear witness to the positive effects that such figures as Nancy Ward have had on the progress made in defining women's roles in American Indian societies. Steer, *Native American Women*, presents an unparalleled examination of the revolutionary growth of these roles. The book traces women's presence from the tribal creation myths through modern American society and the struggle to keep the native cultures alive.

22. "That she was the pioneer in the women's rights movement in America rests on indisputable ground": Lockwood, "Cradle of Women's Rights," 17. See also Yoakam, "Women's Introduction to the American Platform," 157; C. Morris, *Fanny Wright*, 1; C. Morris, "Frances Wright"; Hillbruner, "Frances Wright," 196; and Kendall and Fisher, "Frances Wright on Women's Rights," n. 1.; A. Brown, "Dream of Emancipation;" "The Eccentirc Fanny Wright."

23. Stanton, Anthony, and Gage, *History of Woman Suffrage*.

24. Nanye'hi's speeches are preserved in various manuscripts (including the Draper Papers, Andrew Jackson Papers, *Journal of the Mission of Brainerd*, American State Papers) and have been collated and published recently in Kilcup, *Native American Women's Writing*. Kilcup's book is enormously valuable in its reproduction of speeches (which are at times difficult to decipher in their manuscript form).

25. With respect to "end" and "beginning," I am employing "a little tactic of the habitat" according to Foucault, *Power/Knowledge*, 149. I am, therefore, positioning these women politically and geographically as boundary figures that precede the end and the beginning. Ward is not the *last* Cherokee leader who holds the title of Beloved Woman. But the title had no meaning after the removal of the Cherokee on the Trail of Tears. Recently, Cherokee woman Wilma Mankiller held the title of chief. Wright's speaking is distinguished because she spoke before a mixed or promiscuous audience on the Fourth of July, an occasion calling for a genre of rhetoric called epideictic oratory that traditionally was the province of men. Moreover, before the Civil War, the Fourth of July was

observed by public speeches delivered by prominent members of a community. Wright was a respected member of the utopia community of New Harmony, Indiana; but in the community writ large, a woman would not have been selected, much less considered, to deliver an address on the most important national ceremony. That she did deliver such an important address marks her as a "first" of sorts.

26. See, for example, "Brainerd Journal."

27. F. Wright, "Address, Delivered in the New-Harmony Hall."

28. See, for example, "Female Liberty of Speech."

29. Foreman, *Indian Women Chiefs.*

30. McClary, "Nancy Ward," 353. See also Shenandoah and George, *Skywoman.*

31. J. Brown, *Old Frontiers,* 20.

32. Stiller, *Commune on the Frontier,* 170.

33. Since the 1990s, Aspasia has been "reclaimed" by the rhetorical history as an orator and even early rhetorical theorist. See, for example, Carlson, "Aspasia of Miletus"; and Glenn, *Rhetoric Retold,* 36–44.

34. See, for example, "Female Depravity" and "The Female Pests."

35. Plutarch, *The Lives of the Noble Grecians and Romans,* 20.

36. C. Morris, *Fanny Wright,* 67, 293.

37. Lucy Stone described the difficulties women faced speaking in public: "Think what it would be like to live perpetually in the midst of scorn and reproach; to [hear], 'This Jezebel has come among us.'" L. Stone, "Workers for the Cause."

38. J. Brown, "Nancy Ward, Little Owl's Cousin," 59. For a discussion on the Cherokee and slavery, see Perdue, "Women, Men and American Indian Policy," 102.

39. Ramsey, *The Annals of Tennessee to the End of the Eighteenth Century,* 87.

40. Robbins, "Experiment at Nashoba Plantation," 14.

41. Alderman, *Nancy Ward, Cherokee chieftainess, Dragging Canoe, Cherokee-Chickamauga war chief,* 44, emphasis added.

42. Slotkin, *Regeneration through Violence.*

43. Stiller, *Commune on the Frontier,* 57.

44. Ibid.

45. See, for example, Gage, "Indian Citizenship." In 1876, a New York judge ruled in favor of an Oneida Indian's right to vote in a U.S. presidential election. Gage used this event to argue that "women's political degradation" had reached its lowest depth. The government was willing to observe the authority of a "savage" but not a woman's authority, effectively putting women below civilization, 2.

46. Tropically, the two women meet or come together in the manner of an "X." Each woman's practices, beliefs, and attitudes comprise a series of points to figure a line and as the lines cross ("X"), they configure a meeting. The men motivate the action—the deliberations on the road. Deliberately, I cast each woman embodying her line, so to speak, and moving on a road in a differentiated manner toward the other where they—the two lines embodied as two women—eventually cross. They relate directly to each other by in-

coming and outgoing movement, namely, the nearness and farness of their practices and beliefs. See Bakhtin, *The Dialogic Imagination*, 84. See also "relations of propinquity" in Foucault, "Of Other Spaces."

47. This occurred about five years before the Indian Removal Act of 1830. C. Morris, "Frances Wright"; Robbins, "Experiment at Nashoba Plantation"; Schlesinger, "Jackson's Radical Coalition."

48. *Basic Writings of Thomas Jefferson*, 803.

49. C. Morris, "Frances Wright," 17.

50. "Tells of Frances Wright."

51. Perdue, "Women, Men and American Indian Policy," 108.

52. *The Writings of Thomas Jefferson*, 3:162–63.

53. Clemmer, *Nancy Ward and the Hilderbrand Family of Polk County, Tennessee.*

54. King, *The Wild Rose of Cherokee or Nancy Ward.*

55. Another account that popularized Nanye'hi as Pocahontas was an account given by whites of their canoes. Nanye'hi covered their rifles with corn. She cooperated with the whites to trick her own people. Ramsey, *The Annals of Tennessee to the End of the Eighteenth Century*, 273.

56. Ibid., 157–59.

57. "[Speech to the Cherokee National Council] Cherokee Women and Ward, May 2, 1817."

58. Ibid. As the Cherokee situation grew bleaker, they began to centralize their government, which permitted them to negotiate as a single unit with the whites. However, in doing so, the Cherokee began to adopt the white form of deliberation, and as a result, Cherokee women were encouraged to enter a domestic sphere and be silent.

59. "Cyrus Kingsbury Journal."

60. Wagner, *The Untold Story of the Iroquois Influence on Early Feminists*, argues that the feminist movement did not erupt in a vacuum and that it is derived from Native American role models.

61. F. Wright, *Course of Popular Lectures*, 32; Kilcup, *Native American Women's Writing*, 27.

62. Matilda Joslyn Gage obtained the name Karonienhawi (She Who Holds the Sky). See Wagner, *Matilda Joslyn Gage*, 34; and Wagner, *The Untold Story of the Iroquois Influence on Early Feminists.*

63. See chapter 3, note 25.

64. F. Wright, "An Address to Young Mechanics," 11–12.

65. Kilcup, *Native American Women's Writing*, 411.

66. "Female Depravity."

67. See, for example, Goldenberg, *Madam President*; Gutgold, *Paving the Way for Madam President*; Han and Heldman, *Rethinking Madam President*; and Winik, "Is It Time for a Woman President?"

68. Perelman and Olbrechts-Tyteca, *The New Rhetoric*, 15.

69. Foreman, *Indian Women Chiefs*, 73. Also, the Wahenauhi manuscript tells the

story of a Cherokee woman named Cuhtahlatah who took up her husband's tomahawk. Kidwell, "Indian Women as Cultural Mediators," 102; Shanahan, "Women of the Revolution Were Active in Business and on the Field of Battle"; Tucker, "Nancy Ward," 192.

70. Gridley, *American Indian Women*, 42.

71. Kidwell, "Indian Women as Cultural Mediators," 102.

72. Alderman, *Nancy Ward, Cherokee chieftainess, Dragging Canoe, Cherokee-Chickamauga war chief*, 6.

73. See Cass, "Sacred Fires of the Indians."

74. J. Brown, "Nancy Ward, Little Owl's Cousin," 57; Foreman, *Indian Women Chiefs*.

75. In 1775 Richard Henderson and his Transylvania Company "purchased," so they said, twenty million acres of hunting land from the Cherokee near the banks of the Watauga River (Elizabethtown, Tennessee). The transaction was not without opposition among the Cherokee. One Cherokee band captured Mrs. William Bean and took her to Toqua, a town near Chota, where Nanye'hi lived. Mrs. Bean was condemned to be burned alive. After she was tied to a pole and branches were laid around her feet and lit, Nanye'hi appeared, kicked the burning branches away, and spoke: "It revolts my soul that Cherokee warriors would stoop so low as to torture a squaw. No woman shall be tortured or burned at the stake while I am *Ghighau*." Alderman, *Nancy Ward, Cherokee chieftainess, Dragging Canoe, Cherokee-Chickamauga war chief*, 48. After the highly contested Transylvania deed, Dragging Canoe began leading attacks on white settlers.

76. Nuttall, *A Journal of Travels into the Arkansas Territory, 1819*, 17–18.

77. Foreman, *Indian Women Chiefs*, 14.

78. Martin, "Hillsborough July 12."

79. "April 2, 1871, Talk of Cherokee Chiefs to Col. Martin."

80. Kilcup, *Native American Women's Writing*, 27.

81. Christian, "Response to Nancy Ward [Mothers], Long Island Treaty, 1781."

82. J. Brown, "Nancy Ward, Little Owl's Cousin," 59.

83. J. Brown, *Old Frontiers*; Tucker, "Nancy Ward."

84. Roosevelt, *The Winning of the West*, 196.

85. Ibid.

86. Kilcup, *Native American Women's Writing*, 28.

87. "In the Council Chamber Minutes, Feb. 9, 1757."

88. "In the Council Chamber Minutes, Feb. 12, 1757."

89. Tassel, "Treaty of Long Island of Holston."

90. Ibid.

91. Ibid.

92. Griffin, "The Edifice Metaphor in Rhetorical Theory."

93. See Boyd, "Farewell, Mrs. Parks"; "Dignitaries Honor Rosa Parks"; Dvorak and Harris, "U.S. Bestows Honor on Rosa Parks"; "The Fight for Rosa Continues"; Harris and Holmes, "Services for King to Be Held in Ga."; Haskell and Parnell, "Guardsmen Help Honor Civil Rights Pioneer Rosa Parks"; Ivey, "Rep. Rush Leads Effort for Stamp"; Merida and Harris, "50 Years Later in the Shadow of Jim Crow"; Overton, "Viewing Rosa

Parks at the Capitol Rotunda"; "Pelosi: 'We Mourn the Death of Rosa Parks'"; Pressley and Dvorak, "Thousands Honor Courage of Rosa Parks"; "Reflecting on a Hero"; "Senate Passes Frist, Reid Resolution Allowing Rosa Parks to Lie in Honor in the Rotunda of the Capitol"; Thomas, "Senate OKs Parks Honor"; "The Year in Review"; Younge, "Rosa Parks Given Unprecedented Honour."

94. "Rosa Parks to Lie in Honor at Capitol Rotunda."

95. In fact, until May 1997, when the Portrait Monument to Lucretia Mott, Elizabeth Cady Stanton, and Susan B. Anthony was moved from the crypt (where by House resolution the stone statue had been put on "public display" since 1921), there had not been a statue of a woman in the Rotunda. See, for example, Schiavone, "Even in Stone, Suffragettes Cause a Stir on Capitol Hill." The intensity of Parks's lying in state is also exhibited by the desire to commemorate her in yet another manner reserved only for U.S. presidents—issuing postage stamps within a year of death. Normally, someone must be dead for ten years. See Ivey, "Rep. Rush Leads Effort for Stamp."

96. Jacob Chestnut was the first black to be so honored, according to Senate historian Richard Baker. Chestnut was one of two U.S. Capitol police officers killed in the 1998 Capitol shooting. Andrew J. Broach, "Rosa Parks to Be Honored in Formal Ceremony in U.S. Capitol Building," Voice of America, http://www.voanews.com/english/archive/2005-10/2005-10-30-voal.cfm?CFID=1359430 (accessed October 30, 2005).

97. Or, as Catt, "Gregory Bateson's 'New Science' in the Context of Communicology," 155, puts it, "communicative embodiment materializes the message-code relation giving it spatial dimension."

98. Verene, *Symbol, Myth, and Culture,* 288.

99. Cassirer says we are forming animals. See ibid., 39. This accords with Catt, "Gregory Bateson's 'New Science' in the Context of Communicology," 166–70.

100. For a similar view but a different case, see Sutton and Mpofu, "Figuring Reconciliation."

101. Ovid, *Metamorphosis,* 15.

102. Bachelard, *The Poetics of Space,* 12.

References

Adams, Henry. *The Education of Henry Adams.* Ed. Ira B. Nadel. Oxford: Oxford University Press, 1999.

Adams, John Quincy. *Lectures on Rhetoric and Oratory (1810): A Facsimile Reproduction with an Introduction by Charlotte Downey.* Delmar, NY: Scholars' Facsimiles and Reprints, 1997.

Adams, Mark. "Not in Kansas: Senator Hillary Clinton's Disclosure That the *Wizard of Oz* Was One of Her Favorite Movies Set the Week's Tone in the Emerald City." *New York Magazine,* 5 February 2007.

Aeschylus. *The Oresteia: Agamemnon, Choephoroe, Eumenides.* Trans. George Thomson. New York: Alfred A. Knopf, 2004.

Alderman, Pat. *Nancy Ward, Cherokee chieftainess, Dragging Canoe, Cherokee-Chickamauga war chief.* 2nd ed. Johnson City, TN: Overmountain Press, 1978.

Allen, Danielle. *Talking to Strangers.* Chicago: University of Chicago Press, 2004.

Allen, Prudence. *The Concept of Woman: The Aristotelian Revolution, 750 B.C.–A.D. 1250.* Grand Rapids, MI: William B. Eerdmans, 1985.

Anaximenes. *Rhetorica Ad Alexandrum.* Trans. H. Rackman. 2 vols. Vol. 2. Loeb Classical Library. Cambridge, MA: Harvard University Press, 1957.

Anderson, Bonnie S. *Joyous Greetings: The First International Women's Movement, 1830–1860.* Oxford: Oxford University Press, 2000. 89 p. Micro ATLA F2003 microfiche. Penn St. U.

Anderson, Judith. "Sexual Politics: Chauvinism and Backlash?" *Today's Speech* 21 (1971): 11–16.

Anderson, R. Dean, Jr. *Glossary of Greek Rhetorical Terms Connected to Methods of Argumentation, Figures and Tropes from Anaximenes to Quintilian.* Peeters: Leuven, 2000.

Anderson, Samuel Gilmore. *Woman's Sphere and Influence.* [Toledo, OH]: Franklin Printing and Engraving Company, 1898.

"Another Woman Orator." *Woman's Journal*, 12 March 1870.

Apollodorus. *The Library*. Trans. Sir James George Frazer. 2 vols. Vol. 2. Loeb Classical Library. Cambridge, MA: Harvard University Press, 1921.

"April 2, 1871, Talk of Cherokee Chiefs to Col. Martin." Draper Manuscripts Tennessee Papers, ser. xx, vols. 1–4, reel 177, Carlisle, PA, 1781.

"The Aristotelian Renaissance in Contemporary Rhetorical Theory." *Spectra* 32, no. 5 (1996): 16.

Aristotle. *Eudemian Ethics*. Trans. H. Rackman. Loeb Classical Library. Cambridge, MA: Harvard University Press, 1961.

———. *Generation of Animals*. Trans. A. L. Peck. Loeb Classical Library. Cambridge, MA: Harvard University Press, 1942.

———. *Historia Animalium*. Trans. A. L. Peck. 3 vols. Loeb Classical Library. Cambridge, MA: Harvard University Press, 1965–91.

———. *Metaphysics*. Trans. Hugh Tredennick. 2 vols. Loeb Classical Library. Cambridge, MA: Harvard University Press, 1933–96.

———. *Politics*. Trans. H. Rackman. Loeb Classical Library. Cambridge, MA: Harvard University Press, 1944.

———. *Rhetoric*. Trans. John Henry Freese. Loeb Classical Library. Cambridge, MA: Harvard University Press, 1926–94.

Atwill, Janet M. *Rhetoric Reclaimed*. Ithaca: Cornell University Press, 1998.

Atwill, Janet M., and Janice M. Lauer, eds. *Perspectives on Rhetorical Invention*. Knoxville: University of Tennessee Press, 2002.

Atwood, Margaret. *Negotiating with the Dead*. New York: Cambridge University Press, 2002.

Bachelard, Gaston. *The Poetics of Space*. Trans. Maria Jolas. Boston: Beacon Press, 1994.

Badger, Reid. *The Great American Fair: The World's Columbian Exposition and American Culture*. Chicago: N. Hall, 1979.

Bakhtin, M. M. *Art and Answerability*. Trans. V. Liapunov. Austin: University of Texas Press, 1990.

———. *The Dialogic Imagination*. Trans. Caryl Emerson and Michael Holquist. University of Texas Press Slavic Series, No. 1. Ed. Michael Holquist. Austin: University of Texas Press, 1981.

Ballif, Michelle. *Seduction, Sophistry, and the Woman with the Rhetorical Figure*. Carbondale: Southern Illinois University Press, 2001.

Ballif, Michelle, and Michael G. Moran. Introduction to *Critical Rhetorics and Rhetoricians*, ed. Michelle Ballif and Michael G. Moran, 1–13. Westport, CT: Praeger, 2005.

Barthes, Roland. *Mythologies*. Trans. Annette Lauers. New York: Noonday Press, 1972.

———. *The Semiotic Challenge*. Trans. Richard Howard. New York: Hill and Wang, 1988.

Basic Writings of Thomas Jefferson. Ed. Philip S. Foner. New York: Willey Book Company, 1944.

Baxter, Sylvester. "The Telephone Girl." *The Outlook*, 26 May 1906, 231–39.

Beauvoir, Simone de. *The Second Sex*. Trans. H. M. Parshley. New York: Bantam Books, 1965.

Becker, Stephen W. "The Rhetoric of Architecture: Civic Republican Space in Early Boston." Ph.D. diss., Northwestern University, 2000.

Bender, John, and David W. Wellbery, eds. *The Ends of Rhetoric: History, Theory, and Practice*. Stanford: Stanford University Press, 1990.

Benedict, Burton, ed. *The Anthropology of World's Fairs*. Berkeley: Lowie Museum of Anthropology, University of California, 1983.

Benveniste, Emile. *Indo-European Language and Society*. Trans. Elizabeth Palmer. Coral Gables, FL: University of Miami Press, 1973.

Berg, Barbara J. *The Remembered Gate: Origins of American Feminism*. New York: Oxford University Press, 1978.

Bialostosky, Don. "Architectonics, Rhetoric, and Poetics in the Bakhtin School's Early Phenomenological and Sociological Texts." *Rhetoric Society Quarterly* 36 (2006): 355-76.

———. "Aristotle's *Rhetoric* and Bakhtin's Discourse Theory." In *A Companion to Rhetoric and Rhetorical Criticism*, ed. Walter Jost and Wendy Olmstead, 393-408. London: Blackwell, 2004.

Biesecker, Barbara A. "Coming to Terms with Recent Attempts to Write Women into the History of Rhetoric." *Philosophy and Rhetoric* 25 (1992): 140-61.

———. "Michel Foucault and the Question of Rhetoric." *Philosophy and Rhetoric* 25 (1992): 351-64.

———. "Negotiating with Our Tradition: Reflecting Again (without Apologies) on the Feminization of Rhetoric." *Philosophy and Rhetoric* 26 (1993): 234-42.

Bingham, Caleb. *The Columbian Orator: A Variety of Original and Selected Pieces Calculated to Improve Youth and Others in the Ornamental and Useful Art of Eloquence*. Stereotype ed. Philadelphia: J. B. Lippincott, 1860.

Bizzell, Patricia. "Feminist Methods of Research in the History of Rhetoric: What Difference Do They Make?" *Rhetoric Society Quarterly* 30 (2000): 5-17.

Blackwell, Alice Stone. *Lucy Stone: Pioneer of Women's Rights*. Boston: Little, Brown, and Company, 1930.

Blair, Carole, Julie R. Brown, and Leslie H. Baxter. "Disciplining the Feminine." *Quarterly Journal of Speech* 80 (1994): 383-409.

Booth, Wayne C. *The Rhetoric of Rhetoric: The Quest for Effective Communication*. Oxford: Blackwell, 2004.

Boswell, James. *The Life of Samuel Johnson*. Ed. Roger Ingpen. Boston: Charles E. Laurant Company, 1925.

Bourdieu, Pierre. *Masculine Domination*. Trans. Richard Nice. Stanford: Stanford University Press, 2001.

Bourdieu, Pierre, and Alain Darbel. *L'amour de l'art: Les musée d'arte européens et leur public*. Paris, 1969.

Boyd, Herb. "Farewell, Mrs. Parks." *New York Amsterdam News*, 3 November 2005, 1.

"Brainerd Journal. To S. Worcester, June 30, 1818." In Brainerd Mission (Tenn.), *Cherokee Mission: Joint Communications and Papers Relating to the Mission Generally: Received before Sep. 1, 1824.* Papers of the American Board of Commissioners for Foreign Missions, John D. Rockefeller Jr. Library, Brown University.

Brake, Robert J. "Women Orators: More Research?" *Today's Speech* 15 (1967): 20–22.

Brake, Robert, and R. D. Neuleib. "Famous Women Orators: An Opinion Survey." *Today's Speech* 21 (1973): 33–37.

Brandell, Susan. "Out of the Broom Closet and into the Rotunda." http://feminist.com/resources/artspeech/wword/ww3.htm (accessed August 2001).

Bronson, Minnie. *The Wage-Earning Woman and the State.* Boston: Massachusetts Association Opposed to the Further Extension of Suffrage to Women, 1913.

Brown, Anna B. A. "Dream of Emancipation." *New England Magazine* 30 (June 1904): 494–99.

Brown, Carla. *Dynamic Communication Skills for Women.* Shawnee Mission, KS: National Press Publications, 1989.

Brown, J. P. "Nancy Ward, Little Owl's Cousin." *Flower and Feather* 13 (1957): 57–59.

Brown, John P. *Old Frontiers.* Kingsport, TN: Southern Publishers, 1938.

Brownmiller, Susan. *Femininity.* New York: Fawcett Columbine, 1984.

Burg, David F. *Chicago's White City of 1893.* Lexington: University of Kentucky Press, 1976.

Burke, Kenneth. *The Philosophy of Literary Form.* 3rd ed. Berkeley: University of California Press, 1973.

Burnham, Clara Louise. *Sweet Clover: A Romance of the White City.* Chicago: Laird & Lee, 1893.

Burns, Annie Walker. *Military and Genealogical Records of the Famous Indian Woman: Nancy Ward.* Washington, DC, n.d.

Butler, Jessie Haven. *Time to Speak Up: A Speaker's Handbook for Women.* New York: Harper and Brothers, 1946.

Campbell, Karlyn Kohrs. "Biesecker Cannot Speak for Her Either." *Philosophy and Rhetoric* 26, no. 2 (1993): 153–59.

———. "The Communication Classroom: A Chilly Climate for Women?" *ACA Bulletin* 51 (1988): 68–72.

———. "Feminist Rhetoric." In *Encyclopedia of Rhetoric,* ed. Thomas O. Sloane, 301–9. Oxford: Oxford University Press, 2001.

———. "Hearing Women's Voices." *Communication Education* 40 (1991): 33–48.

———. *Man Cannot Speak for Her.* 2 vols. New York: Greenwood Press, 1989.

———. "The Rhetoric of Women's Liberation: An Oxymoron." *Quarterly Journal of Speech* 59 (1973): 74–86.

———. "The Sound of Women's Voices." *Quarterly Journal of Speech* 75 (1989): 212–20.

———. "Style and Content in the Rhetoric of Early African-American Feminists." *Quarterly Journal of Speech* 72 (1986): 434–45.

Carlson, A. Cheree. "Aspasia of Miletus: How One Woman Disappeared from the History of Rhetoric." *Women's Studies in Communication* 17 (1994): 26–44.

Cass, Lewis. "Sacred Fires of the Indians." *Philadelphia Album and Ladies' Literary Portfolio*, 3 December 1831, 49.

Cassirer, Ernest. *The Myth of the State*. New Haven: Yale University Press, 1946.

———. "Mythic, Aesthetic, and Theoretical Space." *Man and World* 2, no. 1 (1969): 3–17.

Catt, Isaac E. "Gregory Bateson's 'New Science' in the Context of Communicology." *American Journal of Semiotics* 19, nos. 1–4 (2003): 153–72.

Chamberlain, Charles. "From 'Haunts' to 'Character': The Meaning of Ethos and Its Relation to Ethics." *Helios* 11 (1984): 97–108.

Chantraine, Pierre. *Dictionnaire étymologique de la langue grecque*. 5 vols. Paris: Éditions Klincksieck, 1968.

Chapman, John Gadsby. *The Picture of the Baptism of Pocahontas: Painted by the Order of Congress for the Rotunda of the Capitol*. Washington, DC: P. Force, 1840.

"The Cherokees." *Liberator*, 28 February 1835.

Christian, Colonel William. "Response to Nancy Ward [Mothers], Long Island Treaty, 1781." Draper Manuscripts Tennessee Papers, ser. xx, vols. 1–4, reel 116, Army War College, U.S. Army Military History Institute, Carlisle, PA, 1781.

Cicero. *De Inventione*. Trans. H. M. Hubbell. 28 vols. Vol. 2. Loeb Classical Library. Cambridge, MA: Harvard University Press, 1968.

Cixous, Hélène, and Catherine Clément. *The Newly Born Woman*. Trans. Betsy Wing. Minneapolis: University of Minnesota Press, 1986.

Clark, Suzanne. "Rhetoric, Social Construction, and Gender: Is It Bad to Be Sentimental?" In *Writing Theory and Critical Theory*, ed. John Clifford and John Schilb, 96–108. New York: Modern Language Association of America, 1994.

Clemmer, Sudie. *Nancy Ward and the Hilderbrand Family of Polk County, Tennessee: Reprinted Newspaper Clippings from the J. D. Clemmer Scrapbooks*. Benton, TN: Polk County News, 1962.

Cleyre, Voltairine de. "Sex Slavery." In *Selected Works of Voltairine de Cleyre*, ed. Alexander Berkman, 342–58. New York: Mother Earth Publishing, 1914.

Clinton, Hillary. "Hillary's Remarks in Washington, DC, June 7, 2008." Hillary for President, 2008, http://www.hillaryclinton.com/news/speech/view/?id=7903 (accessed 7 June 2008).

Cmiel, Kenneth. *Democratic Eloquence: The Fight over Popular Speech in Nineteenth-Century America*. New York: William Morrow, 1990.

Code, Lorraine. *Rhetorical Spaces: Essays on Gendered Locations*. New York: Routledge, 1995.

Condit, Michelle Celeste. "Opposites in an Oppositional Practice: Rhetorical Criticism and Feminism." In *Transforming Vision: Feminist Critiques in Communication Studies*, ed. Nancy Wyatt. Cresskill, NJ: Hampton Press, 1993.

Conners, Robert J. "The Exclusion of Women from Classical Rhetoric." In *A Rhetoric of Doing: Essays on Written Discourse in Honor of James L. Kinneavy*, ed. Stephen P. Witte, Neil Nakadate, and Roger D. Cherry, 65–78. Carbondale: Southern Illinois University Press, 1992.

Cope, Edward Meredith. *The Rhetoric of Aristotle.* Ed. John Edwin Sandys. 3 vols. Cambridge: W. C. Brown Reprint Library Press, 1877. Reprint, 1966.

Couric, Katie. "One-on-One with Sarah Palin." http://www.youtube.com/watch?v=rs05mjFQF0Q (accessed 24 September 2008).

Cox, J. Robert. "Memory, Critical Theory, and the Argument from History." *Argumentation and Advocacy* 27 (1990): 1–13.

Crawford, Deborah. *Four Women in a Violent Time.* New York: Crown, 1970.

Croix, G.E.M. de Ste. *The Class Struggle in the Ancient Greek World from the Archaic Age to the Arab Conquests.* London: Duckworth, 1981.

Crosby, John F. "The Advisability of Inserting the Word *Sex* before the Word *Race* in the Fifteenth Amendment to the Constitution of the United States." Washington, DC: Georgetown University, 1910. Microfilm D285, reel 952. News and Microforms Library, Pennsylvania State University.

Cutter, Martha J. *Unruly Tongue: Identity and Voice in American Women's Writing, 1850–1930.* Jackson: University Press of Mississippi, 1999.

"Cyrus Kingsbury Journal: 13 February 1817." Papers of the American Board of Commissioners for Foreign Missions, Houghton Library, Harvard University.

Danielian, N. R. *A.T.&T: The Story of Industrial Conquest.* New York: Vanguard Press, 1939.

Demosthenes. "First Philippic." In *Demosthenes.* Cambridge, MA: Harvard University Press, 1929.

Deslauriers, Marguerite. "Sex and Essence in Aristotle's *Metaphysics* and Biology." In *Feminist Interpretations of Aristotle,* ed. Cynthia A. Freeland, 138–67. University Park: Pennsylvania State University Press, 1998.

Detienne, Marcel. *The Masters of Truth in Archaic Greece.* Trans. Janet Lloyd. New York: Zone Books, 1996.

Devens, Carol. *Countering Colonization: Native American Women and Great Lakes Missions, 1630–1900.* Berkeley: University of California Press, 1992.

"The Diary of a Telephone Girl: The Work of a Human Spider in a Web of Talking Wires." *Saturday Evening Post,* 19 October 1907, 6–8ff.

"Dignitaries Honor Rosa Parks; First Woman to Lie in Capitol Rotunda." *Miami Times,* 2 November 2005, A1.

"Dissoi Logoi." In *The Rhetorical Tradition,* ed. Patricia Bizzell and Bruce Herzberg, 48–55. Bedford: St. Martin's Press, 2001.

Dobbs, Darrell. "Family Matters: Aristotle's Appreciation of Women and the Plural Structure of Society." *American Political Science Review* 90, no. 1 (1996): 74–98.

"The Doctrine of St. Paul Concerning Women." *Woman's Journal,* 22 January 1870.

Dorr, Rheta C. *Susan B. Anthony: The Woman Who Changed the Mind of a Nation.* New York: AMS Press, 1928.

Dow, Bonnie J. "Feminism, Cultural Studies, and Rhetorical Studies." *Quarterly Journal of Speech* 83 (1997): 90–106.

Doxtader, Erik W. "Characters in the Middle of Public Life: Consensus, Dissent, and Ethos." *Philosophy and Rhetoric* 33 (2000): 336–69.

Duncan, Carol, and Alan Wallach. "The Universal Survey Museum." *Art History* 3 (1980): 448–69.

Dupriez, Bernard. *A Dictionary of Literary Devices, A–Z.* Trans. Albert W. Halsall. Toronto: University of Toronto Press, 1991.

Dvorak, Petula, and Hamil R. Harris. "U.S. Bestows Honor on Rosa Parks." *Houston Chronicle,* 29 October 2005, A1.

Eagle, Mary Kavanaugh Oldham, ed. *The Congress of Women Held in the Woman's Building, World's Columbian Exposition, Chicago, U.S.A., 1893.* Kansas City, MO: Thompson and Hood, 1894.

Eakins, Barbara. "The Evolution of Rhetoric: A Cosmic Analogy." *Southern Speech Journal* 35 (1970): 193–203.

"The Eccentric Fanny Wright." *Newsweek,* 11 September 1939, 45.

Ede, Lisa, Cheryl Glenn, and Andrea Lunsford. "Border Crossings: Intersections of Rhetoric and Feminism." *Rhetorica* 13, no. 4 (1995): 401–41.

Egermeier, Elsie E. *Girls' Stories of Great Women.* Anderson, IN: Warner Press, 1951.

Ehrenreich, Barbara, and Lionel Tiger. "Who Needs Men?" *Harper's Magazine,* June 1999, 33–46.

Eicher-Catt, Deborah. "A Communicology of Female/Feminine Embodiment: The Case of Non-Custodial Motherhood." *American Journal of Semiotics* 17, no. 4 (2001): 93–130.

———. "Non-Custodial Mothering: A Cultural Paradox of Competent Performance-Performative Competence." *Journal of Contemporary Ethnography* 33 (2004): 72–108.

Eicher-Catt, Deborah, and Jane Sutton. "A Communicology of the Oval Office as Figural Rhetoric: Women, the Presidency, and a Politics of the Body." In *Communicology: The New Science of Embodied Discourse,* ed. Deborah Eicher-Catt and Isaac E. Catt, 200–234. Madison, NJ: Fairleigh Dickinson University Press, 2010.

"Embattled." *New Yorker,* 26 February 1972, 26, passim.

Enoch, Jessica. *Refiguring Rhetorical Education: Women Teaching African American, Native American, and Chicano/a Students, 1865–1911.* Carbondale: Southern Illinois University Press, 2008.

Enos, Richard Leo. "On the Trail of Ancient Rhetoric: Fieldwork of a Wandering Rhetorician." *Advances in the History of Rhetoric* 6 (2001): 43–51.

Erskine, John. *The Influence of Women and Its Cure.* New York: Merrill Company, 1936.

Euripides. *Euripides.* Trans. Arthur S. Day. 4 vols. Vol. 3. Loeb Classical Library. New York: G. P. Putnam's Sons, 1919.

Fallon, Janet L. "Planning for the Year 2000: Women in Academe." *Association for Communication Administration* 76 (1991): 32–38.

"Fanny Wright." *New York Daily Times,* 18 December 1852.

"Fanny Wright." *Philadelphia Mirror,* 23 July 1836.

Farenga, Vincent. "The Paradigmatic Tyrant: Greek Tyranny and the Ideology of the Proper." *Helios* 8, no. 1 (1981): 1–31.

———. "Periphrasis on the Origin of Rhetoric." *Modern Language Notes* 94 (1979): 1033–55.

Farley, Ronnie, ed. *Women of the Native Struggle: Portrait and Testimony of Native American Women*. New York: Orion Books, 1993.

Farrar-Myers, Victoria. "Money and the Art and Science of Candidate Visibility." In *Rethinking Madam President: Are We Ready for a Woman in the White House?* ed. Lori Cox Han and Caroline Heldman, 113-31. Boulder, CO: Lynne Rienner, 2007.

Farrell, Thomas. *Norms of a Rhetorical Culture*. New Haven: Yale University Press, 1993.

Fay, Elizabeth A. *Eminent Rhetoric*. Ed. Donaldo Macedo. Series in Language and Ideology. Westport, CT: Bergin & Garvey, 1994.

Feld, Rose. "The Crusades of Frances Wright." *New York Times*, 17 September 1939, 4.

"Female Depravity." *Liberator*, 13 August 1836.

"Female Liberty of Speech." *Liberator*, 20 October 1837.

"The Female Pests." *Liberator*, 16 September 1853.

"Female Profanity." *Liberator*, 11 July 1835.

Fernandez, James W. *Persuasions and Performances: The Play of Tropes in Culture*. Bloomington: Indiana University Press, 1986.

"The Fight for Rosa Continues." *Jacksonville Free Press*, 24-30 November 2005, 9.

Findling, John E. *Chicago's Great World's Fairs*. Manchester: Manchester University Press, 1994.

Flexner, Eleanor, and Ellen Fitzpatrick. *Century of Struggle: The Woman's Rights Movement in the United States*. Cambridge, MA: Harvard University Press, 1996.

Foreman, Carolyn Thomas. *Indian Women Chiefs*. Washington, DC: Zenger Publishing, 1954.

Fortenbaugh, W. W. *Aristotle on Emotion*. New York: Barnes and Noble, 1975.

———. "Aristotle on Slaves and Women." In *Articles on Aristotle: Ethics and Politics*, ed. Malcolm Schofield, Jonathan Barnes, and Richard Sorabji, 135-39. London: Duckworth, 1977.

Foss, Karen A., and Sonja J. Foss. *Inviting Transformation: Presentational Speaking for a Changing World*. Boulder, CO: Waveland Press, 1994.

Foss, Sonja A., and Cindy L. Griffin. "A Feminist Perspective on Rhetorical Theory: Toward a Clarification of Boundaries." *Western Journal of Communication* 56 (1992): 330-49.

Foucault, Michel. "Of Other Spaces." *Diacritics* 16 (1986): 22-27.

———. *Power/Knowledge*. Trans. L. Marshall C. Gordon, J. Mepham, and K. Soper. Brighton: Harvester, 1980.

Fox-Genovese, Elizabeth, ed. *Augusta Jane Evans: Beulah*. Baton Rouge: Louisiana University Press, 1992.

Freud, Sigmund. "Femininity." In *The Standard Edition of the Complete Psychological Works of Sigmund Freud*, ed. James Strachey, 112-35. London: Hogarth Press, 1953-74.

Furley, David J., and Alexander Nehamas, eds. *Aristotle's Rhetoric: Philosophical Essays*. Princeton: Princeton University Press, 1994.

Gage, Matilda Joslyn. "Indian Citizenship." *National Citizen and Ballot Box*, May 1878.

———. *Woman, Church and State*. New York: Arno Press, 1972.

Gale, Xin Liu. "Historical Studies and Postmodernism: Reading Aspasia of Miletus." *College English* 62 (2000): 361–86.

Gaonkar, Dilip Parameshwar. "Contingency and Probability." In *Encyclopedia of Rhetoric,* ed. Thomas O. Sloane, 151–66. Oxford: Oxford University Press, 2001.

Gardner, Anna. *Woman Suffrage, Association for the Advancement of Women: Papers Read at the Fourth Congress of Women, Philadelphia, Oct. 1876.* Washington, DC: Todd Brothers, 1877.

Garland, J. V. *Public Speaking for Women.* New York: Harper and Brothers, 1938.

Garver, Eugene. *Aristotle's Rhetoric: An Art of Character.* Chicago: University of Chicago Press, 1994.

Gearhart, Sally Miller. "The Womanization of Rhetoric." *Women's Studies International Quarterly* 2 (1979): 195–201.

Genung, John F., ed. *Handbook of Rhetorical Analysis.* Boston: Ginn & Company, 1893.

George, Andrew A. *Woman Suffrage: Argument of Mrs. Andrew A. George before the Committee on Woman Suffrage, United States Senate.* Washington, DC: GPO, 1913.

Gibbs-Smith, C. H. *The Great Exhibition of 1851.* Rev. ed. London: Victoria and Albert Museum, 1964.

Gilbert, Amos. *Memoir of Frances Wright: The Pioneer Woman in the Cause of Human Rights.* Cincinnati: Longley Bros., 1855.

Gilman, Sander L., Carole Blair, and David J. Parent, eds. *Friedrich Nietzsche on Rhetoric and Language.* New York: Oxford University Press, 1989.

"The Girl Schauer Is Set Free." *New York Times,* 10 December 1895.

Gitelman, Lisa. *Always Already New: Media, History, and the Data of Culture.* Cambridge, MA: MIT Press, 2006.

Glenn, Cheryl. "Comment: Truth, Lies, and Method: Revising Feminist Historiography." *College English* 62 (2000): 387–89.

———. *Rhetoric Retold.* Carbondale: Southern Illinois University Press, 1997.

Goffman, Erving. "The Arrangement between the Sexes." *Theory and Society* 4 (1977): 301–31.

Goldenberg, Suzanne. *Madam President: Is America Ready to Send Hillary Clinton to the White House?* London: Guardian Books, 2007.

Goode, G. Brown. *The Museums of the Future: A Lecture Delivered before the Brooklyn Institute, February 28, 1889, from the Report of the National Museum, 1888–89, Pages 427–445.* Washington, DC: GPO, 1891.

Grassi, Ernesto. *Rhetoric as Philosophy.* Trans. John Michael Krois and Azizeh Azodi. University Park: Pennsylvania State University Press, 1980.

"Greek Women." *Woman's Journal,* 22 January 1870.

Green, Venus. "The Impact of Technology upon Women's Work in the Telephone Industry." Ph.D. diss., Columbia University, 1990.

Gridley, Marion E. *American Indian Women.* New York: Hawthorn Books, 1974.

Griffin, Leland M. "The Edifice Metaphor in Rhetorical Theory." *Speech Monographs* 27 (1960): 279–92.

Grimaldi, William, S.J. *Aristotle, Rhetoric I: A Commentary.* New York: Fordham Press, 1980.

———. *Studies in the Philosophy of Aristotle's Rhetoric.* Wiesbaden: Franz Steiner, 1972.

Gross, Alan G. "Renewing Aristotelian Theory: The Cold Fusion Controversy as a Test Case." *Quarterly Journal of Speech* 81 (1995): 48–62.

Gross, Alan G., and Arthur E. Walzer, eds. *Rereading Aristotle's Rhetoric.* Carbondale: Southern Illinois University Press, 2000.

Gutgold, Nichola D. *Paving the Way for Madam President.* Lanham, MD: Rowman and Littlefield, 2006.

Hahn, Dan F., and Deborah Borisoff. "How Do We Keep Women in their Place if Woman Is Place?" *Qualitative Research Reports in Communication* 1 (2000): 14–17.

Hamilton, W. *The Time-Saver: A Book Which Names and Locates 5,000 Things at the World's Fair That Visitors Should Not Fail to See.* Chicago: W. E. Hamilton, 1893.

Han, Lori Cox, and Caroline Heldman, eds. *Rethinking Madam President: Are We Ready for a Woman in the White House?* Boulder, CO: Lynne Rienner, 2007.

Hariman, Robert, ed. *Popular Trials: Rhetoric, Mass Media, and the Law.* Tuscaloosa: University of Alabama Press, 1990.

Harris, Hamil R., and Steven A. Holmes. "Services for King to Be Held in Ga.; No Viewing Planned at U.S. Capitol." *Washington Post,* 3 February 2006, A06.

Harrison, Fairfax. "An Address before the Alabama Girls' Technical Institute, Montevallo, Alabama, Oct. 17, 1914." [Montevallo]: n.p., 1914.

Haskell, Bob, and Lorenzo Parnell. "Guardsmen Help Honor Civil Rights Pioneer Rosa Parks." *National Guard,* 1 December 2005, 34.

Hauser, Gerard A. "Aristotle on Epideictic: The Formation of Public Morality." *Rhetoric Society Quarterly* 29 (1999): 5–23.

Hauser, Gerard A., and Amy Grim, eds. *Rhetorical Democracy: Discursive Practices of Civic Engagement.* Mahwah, NJ: Lawrence Erlbaum Associates, 2004.

Hawhee, Debra. *Bodily Arts: Rhetoric and Athletics in Ancient Greece.* Austin: University of Texas Press, 2004.

Hays, Elinor. *Lucy Stone: One of America's First and Greatest Feminists.* New York: Tower Publications, 1961.

Heidegger, Martin. "Building Dwelling Thinking." In *Basic Writings,* ed. David Ferrell Krell, 323–39. New York: Harper and Row, 1977.

Heinrichs, Jay. *Figures of Speech Served Fresh.* Figaro, 2005, http://www.figarospeech.com/ (accessed 14 February 2007).

———. "How Harvard Destroyed Rhetoric." *Harvard Magazine,* July–August 1995, 37–42.

Hennessey, Joseph B. "A Theory of Memory as Applied to Speech." *Today's Speech* 7 (1959): 15–19.

Hill, Joseph A. "Women in Gainful Occupations, 1870 to 1920." Washington, DC: GPO, 1929.

Hillbruner, Anthony. "Frances Wright: Egalitarian Reformer." *Southern Speech Journal* 23 (1958): 193–203.

Hirschman, Albert O. *The Rhetoric of Reaction*. Cambridge, MA: Belknap Press of Harvard University Press, 1991.

Holly, Marietta. *Samantha at the World's Fair*. New York: Funk and Wagnall's, 1983.

Homer. *The Odyssey*. Trans. Walter Shewring. Oxford: Oxford University Press, 1980.

———. *Odyssey*. Trans. A. T. Murphy. 2nd ed. 2 vols. Cambridge, MA: Harvard University Press, 1995.

Hoogestraat, Wayne E. "Memory: The Lost Canon?" *Quarterly Journal of Speech* 46 (1960): 141-47.

Horowitz, Maryanne Cline. "Aristotle and Woman." *Journal of the History of Biology* 9 (1993): 183-213.

Howells, William Dean. *Letters of an Altrurian Traveller (1893-94)*. Gainesville, FL: Scholars' Facsimiles & Reprints, 1961.

Hyman, Linda. "The Greek Slave by Hiram Powers: High Art as Popular Culture." *Art Journal* 35 (1976): 216-23.

Hyperides. "Funeral Speech." In *Minor Attic Orators*, 536-59. Cambridge, MA: Harvard University Press, 1962.

An Ideal Occupation for Women. [New York]: New York Telephone Company, [191?].

"In the Council Chamber Minutes, Feb. 9, 1757." *South Carolina Council Journal, 1757-1758*. Columbia: South Carolina Department of Archives and History, 1757.

"In the Council Chamber Minutes, Feb. 12, 1757." *South Carolina Council Journal, 1757-1758*. Columbia: South Carolina Department of Archives and History, 1757.

"Insult to Woman." *Liberator*, 23 September 1852.

Irigaray, Luce. *The Forgetting of Air in Martin Heidegger*. Trans. Mary Beth Mader. Austin: University of Texas Press, 1999.

———. "Place, Interval: A Reading of Aristotle, *Physics IV*." In *Feminist Interpretations of Aristotle*, ed. Cynthia A. Freeland, 41-58. University Park: Pennsylvania State University Press, 1998.

Irwin, Clark T. "Rhetoric Remembers: Richard Weaver on Memory and Culture." *Today's Speech* 21 (1973): 2126.

Irwin, Inez Haynes. *Angels and Amazons*. Garden City, NJ: Doubleday, 1933.

Isocrates. "Antidosis." In *Isocrates*. New York: Putnam, 1928-80a.

———. "Nicocles or the Cyprians." In *Isocrates*. Cambridge, MA: Harvard University Press, 1928-80b.

———. "Panegyricus." In *Isocrates*, ed. G. P. Goold, 120-241. Cambridge, MA: Harvard University Press, 1980.

Ivey, Steve. "Rep. Rush Leads Effort for Stamp; Bill Seeks Exemption to Honor Rosa Parks." *Chicago Tribune*, 16 December 2005, 26.

Ivie, Robert L. "Democratic Deliberation in a Rhetorical Republic." *Quarterly Journal of Speech* 84 (1998): 491-530.

———. "Rhetorical Deliberation and Democratic Politics in the Here and Now." *Rhetoric & Public Affairs* 5 (2002): 277-85.

Jakobson, Roman. "The Metaphoric and Metonymic Poles." In *Critical Theory since Plato*, ed. Hazard Adams, 1113-16. New York: Harcourt Brace Jovanovich, 1971.

James, Henry. *The Question of Our Speech.* Boston: Houghton Mifflin, 1905.

Jamieson, Kathleen Hall. *Beyond the Double Bind: Women and Leadership.* Oxford: Oxford University Press, 1995.

———. *Eloquence in an Electronic Age: The Transformation of Political Speechmaking.* New York: Oxford University Press, 1988.

Janieson, Duncan R. "Women's Rights at the World's Fair, 1893." *Illinois Quarterly* 37, no. 2 (1974): 5-20.

Jarratt, Susan C. "Comment: Rhetoric and Feminism: Together Again." *College English* 62 (2000): 390-93.

———. "Sappho's Memory." *Rhetoric Society Quarterly* 32 (2002): 11-43.

Johnson, Adelaide. "Memories of a Pioneer Feminist, 1848-1948." *Equal Rights* 34, no. 4 (1948): 50.

Johnson, Nan. *Gender and Rhetorical Space in American Life, 1866-1910.* Studies in Rhetorics and Feminisms. Carbondale: Southern Illinois University Press, 2002.

———. "Reigning in the Court of Silence: Women and Rhetorical Space in Postbellum America." *Philosophy and Rhetoric* 33 (2000): 221-42.

Johnson, Rossiter. *A History of the World's Columbian Exposition Held in Chicago in 1893.* Vol. 4. New York: D. Appleton & Company, 1897.

Jones, Rachel. "Monument to Suffragists Stuck in Basement for Now: Feminists Are Upset over Low Priority for Moving the Statue." *Philadelphia Inquirer,* 16 August 1995, A04.

———. "Suffrage Statue to Miss Ceremony." *The State,* 20 August 1995.

Jorgensen-Earp, Cheryl R. "The Lady, the Whore, and the Spinster: The Rhetorical Use of Victorian Images of Women." *Western Journal of Communication* 54 (1990): 82-98.

Kamensky, Jane. *Governing the Tongue: The Politics of Speech in Early New England.* New York: Oxford University Press, 1997.

Kasee, Cynthia. "Ward, Nancy [Nanye-Hi, One Who Goes About]." In *Native American Women: A Biographical Dictionary,* ed. Gretchen M. Bataille and Laurie Lisa, 327-28. New York: Routledge, 2001.

Kasson, Joy S. *Marble Queens and Captives: Women in Nineteenth-Century American Sculpture.* New Haven: Yale University Press, 1990.

Katz, Jane B., ed. *I Am the Fire of the Time: The Voices of Native American Women.* New York: Dutton, 1977.

Katz, Marilyn. "Ideology and 'the Status of Women' in Ancient Greece." *History & Theory* 31, no. 4 (1992): 70-97.

Kendall, Kathleen Edgerton, and Jeanne Y. Fisher. "Frances Wright on Women's Rights: Eloquence versus Ethos." *Quarterly Journal of Speech* 64 (1974): 58-68.

Kern, Stephen. *The Culture of Time and Space, 1889-1918.* Cambridge, MA: Harvard University Press, 1983.

Kerr, Andrea More. *Lucy Stone Speaking Out for Equality.* New Brunswick, NJ: Rutgers University Press, 1992.

Kidwell, Clara Sue. "Indian Women as Cultural Mediators." *Ethnohistory* 39 (1992): 97-107.

Kilcup, Karen L., ed. *Native American Women's Writing, c. 1800–1924*. Oxford: Blackwell, 2000.

Kilian, Michael. "Out of Capitol Cellar, Statue of Feminists Returns to Glory." *Chicago Tribune*, 27 June 1997, 3.

King, E. Sterling. *The Wild Rose of Cherokee or Nancy Ward*. 1895. Reprint, Etowah, TN: Myrtle King Tatum, 1938.

Kirby, Kathleen M. *Indifferent Boundaries: Spatial Concepts of Human Subjectivity*. New York: Guilford Press, 1996.

Klein, Jacob. *Lectures and Essays*. Ed. Robert B. Williamson and Elliott Zuckerman. Annapolis: St. John's College Press, 1985.

Kleinberg, S. J. *Women in the United States–1839–1945*. New Brunswick, NJ: Rutgers University Press, 1999.

Knox, Bernard. *Backing into the Future: The Classical Tradition and Its Renewal*. New York: Norton, 1994.

Komblut, Anne E. "So What Is Fair Game with Sarah Palin? Look at the Rules Hillary Clinton Had to Play By." *Washington Post*, 7 September 2008, B01.

Kramer, Jane. "Liberty, Equality, Sorority." *The New Yorker*, 29 May 2000, 112–23.

Krippendorff, Klaus. *On Communicating: Otherness, Meaning, and Information*. Ed. Fernando Bermejo. New York: Routledge, 2009.

Lacan, Jacques. "The Agency of the Letter in the Unconscious or Reason since Freud." In *Écrits: A Selection*, 146–78. New York: Norton, 1977.

Lakoff, George and Mark Johnson. *Philosophy in the Flesh: The Embodied Mind and Its Challenges to Western Thought*. New York: Basic Books, 1999.

Lamb, Ruth DeForest. "Frances Wright: Looking Back across the Century at a 'Radical.'" *Woman's Journal* 15 (November 1930): 47.

Lang, Marlene. "Rosa Parks Deserves Memorial, But Not on Portrait Monument." *Daily Southtown (Chicago)*, 6 November 2005.

Langer, Suzanne K. "The Primary Illusions and the Great Orders of Art." *Hudson Review* 3, no. 2 (1950): 219–33.

Lanham, Richard A. *A Handlist of Rhetorical Terms, 2nd Ed*. Berkely: University of California Press, 1991.

Lanzi, Beatrice. "Uncle Sam Needs You." *Glamour*, May 2000, 184.

"Late Debut for Statute," Pittsburgh Post-Gazette, 27 June 1997, A-12.

Lausberg, Heinrich. *Handbook of Literary Rhetoric; with a Foreword by George A. Kennedy*. Trans. Matthew T. Bliss, Annemiek Jansen, and David E. Orton. Ed. David E. Orton and R. Dean Anderson. Leiden: Brill, 1998.

Lentz, Tony M. "From Recitation to Memory." *Southern Speech Communication Journal* 51 (1985): 49–70.

Lerner, Gerda. *The Woman in American History*. Menlo Park, CA: Addison-Wesley, 1971.

Levander, Caroline Field. *Voices of the Nation: Women and Public Speech in Nineteenth-Century American Literature and Culture*. Cambridge: Cambridge University Press, 1998.

Levy, Harold L. "Does Aristotle Exclude Women from Politics?" *Review of Politics* 52 (1990): 397–416.

Lévy-Bruhl, Lucien. *How Natives Think*. Trans. Lilian A. Clarke. Princeton: Princeton University Press, 1985.

Lillard, Roy G. "The Story of Nancy Ward, 1738–1822." *Daughters of the American Revolution Magazine* 110, no. 1 (1976): 42–43, 158.

Lipartito, Kenneth. "When Women Were Switches: Technology, Work and Gender in the Telephone Industry, 1890–1920." *American Historical Review* 99 (1995): 1075–1111.

Liu, Yameng. "Disciplinary Politics and the Institutionalization of the Generic Triad in Classical Rhetoric." *College English* 57, no. 1 (1995): 9–26.

Lockwood, George B. "Cradle of Women's Rights." *National Republic*, January 1931, 16–17.

Logan, Shirley Wilson. *"We Are Coming": The Persuasive Discourse of Nineteenth-Century Black Women*. Carbondale: Southern Illinois University Press, 1999.

———, ed. *With Pen and Voice: A Critical Anthology of Nineteenth-Century African-American Women*. Carbondale: Southern Illinois University Press, 1995.

Malloux, Steven. "Afterword: A Pretext for Rhetoric: Dancing 'Round the Revo-lution" in *Pre/Text: The First Decade*, ed. Victor J. Vitanza, 299–314. Pittsburgh, Pittsburgh Univ. Press, 1993.

Mandziuk, Roseann M. "Dressing Down Hillary." *Communication and Critical/Cultural Studies* 5 (2008): 312–16.

Marback, Richard. "The Rhetorical Space of Robben Island." *Rhetoric Society Quarterly* 34 (2004): 7–27.

Martin, Joseph. "Hillsborough July 12." Draper Manuscripts Tennessee Papers, ser. xx, vols. 1–4, reel 116, Carlisle, PA, 1775.

Marvin, Carolyn. *When Old Technologies Were New*. Oxford: Oxford University Press, 1988.

Massa, Ann. "Black Women in the 'White City.'" *Journal of American Studies* 8, no. 3 (1974): 319–37.

Matthews, Glenna. *The Rise of Public Woman*. Oxford: Oxford University Press, 1992.

McClary, Ben Harris. "Nancy Ward: The Last Beloved Woman of the Cherokee." *Tennessee Historical Quarterly* 21 (1962): 352–64.

McEwen, Indra Kagis. *Socrates' Ancestor*. Cambridge, MA: MIT Press, 1993.

McGee, Michael Calvin. "Ideograph." In *Encyclopedia of Rhetoric*, ed. Thomas O. Sloane, 378–81. Oxford: Oxford University Press, 2001.

McKeon, Richard. "Introduction: The Philosophy of Aristotle." In *The Basic Works of Aristotle*, ed. Richard McKeon, i–xx. New York: Random House, 1941.

Mele, Kate. "Legal Subjects: The Tropological Discussion of 'Woman' in Legal Narratives." Ph.D. diss., University of Rhode Island, 2001.

Merida, Kevin, and Hamil R. Harris. "50 Years Later in the Shadow of Jim Crow; After Rosa Parks, a Struggle So Different and Yet the Same." *Washington Post*, 6 November 2005, D01.

Meyer, Michaela D. E. "Women Speak(ing): Forty Years of Feminist Contributions to Rhetoric and an Agenda for Feminist Rhetorical Studies." *Communication Quarterly* 55 (2007): 1–17.

"Michelle Obama Honors Sojourner Truth, Wears Striped Skirt." Huffington Post, 2009,

http://www.huffingtonpost.com/2009/04/28/michelle-obama-honors-soj_n_192427
.html (accessed 29 April 2009).

Michelstaedter, Carlo. *Persuasion and Rhetoric.* Trans. Russell Scott Valentino, Cinzia Sartini Blum, and David J. Depew. New Haven: Yale University Press, 2004.

Midway Types. Chicago: American Engraving Company, 1894.

Mifsud, Mari Lee, Jane S. Sutton, and Lindsey Fox. "Configurations: Encountering Ancient Athenian Spaces of Rhetoric, Democracy, and Woman." *Journal of International Women's Studies* 7 (2005): 36–52.

Miller, Diane Helene. "The Future of Feminist Rhetorical Criticism." In *Listening to Their Voices: The Rhetorical Activities of Historical Women,* ed. Molly Meijer Wertheimer, 359–80. Columbia: University of South Carolina Press, 1997.

Miller, Florence Fenwick. "Art in the Women's Section of the Chicago Exhibit." *Art Journal* 55 (1893): xiii–xvi.

Miller, Nancy K. "Rereading as a Woman: The Body in Practice." *Poetics Today* 6, nos. 1–2 (1985): 291–99.

Morison, Samuel Eliot, and Henry Steele Commager. *The Growth of the American Republic.* 2 vols. New York: Oxford University Press, 1942.

Morris, Celia. *Fanny Wright: Rebel in America.* Cambridge, MA: Harvard University Press, 1984.

———. "Frances Wright: She Fought the Major Battles of Her Time and Ours." *Ms.* 4 (1976): 15–18.

Morris, Tom. *If Aristotle Ran General Motors.* New York: Henry Holt, 1997.

Morsink, Johannes. "Was Aristotle's Biology Sexist?" *Journal of the History of Biology* 12, no. 1 (1979): 83–112.

Mosley, Shelly. *The Suffragists in Literature for Youth: The Fight for the Vote.* Lanham, MD: Scarecrow Press, 2006.

Mouffe, Chantal. *The Return of the Political.* London: Verso, 1993.

Mountford, Roxanne. "On Gender and Rhetorical Space." *Rhetoric Society Quarterly* 30 (2001): 41–71.

———. *The Gendered Pulpit: Preaching in American Protestant Spaces.* Carbondale: Southern Illinois University Press, 2003.

"Mrs. Frances Wright Darusmont." *York Gazette,* 16 August 1836.

"Mrs. Palmer's Address to the Fortnightly Club of Chicago." In *Addresses and Reports of Mrs. Potter Palmer, President, to the Board of Lady Managers, September 2, 1891,* 41–50. Chicago: Rand McNally, 1894.

Mrs. Willard Reviewed, or a Short Examination of the Proceedings of the Society for the Advancement of Female Education in Greece. Albany, 1838.

Mueller, Lisel. "Aphasia." In *Alive Together.* Baton Rouge: Louisiana University Press, 1996.

"Must Go to the Workhouse." *New York Times,* 7 December 1895.

Neel, Jasper. *Aristotle's Voice: Rhetoric, Theory, and Writing in America.* Carbondale: Southern Illinois University Press, 1994.

Nietzsche, Friedrich. "History of Greek Eloquence (1872-1873)." In S. L. Gilman, Carole Blair, and David Parent, 213-242. New York: Oxford Univ. Press, 1989.

———. "On Truth and Lies in a Nonmoral Sense." In *Friedrich Nietzsche on Rhetoric and Language*, ed. S. L. Gilman, Carole Blair, and David J. Parent, 246-57. New York: Oxford University Press, 1989.

———. *The Twilight of the Idols.* Trans. Anthony M. Ludovici. Ed. Dr. Oscar Levy. Vol. 16 of *The Complete Works of Friedrich Nietzsche.* New York: Gordon Press, 1974.

"The Night of Horror." *New York World,* 6 December 1895.

Noble, David. *A World Without Women.* Oxford: Oxford University Press, 1992.

Norton, Janice. "Rhetorical Criticism as Ethical Action: Cherchez la Femme." *Southern Communication Journal* 61 (1995): 29-45.

Nuttall, Thomas. *A Journal of Travels into the Arkansas Territory, during the Year 1819 with Occasional Observations on the Manners of the Aborigines; Illustrated by a Map and Other Engravings.* Philadelphia: T. H. Palmer, 1821.

Nuyen, A. T. "The Rhetoric of Feminist Writings." *Philosophy and Rhetoric* 28 (1995): 69-82.

O'Conner, Lillian. *Pioneer Women Orators.* New York: Vantage Press, 1952.

O'Connor, Thomas H. *The Athens of America.* Amherst: University of Massachusetts Press, 2006.

Official Directory of the World's Columbian Exposition, May 1 to October 30, 1893. Chicago: Conkey, 1893.

Oliver, Robert T. *The History of Public Speaking.* Boston: Allyn and Bacon, 1965.

On Rhetoric: A Theory of Civic Discourse. Trans. George A. Kennedy. New York: Oxford University Press, 1991.

O'Rourke, Sean Patrick. "Anaximenes, *Rhetorica Ad Alexandrum.*" In *Classical Rhetorics and Rhetoricians,* ed. Michelle Ballif and Michael G. Moran, 19-23. Westport, CT: Praeger, 2005.

Overton, Spencer. "Viewing Rosa Parks at the Capitol Rotunda," 2005, http://www.blackprof.com/ (accessed 31 October 2005).

Ovid. *Metamorphoses.* Trans. Frank Justus Miller. Ed. G. P. Goold. 2 vols. Vol. 1. Loeb Classical Library. Cambridge, MA: Harvard University Press, 1984.

"Paul Concerning Women." *Woman's Journal,* 11 March 1871.

Pausanias. *Description of Greece.* Trans. W.H.S. Jones. 5 vols. Cambridge, MA: Harvard University Press, 1935.

Peeren, Esther. *Intersubjectivities and Popular Culture: Bakhtin and Beyond.* Stanford: Stanford University Press, 2008.

"Pelosi: 'We Mourn the Death of Rosa Parks, But We Celebrate an America That's More Just Because of the Life of Rosa Parks.'" 3-9 November 2005, http://www.encyclopedia.com/doc/1P2-13209122.html.

Perdue, Theda. "Cherokee Women and the Trail of Tears." *Journal of Women's History* 1 (1989): 14-30.

———. "Women, Men and American Indian Policy: The Cherokee Response to 'Civilization.'" In *Negotiators of Change*, ed. Nancy Shoemaker, 90–114. New York: Routledge, 1995.

Perelman, Chaim, and Lucie Olbrechts-Tyteca. *The New Rhetoric: A Treatise on Argumentation*. Trans. John Wilkinson and Purcell Weaver. Notre Dame: University of Notre Dame Press, 1969.

Perkins, A.J.G., and Theresa Wolfson. *Frances Wright, Free Enquirer: The Study of a Temperament*. Philadelphia: Porcupine Press, 1972.

Peters, F. E. *Greek Philosophical Terms: A Historical Lexicon*. New York: New York University Press, 1967.

Peyser, Andrea. "Ok, I Give Up—She Just Won't Die." *New York Post*, 24 January 2007, Metro Section 2.

Pirsig, Robert. *Zen and the Art of Motorcycle Maintenance: An Inquiry into Values*. New York: Harper Collins, 1974.

Plato. *Phaedrus*. Trans. H. N. Fowler. 12 vols. Vol. 1. Cambridge, MA: Harvard University Press, 1914.

———. *Protagoras*. Trans. W.R.M. Lamb. 12 vols. Vol. 2. Cambridge, MA: Harvard University Press, 1924.

———. *Theaetetus*. Trans. H. N. Fowler. 12 vols. Vol. 7. Cambridge, MA: Harvard University Press, 1921.

Platz, Mabel. *The History of Public Speaking: A Comparative Study of World Oratory*. New York: Noble and Noble Publishers, 1935.

Plutarch. *The Lives of the Noble Grecians and Romans*. Trans. John Dryden. New York: Modern Library, 1932.

Pohl, Frances K. "Historical Reality or Utopian Ideal? The Woman's Building at the World's Columbian Exposition, Chicago, 1893." *International Journal of Women Studies* 5, no. 4 (1982): 289–311.

Portnoy, Alisse. *Their Right to Speak: Women's Activism in the Indian and Slave Debates*. Cambridge, MA: Harvard University Press, 2005.

Poster, Carol. "Being and Becoming: Rhetorical Ontology in Early Greek Thought." *Philosophy and Rhetoric* 29 (1996): 1–14.

———. "(Re)Positioning Pedagogy: A Feminist Historiography of Aristotle's *Rhetorica*." In *Feminist Interpretations of Aristotle*, ed. Cynthia A. Freeland, 327–49. University Park: Pennsylvania State University Press, 1998.

Preminger, Alex, ed. *Princeton Encyclopedia of Poetry and Poetics*. Enlarged ed. Princeton: Princeton University Press, 1974.

"President Obama Speaks at Signing of Executive Order Creating White House Council on Women and Girls." 11 March 2009, http://www.whitehouse.gov/the_press_office/Executive-Order-Creating-the-White-House-Council-on-Women-and-Girls/ (accessed 2009).

Pressley, Sue Anne, and Petula Dvorak. "Thousands Honor Courage of Rosa Parks; A Gathering of Gratitude for Movement's Inspiration." *Washington Post*, 31 October 2005, A01.

"Province of Woman: The Pastoral Letter." *Liberator*, 6 October 1837.

Pyle, Joseph Gilpin. *Should Women Vote? Remarks by Joseph Gilpin Pyle at a Meeting of the Informal Club, St. Paul, March 25, 1913*. [St. Paul?], [1913?].

Quintilian. *The Institutio Oratoria of Quintilian*. Trans. H. E. Butler. 4 vols. New York: G. P. Putnam's Sons, 1921.

Rabe, Hugo, ed. *Prolegomenon Sylloge*. Editio stereotypa editionis primae (1931). Vol. 14, *Bibliotheca Scriptorum Graecorum Et Romanorum*. Stutgardiae: Teubner, 1995.

Ramsey, J.G.M., A.M., M.D. *The Annals of Tennessee to the End of the Eighteenth Century*. Philadelphia: Lippincott, Grambo & Company, 1853.

Ratcliffe, Krista. *Anglo-American Feminist Challenges to the Rhetorical Tradition*. Carbondale: Southern Illinois University Press, 1996.

"Reflecting on a Hero." *USA Today*, 3 November 2005, A4.

Reid, R. F., ed. *Three Centuries of American Rhetorical Discourse: An Anthology and a Review*. Prospect Heights, IL: Waveland Press, 1989.

Report of Mrs. Potter Palmer, President, to the Board of Lady Managers, September 2, 1891. Chicago, 1891.

Richardson, Eudora Ramsay. *The Woman Speaker: A Handbook and Study Course on Public Speaking*. Richmond, VA: Whittet & Shepperson, 1936.

Ricoeur, Paul. *The Rule of Metaphor: Multidisciplinary Studies of the Creation of Meaning in Language*. Trans. Robert Czerny. Toronto: Univ. of Toronto Press, 1977.

Robbins, Peggy. "Experiment at Nashoba Plantation [1825]." *American History Illustrated* 15 (1980): 12–19.

Roosevelt, Theodore. *The Winning of the West*. Part III: *The War in the Northwest*. New York: Current Literature Publishing Company, 1905.

Rorty, Amélie, ed. *Essays on Aristotle's Rhetoric*. Berkeley: University of California Press, 1996.

"Rosa Parks to Lie in Honor at Capitol Rotunda." Find Law: Legal News and Commentary, 2005, http://news.findlaw.com/ (accessed 1 November 2005).

Rudwick, Elliot M., and August Meier. "Black Man in the 'White City': Negroes and the Columbian Exposition." *Phylon* 26, no. 4 (1965): 354–61.

Rupp, Leila J., and Verta Taylor. *Survival in the Doldrums: The American Women's Rights Movement, 1945 to the 1960s*. New York: Oxford University Press, 1987.

Rushing, Janice Hocker. *Erotic Mentoring: Women's Transformations in the University*. Walnut Creek, CA: Left Coast Press, 2006.

———. "Evolution of 'the New Frontier' in *Alien* and *Aliens*: Patriarchal Co-optation of the Feminine Archetype." *Quarterly Journal of Speech* 75 (1989): 1–24.

———. "Introduction to 'Feminist Criticism.'" *Southern Communication Journal* 57 (1992): 83–85.

———. "Power, Other, and Spirit in Cultural Texts." *Western Journal of Communication* 57 (Spring 1993): 159–68.

———. "Putting Away Childish Things: Looking at Diana's Funeral and Media Criticism." *Women's Studies in Communication* 21, no. 2 (1998): 150–67.

Rydell, Robert W. "All the World's a Fair: America's International Expositions, 1876–1916." Ph.D. diss., University of California, Los Angeles, 1980.

———, ed. *The Reason Why the Colored American Is not in the World's Columbian Exposition: Ida B. Wells, Frederick Douglass, Irvine Garland Penn, and Ferdinand L. Barnett.* Urbana: University of Illinois Press, 1999.

Rykwert, Joseph. *The Dancing Column: On Order in Architecture.* Cambridge, MA: MIT Press, 1996.

Sachs, Joe. *Aristotle's Physics.* Ed. Harvey M. Flaumenhaft. Guided Studies of Great Texts in Science. New Brunswick, NJ: Rutgers University Press, 1995.

Salkever, Stephen. "Women, Soldiers, Citizens: Plato and Aristotle on the Politics of Virility." *Polity* 19 (1986): 232–53.

Sanford, J. B. *Extracts from a Speech against Woman's Suffrage in the California State Senate.* N.p., [1911?].

Saxonhouse, Arlene W. "Family, Polity and Unity: Aristotle on Socrates' Community of Wives." *Polity* 15 (1982): 202–19.

Schiavone, Louise. "Even in Stone, Suffragettes Cause a Stir on Capitol Hill." CNN, 10 May 1997, http://www.cnn.com/US/9705/10/womens.statue/ (accessed 1998).

Schlesinger, Arthur M. Jr. "Jackson's Radical Coalition." *New Republic* 114 (1946): 578–81.

Schmitt, Katherine M. "I Was Your 'Hello Girl.'" *Saturday Evening Post,* 12 July 1930, 18ff.

Scott, Joan Wallach. *Gender and the Politics of History.* New York: Columbia University Press, 1999.

Scull, Danielle. "Women, Art and the Capitol." U.S. Capitol Historical Society, 1999, http://www.uschs.org/04_history/subs_articles/04e_07.html (accessed 2004).

———. "Women Members of Congress." U.S. Capitol Historical Society, 1999, http://www.uschs.org/CapitolandCongress/FeatureArticles/womenincongress.htm (accessed 2001).

"Senate Passes Frist, Reid Resolution Allowing Rosa Parks to Lie in Honor in the Rotunda of the Capitol." *Tennessee Tribune,* 3 November 2005, C1.

"A Sermon of the Public Function of Woman by Theodore Parker Preached at Music Hall of Boston, March 27, 1853." *Liberator,* 15 April 1853.

Shanahan, Eileen. "Women of the Revolution Were Active in Business and on the Field of Battle." *New York Times,* 28 July 1975.

Shenandoah, Joanne, and Douglas M. George. *Skywoman.* Santa Fe: Clear Light Publishers, 1998.

Shoemaker, Nancy, ed. *Negotiators of Change: Historical Perspectives on Native American Women.* New York: Routledge, 1995.

Shugart, H. A. "Counterhegemonic Acts: Appropriation as a Feminist Rhetorical Strategy." *Quarterly Journal of Speech* 83 (1997): 210–29.

Sloane, Thomas O. Preface to *Encyclopedia of Rhetoric,* ed. Thomas O. Sloane, ix–xii. Oxford: Oxford University Press, 2001.

Slotkin, Richard. *Regeneration through Violence: The Mythology of the American Frontier, 1600–1860.* Middletown, CT: Wesleyan University Press, 1973.

Smith, Nicholas. "Plato and Aristotle on the Nature of Women." *Journal of the History of Philosophy* 21 (1983): 467–78.

Snyder-Ott, Joelynn. "Woman's Place in the Home (That She Built)." *Feminist Art Journal* 3 (1974): 7–8, 18.

Sobol, D. J. *The Amazons of Greek Mythology.* London: Thomas Yoseloff, 1972.

"Society of Females." *Liberator,* 4 August 1837.

Sparshott, Francis. "Aristotle on Women." *Philosophical Inquiry* 7, nos. 3–4 (1985): 177–200.

"[Speech to the Cherokee National Council] Cherokee Women and Ward, May 2, 1817." In Presidential Papers Microfilm: Andrew Jackson Papers, ser. 1, reel 22, Library of Congress, Washington, DC.

Spence, Sarah. *Figuratively Speaking: Rhetoric and Culture from Quintilian to the Twin Towers.* London: Duckworth, 2007.

Spitzack, Carole, and Kathryn Carter. "Women in Communication Studies: A Typology for Revision." *Quarterly Journal of Speech* 73 (1987): 401–23.

Sprague, Rosamond Kent, ed. *The Older Sophists: A Complete Translation by Several Hands of the Fragments in "Die Fragmente Der Vorsokratiker."* Ed. Diels-Kranz. Columbia: University of South Carolina Press, 1972.

"St. Paul Once More." *Woman's Journal,* 26 March 1870.

Stanton, Elizabeth Cady. *Solitude of Self: House Judiciary Committee.* New York: Caedmon, 1892.

Stanton, Elizabeth Cady, Susan B. Anthony, and Matilda Joslyn Gage. *History of Woman Suffrage.* 5 vols. Vol. 1. New York: Arno, 1969.

Steer, Diana. *Native American Women.* New York: Barnes and Noble Books, 1996.

Steinem, Gloria. "What Women Need to Rise." 2009, http://www.emilyslist.org/ (accessed 21 July 2009).

Stevenson, L.M.N. "Miss Willard as University Woman & Educator." *Union Signal and World's White Ribbon,* 10 March 1898, 153–54.

Stiller, Richard. *Commune on the Frontier: The Story of Frances Wright.* New York: Thomas Y. Crowell Company, 1972.

Stone, Francis Jr. "Letter to Lucy Stone." Blackwell Family Collection, Library of Congress, Washington, DC, 1847.

Stone, I. F. "Nineteenth-Century Bogywoman." *The Nation,* 14 October 1939, 418.

Stone, Janet, and Jane Bachner. *Speaking Up: A Book for Every Woman Who Talks.* New York: Carroll & Graf, 1994.

Stone, Lucy. "The Condition of Women." Blackwell Family Collection, Washington, DC, c. 1887.

———. "Letter to Francis and Hannah Stone." Blackwell Family Collection, Library of Congress, Washington, DC, 1843.

———. "Letter to Francis and Hannah Stone." Blackwell Family Collection, Library of Congress, Washington, DC, 1847.

———. "Letter to Hannah Stone." Blackwell Family Collection, Library of Congress, Washington, DC, 1847.

———. "Workers for the Cause." Blackwell Family Collection, Library of Congress, Washington, DC, n.d.

Struever, Nancy S. "Rhetoric: Time, Memory, Memoir." In *A Companion to Rhetoric and Rhetorical Criticism*, ed. Walter Jost and Wendy Olmsted, 425–41. London: Blackwell, 2004.

Sullivan, Louis. *The Autobiography of an Idea*. New York: Norton, 1935.

Sunstein, Cass R. *Why Societies Need Dissent*. Cambridge, MA: Harvard University Press, 2003.

Sutherland, Christine, and Rebecca Sutcliffe, eds. *The Changing Tradition: Women in the History of Rhetoric*. Calgary: University of Calgary Press, 1999.

Sutton, Jane S. "The Death of Rhetoric and Its Rebirth in Philosophy." *Rhetorica* 4 (1986): 203–26.

———. "Hippias of Elis." In *Classical Rhetorics and Rhetoricians: Critical Studies and Sources*, ed. Michelle Ballif and Michael G. Moran, 199–203. Westport, CT: Greenwood, 2005.

———. "Intersections: Woman, Rhetoric, and Domination." *American Journal of Semiotics* 22 (2006): 129–46.

———. "On the Structure of Rhetoric in Aristotle: The Space of Speech, Self, and Other." In *The Philosophy of Communication*, ed. Konstantine Boudouris and Takis Poulakos, 204–12. Athens: Ionia Publications, 2002.

———. "Rhetoric and the Peacock: An Antiphonic Spectacle of Preconceptual Linguistic Equipment for an Art of Rhetoric." *Canadian Journal for Rhetorical Studies* 4 (1994): 123–42.

———. "The Taming of the *Polos/Polis*: Rhetoric as an Achievement without Woman." *Southern Communication Journal* 57 (1992): 97–119.

Sutton, Jane, and Mari Lee Mifsud. "Figuring Rhetoric: From Antistrophe to Apostrophe through Catastrophe." *Rhetoric Society Quarterly* 32 (2002): 29–49.

———. "Translating Tropes and Theorizing Rhetoric." Paper presented at the American Society for the History of Rhetoric Preconference, Chicago, 2006.

Sutton, Jane S., and Nkanyiso Mpofu. "Figuring Reconciliation: Dancing with the Enemy." *Windsor Yearbook of Access to Justice* 25, no. 2 (2007): 291–311.

Swanson, Judith A. *The Public and the Private in Aristotle's Philosophy*. Ithaca: Cornell University Press, 1992.

Tassel, Corn. "Treaty of Long Island of Holston." Draper Manuscripts Tennessee Papers, ser. xx, vols. 1–4, reel 177, Carlisle, PA, 1781.

Taylor, Charles. *Modern Social Imaginaries*. Durham: Duke University Press, 2004.

"Tells of Frances Wright: Miss Perkins Speaks to Equal Franchise Society of Her Public Career." *New York Times*, 17 February 1911.

Templin, C. "Hillary Clinton as a Threat to Gender Norms: Cartoon Images of the First Lady." *Communication Inquiry* 23, no. 1 (1999): 20–36.

Thomas, Ken. "Senate OKs Parks Honor: Rotunda Stop Would Be a First for a Woman." *Chicago Tribune*, 28 October 2005, 13.

Truth, Sojourner. *The Women Want Their Rights!: Broadway Tabernacle.* New York: Caedmon, 1853.

Tuchman, Gaye, Arlene Kaplan Daniels, and James Benét, eds. *Hearth and Home: Images of Women in the Mass Media.* New York: Oxford University Press, 1978.

Tucker, Norma. "Nancy Ward, Ghighau of the Cherokees." *Georgia Historical Quarterly* 53 (1969): 192-200.

Turner, Frederick Jackson. "The Significance of the Frontier in American History." In *Milestones of Thought in the History of Ideas,* ed. Hans Kohn, 27-58. New York: Frederick Ungar Publishing, 1963.

Turner, Victor. *Blazing the Trail: Waymarks in the Exploration of Symbols.* Tucson: University of Arizona Press, 1992.

"U.S. Military Women Cast Off Abayas: No Longer Required to Wear Veil When Off-Base in Saudi Arabia." CBS, 2002, http://www.cbsnews.com/stories/2002/01/22/national/main325246.shtml (accessed 4 June 2003).

Valian, Virginia. *Why So Slow? The Advancement of Women.* Cambridge, MA: MIT Press, 2000.

van Zoonen, Liesbet. "The Personal, the Political, and the Popular: A Woman's Guide to Celebrity Politics." *European Journal of Cultural Studies* 9 (2006): 287-301.

Verene, Donald Phillip, ed. *Symbol, Myth, and Culture: Essays and Lectures of Ernst Cassirer, 1935-1945.* New Haven: Yale University Press, 1979.

Vitanza, Victor J. *Negation, Subjectivity, and the History of Rhetoric.* Albany: SUNY Press, 1996.

Vonnegut, Kristin S. "Listening for Women's Voices: Revisioning Courses in American Public Address." *Communication Education* 41 (1992): 26-39.

Vrato, Elizabeth, and Bill Clinton. *The Counselors: 18 Courageous Women Who Have Changed the World.* Philadelphia: Running Press, 2002.

Wagner, Sally Roesch. *Matilda Joslyn Gage: She Who Holds the Sky.* Aberdeen, SD: Sky Carrier Press, 1998.

———. *The Untold Story of the Iroquois Influence on Early Feminists.* Fayetteville, NY: Sky Carrier Press, 1996.

Waldenfels, Bernhard. *Order in the Twilight.* Trans. David J. Parent. Athens: Ohio University Press, 1996.

Walker, Jeffery. "Before the Beginnings of 'Poetry' and 'Rhetoric': Hesiod on Eloquence." *Rhetorica* 14 (1996): 243-64.

Ward, John. "Women and Latin Rhetoric: From Hortsvit to Hildegard." In *The Changing Tradition: Women in the History of Rhetoric,* ed. Christine Mason and Rebecca Sutcliffe Sutherland, 121-32. Calgary: University of Calgary Press, 1999.

Wardy, Robert. *The Birth of Rhetoric.* New York: Routledge, 1996.

———. "Mighty Is the Truth and It Shall Prevail?" In *Essays on Aristotle's Rhetoric,* ed. Amélie Oksenberg Rorty. Berkeley: University of California Press, 1996.

Waterman, William Randall. *Frances Wright.* New York: AMS Press, 1967.

Weaver, Richard. *Visions of Order.* Baton Rouge: Louisiana State University Press, 1964.

Webster, Sally. "Writing History/Painting History." In *Critical Issues in Public Art: Content, Context, and Controversy*, ed. Harriet F. Senie and Sally Webster, 33–43. Washington, DC: Smithsonian Institution Press, 1992.

Weimann, Jeanne Madeline. *The Fair Women*. Chicago: Academy, 1981.

Wertheimer, Molly Meijer, ed. *Listening to Their Voices: The Rhetorical Activities of Historical Women*. Columbia: University of South Carolina Press, 1997.

Whately, Richard. *Elements of Rhetoric (1846): A Facsimile Reproduction with Introductions by Charlotte Downey and Howard Coughlin*. Delmar, NY: Scholars' Facsimiles & Reprints, 1991.

White, Hayden. *Figural Realism: Studies in the Mimesis Effect*. Baltimore: Johns Hopkins University Press, 1999.

———. *Metahistory: The Historical Imagination in Nineteenth-Century Europe*. Baltimore: Johns Hopkins University Press, 1973.

"Who's Still Talking." White House Project, 2002, http://www.whitehouseproject.org/ (accessed 10 July 2006).

Who's Talking? An Analysis of Sunday Morning Talk Shows. White House Project, 2001, http://www.whitehouseproject.org/.

"Who's Talking Now: A Followup Analysis of Guest Appearances by Women on the Sunday Morning Talk Shows." White House Project, 2005, http://www.whitehouseproject .org/ (accessed 10 July 2006).

"Why Whitewashed Inscription Was Turned to the Wall." *Woman Patriot* 5, no. 8 (1921): 8.

Wilcox, Stanley. "Corax and the Prolegomena." *American Journal of Philology* 64, no. 1 (1943): 1–23.

Willard, Frances E., and Mary A. Livermore, eds. *A Woman of the Century: Fourteen Hundred Seventy Biographical Sketches of Leading American Women*. Buffalo: Charles Wells Moulton, 1893.

Winik, Lyric Wallwork. "Is It Time for a Woman President?" *Parade*, 30 April 2006, http:// www.parade.com/articles/editions/2006/edition_04-30-2006/Women_Candidates (accessed 21 March 2008).

Winslow, Hubbard. *Woman as She Should Be*. Boston: T. H. Carter, 1838.

"Woman on the Platform." *Liberator*, 4 November 1853.

"Woman's Sphere." *Liberator*, 25 February 1852.

"Women behind the Throne." *Woman's Journal*, 30 March 1872.

"Women in Cornell University." *Woman's Journal*, 16 April 1870.

"Women Leaders Decreasing Worldwide." *Ms. Magazine*, 21 October 1997, http:// msmagazine.com/news/uswirestory.asp?id=2678 (accessed 17 November 2008).

"Women on the Grand Jury." *Woman's Journal*, 19 March 1870.

"The Women Orators." *Liberator*, 10 June 1853.

Wood, Andrew F. "Managing the Lady Managers: The Shaping of Heterotopian Spaces in the 1893 Chicago Exposition's Woman's Building." *Southern Communication Journal* 69 (2004): 289–303.

Wood, Norton, ed. *Official Guide: New York World's Fair*. New York: Time-Life Books, 1965.

Woodall, Gina Serignese, and Kim L. Fridkin. "Shaping Women's Chances: Stereotypes and the Media." In *Rethinking Madam President: Are We Ready for a Woman in the White House?* ed. Lori Cox Han and Caroline Heldman, 69–86. Boulder, CO: Lynne Rienner, 2007.

Woolf, Virginia. "Shakespeare's Sister." In *Great Speeches of the 20th Century*, 5–18. London: Preface Publishing, 2008.

Wright, Almroth E. *The Unexpurgated Case against Woman Suffrage.* New York: Paul B. Hoeber, 1913.

Wright, Frances. "Address, Delivered in the New-Harmony Hall, by Frances Wright, at the Celebration of the Fourth of July, 1828, the Fifty-Second Anniversary of American Independence." In *New Harmony's Fourth of July Tradition: Speeches of Robert Owen, William Owen, Frances Wright,* ed. Donald E. Pitzer and Josephine M. Elliott Pitzer, 23–26. New Harmony, IN: Raintree Books, 1976.

———. "An Address to Young Mechanics: As Delivered in the Hall of Science, June 13, 1830." New York, 1830.

———. *Course of Popular Lectures in New York, Philadelphia, Baltimore, Boston, Cincinnati, St. Louis, Louisville, and Other Cities, Towns, and Districts of the United States.* 6th ed. New York: G. W. & A. J. Matsell, 1836.

"Writ for Amelia Schauer." *New York Times,* 8 December 1895.

The Writings of Thomas Jefferson. Ed. Andrew Adgate Lisscomb and Albert Ellery Bergh. 20 vols. Washington, DC: Thomas Jefferson Memorial Association of the United States, 1905.

Wu, Hui. "Historical Studies of Women Here and There: Methodological Challenges to Dominant Interpretive Frameworks." *Rhetoric Society Quarterly* 32 (2002): 81–97.

Yartz, Frank J. "Aristotle on Monsters." *Ancient World* 28, no. 1 (1997): 67–72.

"The Year in Review . . . Highlights of 2005." *Atlanta Inquirer,* 31 December 2005, 1.

Yoakam, Doris G. "An Historical Survey of the Public Speaking Activities of American Women, 1828–1860." Ph.D. diss., University of Southern California, 1935.

———. "Pioneer Women Orators of America." *Quarterly Journal of Speech* 23 (1937): 251–59.

———. "Women's Introduction to the American Platform." In *A History and Criticism of American Public Address,* ed. William Norwood Brigance; Speech Association of America, 1:153–209. New York: Russell & Russell, 1960.

Younge, Gary. "Rosa Parks Given Unprecedented Honour." *The Guardian,* 23 October 2005, 23.

Zaeske, Susan. "The 'Promiscuous Audience' Controversy and the Emergence of the Early Women's Rights Movement." *Quarterly Journal of Speech* 81 (1995): 191–207.

Index

2.